Infighting in the UAW

Recent Titles in
Contributions in Labor Studies

New Trends in Employment Practices
Walter Galenson

Order Against Chaos: Business Culture and Labor Ideology in America, 1880–1915
Sarah Lyons Watts

The Emancipation of Labor: A History of the First International
Kenryk Katz

The Unsettled Relationship: Labor Migration and Economic Development
Demetrios G. Papademetriou and Philip L. Martin, editors

Workers' Participative Schemes: The Experience of Capitalist and Plan-Based Societies
Helen A. Tsiganou

"Parish-Fed Bastards": A History of the Politics of the Unemployed in Britain, 1884–1939
Richard Flanagan

The Social Dimension of 1992: Europe Faces a New EC
Beverly Springer

Farewell to the Self-Employed: Deconstructing a Socioeconomic and Legal Solipsism
Marc Linder

Trade Unionism and Industrial Relations in the Commonwealth Caribbean: History,
Contemporary Practice and Prospect
Lawrence A. Nurse

Eastern's Armageddon
Martha Dunagin Saunders

A State Within a State: Industrial Relations In Israel, 1965–1987
Ran Chermesh

Culture, Gender, Race, and U.S. Labor History
Ronald C. Kent, Sara Markham, David R. Roediger, and Herbert Shapiro, editors

INFIGHTING IN THE UAW

The 1946 Election and the Ascendancy
of
Walter Reuther

BILL GOODE

Contributions in Labor Studies, Number 44

GREENWOOD PRESS
Westport, Connecticut • London

Library of Congress Cataloging-in-Publication Data

Goode, Bill.
     Infighting in the UAW : the 1946 election and the ascendancy of
Walter Reuther / Bill Goode.
       p. cm.—(Contributions in labor studies, ISSN 0886–8239 ;
no. 44)
     Includes bibliographical references and index.
     ISBN 0–313–28904–2 (alk. paper)
     1. International Union, United Automobile, Aerospace, and
Agricultural Implement Workers of America—History. 2. Trade
unions—Automobile industry workers—United States—History.
3. Reuther, Walter, 1907–1970. I. Title. II. Series.
HD6515.A82I5737   1994
331.88′1292′0973—dc20   93–30450

British Library Cataloguing in Publication Data is available.

Library of Congress Catalog Card Number: 93–30450
ISBN: 0–313–28904–2
ISSN: 0886–8239

First published in 1994

Greenwood Press, 88 Post Road West, Westport, CT 06881
An imprint of Greenwood Publishing Group, Inc.

Printed in the United States of America

(∞)™

The paper used in this book complies with the
Permanent Paper Standard issued by the National
Information Standards Organization (Z39.48–1984).

10 9 8 7 6 5 4 3 2 1

Every reasonable attempt has been made to trace the owners of copyright
materials in this book, but in some cases this has proven impossible. The
author and publisher will be glad to receive information leading to
complete acknowledgments in subsequent printings of the book and in the
meantime extend their apologies for any omissions.

To the memory of Charles Watson Goode, my father, and Brendan Sexton, my friend and mentor

CONTENTS

46 & 47

ABBREVIATIONS

AC	Allis-Chalmers Company
ACTU	Association of Catholic Trade Unionists
ACW	Amalgamated Clothing Workers
AFL	American Federation of Labor
AIF	Annual improvement factor
AIWA	Automotive Industrial Workers Association
ATL	Addes-Thomas-Leonard
AWU	Auto Workers Union
CIO	Congress of Industrial Organizations
COLA	Cost-of-living adjustment
CP	Community Party
CPUSA	Communist Party—United States of America
FBI	Federal Bureau of Investigation
FDR	A journal published by the ATL caucus
FE	Farm Equipment Workers
FEWOC	Farm Equipment Workers Organizing Committee
GM	General Motors
HUAC	House Un-American Activities Committee
IAM	International Association of Machinists
IEB	International Executive Board
ILGWU	International Ladies' Garment Workers' Union
ILWU	International Longshoremen's and Warehousemen's Union
IWW	Industrial Workers of the World
KKK	Ku Klux Klan
MESA	Mechanics Educational Society of America
NAACP	National Association for the Advancement of Colored People
NCWC	National Catholic Welfare Conference
NLRB	National Labor Relations Board
NMU	National Maritime Union

NPA	National Planning Association
NYU	New York University
OH	Oral History
OPM	Office of Production Management
PM	A New York daily newspaper (1940–1948)
SLP	Socialist Labor Party
SP	Socialist Party
SUB	Supplemental Unemployment Benefits
SWP	Socialist Workers Party
T-H	Taft-Hartley (Act)
TUEL	Trade Union Educational League
TUUL	Trade Union Unity League
UA, WSU	University Archives, Wayne State University
UAW	United Automobile, Aerospace, and Agricultural Implement Workers of America
UE	United Electrical, Radio, and Machine Workers of America
UMW	United Mine Workers
WERB	Wisconsin Employee Relations Board
WP	Workers Party

PREFACE

One of the exciting aspects of writing about a contemporary problem is that so many people are still alive who have lived through the situation. Some of the information about the 1946 and 1947 United Automobile Workers (UAW) conventions, the minority representation, for example, would have been impossible to have discovered without the evidence of those involved. Cross-checking with several sources produced an astonishing correspondence in their recollections.

It is apparent, and I am delighted to acknowledge the fact, that much is owed to many people who wrote before me. On the Communist Party activities, I am indebted to Irving Howe and Lewis Coser's *The American Communist Party* (1957) and Bert Cochran's *Labor and Communism* (1977) and, for the early days of the Communist Party in the auto industry, Roger Keeran's *The Communist Party and the Auto Workers Unions* (1980). Joseph Rayback's *A History of American Labor* (1966) was of great value to me on early labor history. All have made excellent contributions to the field, and my efforts would have been impoverished without their fine work.

Others spent many hours of their precious time in discussions with me. Their patience and openness added considerably to this study. Notable were Irving Bluestone, Jack Conway, George Merrilli, Ken Morris, Brendan Sexton, and Leonard Woodcock. I am grateful to them.

As important as these contributions were, it is obvious that the major sources for this book were archives and libraries. Every researcher should have at their disposal a collection such as the Archives of Labor and Urban Affairs at Wayne State University. If the researcher were extremely lucky, he or she would also encounter a staff like that of the Wayne State archives, who are outstanding for their knowledge and helpfulness. The Detroit Public Library, the Flint Purdy Library, Wayne State University, the New York Public Library, and the Wagner

Library at New York University also contributed in a significant way to this research. In institutional terms, I am indebted to the Harry A. Van Arsdale, Jr., Center for Labor Studies, Empire State College (State University of New York), for a sabbatical that gave me a year to do much of the research in Detroit, Michigan, at the Wayne State Archives.

Several people read earlier versions of the manuscript and gave me excellent advice. I would like to attribute any errors of fact or interpretation to them, but I do not think they would let me get away with it. Thanks anyway to Jack Conway, my son David Goode, Oscar and Delores Paskal, Warner Pflug, Patricia Cayo Sexton, and B. J. Widick.

Others contributed by their encouragement or in the tedious preparation of the manuscript. When my energy flagged, they were firm. Thanks to Susan Salmansohn, Ray and Reta Schultz, Jim and Stella Goode, Mort Feigenson, Gerald Lazarowitz, Elizabeth McHale, and Sue Wilensky.

These encounters with colleagues were invariably pleasant, but my undying gratitude goes to my many sisters and brothers from the UAW who patiently provided answers to the many problems that I found so confounding. Meeting with them was one of the most pleasurable moments I had while writing this book. My thanks to the following: John Allard, Buddy Battle III, Erwin Baur, John Beneri, Ray Berndt, Willie Brooks, Bob Burkart, Ray Calore, Dan Cassey, Bill Casstevens, Allen Cheesman, Ed Coffey, Leland Cox, Mike Daly, Irene Danowski, Joe Danz, Tom DeLorenzo, Ernie Dillard, Tom Doherty, Don Ellis, Bill English, Mal Evans, James Feeney, Ralph Feliccia, Sam Fishman, Cal Fletcher, Ken Flowers, Dan Forchioni, Clayton Fountain, Doug Fraser, Ken Gidner, William Goldman, Vince Granata, Ed Gray, Pat Greathouse, George Holloway, Art Hughes, Bill Kemsley, Mike Kenjalo, Stan Kuprey, Bob Lent, Jack Livingstone, Florence Maloney, John Markowski, Bill Marshall, Hodges Mason, Bill McLean, Paul McLee, Sam Meyers, May Navarre, Clare Philips, Lloyd Ramel, Vic Ranke, Victor Reuther, Ray Ross, Leonard Selke, Horace Sheffield, Art Shy, Stuart Strachan, Charles Szabo, Shelton Tappes, Joe Tomasi, Michael Vernovai, Ray Wagner, Paul Weber, Mary Anna Wells, Margaret Wells, Jack White, John Wilse, and Jack Zeller.

Finally, on occasion I have felt uneasy about my colleagues who have written on labor because they were not explicit about their involvement in the events they recorded or failed to make clear their biases. In my own case, I worked in UAW shops for a short time prior to World War II and for nearly a decade after the war. I became the Skilled Trades Committee Representative at Local 400. Later I became Educational Director of the UAW. During some of this time, I was also a member of the Socialist Party and the Independent Socialist League, and I proudly acknowledge these affiliations. No one can hope to approach a problem without biases. These experiences helped to form my biases. I can only hope that they did not distort too badly my perception of these events.

Infighting in the UAW

INTRODUCTION

Walter P. Reuther was elected president of the United Automobile Workers (UAW) in April 1946, after a hotly contested campaign, by the narrow margin of 114 votes out of the 8,821 votes cast. The smallness of the victory was an indication of the bitterness of the battle. The UAW and the entire country were at a crossroads. The labor and capital cooperation that existed during the war was frayed, and the repressed conflicts were free to find expression in spite of some of the restrictions that remained. Major strikes erupted just a few months after the cessation of the armed conflict. On the international scene, the coalition that had defeated Nazi Germany was beginning to unravel. Europe lay devastated, as did the Soviet Union, and the Cold War with all of its horrors loomed a few years in the future.

All of the facts in the UAW election seemed to point to a defeat for Reuther. R. J. Thomas, the incumbent president, had enjoyed the support of all the diverse groups in the UAW, including the small but effective cadre of the Communist Party (CP), since he succeeded Homer Martin in 1938. Despite intense factional squabbles, most of the leadership remained solidly in support of Thomas and the popular secretary-treasurer George Addes during the important election. Reuther's overtures to divide the leadership, attempting to capitalize on past differences in the union, were unsuccessful, and Reuther struck out on his own, leaving the majority of the leadership intact and opposed to him. But despite his relative isolation, Reuther won the election. The victory was especially significant because the UAW leadership had shown such great stability for eight years, only to be upset by Reuther's defection.

Ordinarily, the defeat of one union official by another, however unexpected, would not have occasioned any great dispute among political partisans or historians except for the highly charged political atmosphere of the time, including the postwar series of strikes and the presence of the Communist Party as the ideological and organizational mentor of the Addes-Thomas-Leonard (ATL) caucus, Reuther's opponent.

The reasons given for his victory are varied and vigorously disputed, depending on the political orientation of the writers. Early observers had attributed his victory to his exposure of the totalitarian nature of the Communist Party and to his aggressive militancy, not to repression or "turning to reaction." On the other hand, two writers on labor, both self-proclaimed radicals, saw Reuther's success as due to his "red-baiting." Another leftist author concurred about the red-baiting but added several other factors leading to the defeat of the ATL caucus: "red company unionism," government repression, and the "sectarian policies of the communists themselves." All these explanations held the conflict with the CP to be central to the dispute (Howe and Widick, 1949, p. 171; Geschwender, 1977, pp. 50–51; Green, 1980, p. 195; Aronowitz, 1974, p. 246).

The actual conflict and its resolution became obscured by the symbolic value attached to them. The conflict became a battle between good and evil, totalitarianism and democracy, or left-wing politics and reactionary politics. All the horrors of McCarthyism and the Cold War were linked in hindsight to the contest, but it did not deserve such attributions. The elections in 1946 and 1947 were, first and foremost, trade union disputes, and the outcome was predicated on the way that the caucuses conducted themselves on union issues.

In fact, despite the activities of the CP in the ATL caucus, the Communist issue had little currency in the 1946 election. For one, this time span preceded the virulent anticommunism of the 1950s. Winston Churchill had made his "Iron Curtain" speech at Fulton, Missouri, in March 1946, and Harry Truman had immediately supported it. Then Truman had second thoughts and modified his position. *Newsweek* ("Churchill: Home View," 1946, p. 49) reported that British "newspapers generally took the line that Churchill had gone too far in both criticism of Russia and in proposing a virtual British-American alliance." Though the Communist issue was visible in political life, it was hardly the all-consuming concern that it later became.

Even Nat Ganley, a leading Communist in the UAW and an implacable Reuther foe, generally ignored the Communist issue and ascribed Reuther's successful bid for the union's presidency to his militancy during World War II and his fight against the piecework system that the Communists had proposed. Ganley pointed to Reuther's leadership in the 1945–1946 General Motors (GM) strike and the wartime "opportunism" of the Communist Party as other key factors that aided in Reuther's victory (Ganley, 1960, p. 32).

Reuther's anticommunism existed in full measure, but all too often his detractors intentionally confused his anticommunism with nativistic red baiting. According to these critics, all criticism of the Communist Party is by definition red baiting, a view that places the Communist Party beyond the scrutiny that every institution in a democratic society can expect.

Other pro-ATL writers have mentioned Reuther's very real accomplishments. Martin Halperin has written an impressive, sympathetic history of the role of the CP and the ATL covering the time of Reuther's victory. Reuther's achievements are not ignored, nor are some failings of the CP, though usually mentioned in asides, despite their critical relevance to Reuther's success. Halperin poses the immediate cause for Reuther's victory to the desire of the rank and file for a more "pragmatic" leadership who could, for example, comply with the provisions of the Taft-Hartley Act (T-H) calling for anti-Communist affidavits from union officers. The top officers of the UAW regardless of their caucus loyalty could easily have signed the required statements, since none of them were Communists. The effect of the defeat of the CP, according to Halperin, deprived the union and the nation of an effective radical political voice against the Cold War and the McCarthy era. However, careful to avoid the interpretation that the Communists had been repudiated, Halperin states that the defeat of the ATL "was in no sense a victory for Cold War, anti-Communist tactics." That, of course, was true. The Communist issue had no particular potency in the 1946–1947 elections (Halperin, 1988, pp. 104, 233).

One of the most sophisticated and thoughtful books on this period was written by Bert Cochran. Recollecting in tranquillity his past radicalism, Cochran is a determined critic of both the CP and Reuther. These positions reflected his past association with the Trotskyist movement. Although Cochran's Trotskyist past was long behind him, his anti-Reuther and anti-CP positions remained. His knowledge of the connection between the policies of the Soviet Union and the American Communists transcends any of the material on this conflict. As a staunch anti-Communist, Cochran is, nevertheless, quick to explode some of the liberal shibboleths about CP behavior in the unions: for example, the CP's alleged late commitment to the newly established Congress of Industrial Organizations (CIO) in 1936 and the purported political strikes by the CP unions during the Moscow-Berlin Pact. Despite these caveats, the Communists do not fare well in Cochran's hands. Nor does Walter Reuther.

On the proximate cause of Reuther's victory, Cochran is dismissive of Reuther's conduct during the GM strike, labeling it as a "matter of posturing and public relations." While he concedes that the election was democratic and that the ATL caucus failed on the "plane of policy," the long-term cause of Reuther's victory was the "Red issue." Cochran maintains that the ATL caucus, if it had won in 1946, would have eventually divested itself of the CP within two years. It would have been caught in the same Cold War atmosphere that loomed in the future. The effect of the Reuther victory over a CP subservient to the Soviet Union and the subsequent expulsion of the CP unions from the CIO led only, according to Cochran, to the "bureaucratization" of the union movement and proved that the "CIO's crusading days were over" (Cochran, 1977, pp. 263, 278, 279, 315).

Roger Keeran (1980) wrote a sympathetic account of the early role of the CP in organizing the auto industry, excellently researched and informative. Unfortunately, his analysis of the 1946–1947 election contests barely reaches beyond some of the worst fulminations of the anti-Reuther forces for those years.

As might be expected, this dependence on arguments made during the heat of battle tends to be misleading. For example, he asserts, "In large measure, Reuther's victory rested on the support he received from the Association of Catholic Trade Unionists [ACTU]" (p. 253). Leftist writers had noted ACTU's support of Reuther (usually as proof of the "opportunistic, rightist" character of his caucus), but no one had suggested that this support was a major determinant of Reuther's wresting the UAW presidency from R. J. Thomas in 1946 and the virtual destruction of the ATL caucus in 1947. In fact, ACTU did not support Reuther in the crucial 1946 election, holding to a strictly neutral position until after the convention. Keeran further maintains that "ACTU was able to play the same organizational and ideological role for the Reuther-right-wing faction as the Communist Party played for the Addes-left-wing faction" (p. 254). Keeran is right about the role of the CP in the ATL caucus but is sadly amiss in his description of ACTU in relation to the Reuther caucus. ACTU openly supported Reuther after the 1946 election, but it never reached the role ascribed to it by Keeran. On several important issues in the 1947 election, ACTU was at variance with Reuther's leadership.

One UAW activist, an anti-Reutherite, wrote: "The history of the UAW after Reuther made his alliance with the Catholics early in '39 is therefore a history of the Reuther-Catholic power caucus' march to Power" (Haessler, 1959, p. 264). Even three years after the Reuther victory, Kermit Eby ("Labor Priests," 1949, p. 150), respected, retired research director of the CIO, could say, "There are two extreme poles of power attraction in the CIO, the Communist pole and the ACTU pole. Both receive their impetus from without the CIO. Both believe the control of the CIO is part of the larger struggle for the control of the world." Thus, the stage seemed to be set for a monumental world struggle, and the UAW in 1946 and 1947 seemed to be, for some, a symbol of that struggle.

Despite statements from the opposing side regarding ACTU's role in the union movement, it is difficult to determine a definitive "Catholic" position in the conflict. These anti-Catholic opinions reflect the highly ideological nature of the battle in the union movement. ACTU's positions were consonant with the Bishops' statements of 1940 (*The Church and the Social Order,* 1940), which were generally prounion and liberal on economic issues and conservative on social issues. Some Catholics were much more conservative than ACTU regarding the aggressive upsurge of the CIO.

Fr. Charles Coughlin, an influential priest in a Detroit suburb, played a destructive role in the early Chrysler strikes. ACTU was decisive in rallying the Catholic hierarchy to support the UAW's efforts and to rebuke the popular priest. Radical Catholics, such as Richard Deverall, were ruthlessly attacked by conservative coreligionists and victimized by the CP for his alleged fascist beliefs. Even ACTU members in the UAW were divided on Reuther's campaign for president of the UAW. The role of ACTU in the UAW 1946–1947 elections has probably been exaggerated because observers have wanted to highlight the intense ideological nature of the conflict and the high profile of several ACTU leaders. It is certainly true that the Catholic organization held no such leadership position in the Reuther caucus that the CP held in the ATL caucus.

The emphasis on the ideological nature of the battle within the UAW is easy to understand. Many of the principals were clearly identified with leftist political tendencies. Coupled with that, the Cold War was beginning to emerge as a major element in the postwar world. This international realignment did not mean that the union issues were immediately marked by such a cleavage or that the ideological component was a major determinant of the outcome of the UAW elections. Even on matters of foreign affairs, there was no major difference between the two caucuses. If the Reuther forces had wanted to turn the campaign into an anti-Communist tirade, they would certainly have used the international issues and the intraunion disputes with the Communist-led Local 248 of the UAW and the proposed merger with the Communist-led Farm Equipment Workers (FE). But they did not.

One aspect of the Communist ideology that impeded the party's success in the UAW was their millenarianism. Nothing reinforces a political or religious belief more than the certainty that God, History, or Evolution is on the side of the partisan. There develops a surety of purpose, a conviction of the redemptive power of ideology, and the assurance of victory. The negative aspect of such strongly held beliefs is the intolerance of dissent and the self-righteous brutalizing of opponents.

Alarming allegations were made that were not just violations of factual accuracy or literary felicity but smacked of a Gulag mentality. Fifteen members of the CP-dominated Local 51 sent a telegram to R. J. Thomas at the 1946 convention, urging his reelection and calling for a "repudiation of the three axis partners—Lewis, Dubinsky and Reuther." Apparently, on the off-chance that the reference to the three *axis* partners might be lost on the delegates, two of the fifteen signers sent another telegram saying, in part, that "Reuther has diligently memorized Hitler's *Mein Kampf*'s phrases which caused our best sons to give their blood and lives" (UAW Convention Proceedings, 1946, p. 221). Bereft of political analysis and contemptuous of facts, the promiscuous use of political epithets by the communists excited opposition even among those ordinarily defensive of the CP. The level of invective became so high on the part of the ATL caucus that even pro-ATL observers later acknowledged that "when the controversy did become personalized, the anti-Reuther forces lost rather than gained ground" (Halperin, 1988, p. 128).

As a result, apart from organizational skills, the major contribution of the CP to the ATL cause was not a radical program but a matter of style. Its hectoring, inflammatory rhetoric tended to personalize every issue, turning each very often into a reprise of the battles between the Communists and the Socialists in Germany in the 1930s. This stylistic exuberance also masked the essential moderation of their actions on basic union issues.

The history of Communist activity in the UAW differed considerably from that of some other unions. The CP had a long record of organizing in the auto shops prior to the formation of the UAW. Thus, it had created a political base and had experienced cadres in the industry. In the steel-organizing drive, the Communists were very active, having been hired by John L. Lewis because of their proven record as organizers. However, when the steel industry had been organized, Lewis simply dismissed them, leaving them without a political base in the union. Unlike the United Electrical Workers (UE), the Communists in the UAW had no one in a top leadership position and had not had one since 1939. Before that, the CP had been active in unseating Homer Martin, president at that time of the UAW, and had known members active in the top leadership.

The subsequent activities just prior to World War II and during the war itself were mixed. Before the Soviet Union was invaded, the party called a strike at the North American Aviation plant in California against the express orders of the UAW International leadership, including non-Communist members of their own caucus. This militancy gave way to an extremely conservative support of the war effort after the Nazi invasion of the Soviet Union. At the conclusion of the war, Reuther jumped into the leadership of the GM strike, leaving the CP in support of the ATL caucus, that was not distinguishable from the generally conservative union movement, including the Communist-led unions. In all of these maneuvers by the parties involved, there were critical strategic and tactical considerations that were decisive in the 1946 and 1947 elections.

The treatment of major trade union problems became paramount in the outcome of these elections that Reuther won. The proposed merger with the Farm Equipment Workers, the Allis-Chalmers strike, and other internal union matters were concerns that weighed heavily on the outcome of the election. Given that there were many internal and external impediments to the success of the CP's activities in the UAW, is it likely that they, who subsequently became the stage managers of the ATL caucus, could have conducted themselves on simple union matters in a fashion that would have left themselves less vulnerable to the campaign of Walter Reuther? Probably no minor radical group could have survived the massive assault visited on them by the government in the 1950s, but this was not true of 1946–1947 in the UAW.

In the attempt to sift through the factors that led to Reuther's victory in 1946–1947, the emphasis is on the roles of the Reuther caucus, the Communist Party apparatus in the UAW, and least decisive of the three, the role of ACTU. The other concerns of this study of the factional fight in the UAW are with basic union tactics and strategies of the opposing sides, the quality and texture of the exchanges, concern for civil liberties, the use of the local union's press, and the rights of workers in their own union.

1

THE UAW PRIOR TO 1940

THE IMPACT OF LEFT POLITICS

Stephen Spender, the British poet, joined the Communist Party in 1936. Impressed by the leftist orientation of Spender's book *Forward From Liberalism,* Harry Pollitt, secretary of the British Communist Party, asked to meet with Spender. They disputed about the Moscow Trials and defined their other differences, and Pollitt bluntly asked Spender to join the party. It was during the Communist Party's Popular Front period, an attempt to get all anti-Fascist groups into a common alliance against the Nazis. Party discipline was relaxed, and the Iron Man of the British Communist Party was willing to overlook the discrepancies in their positions in order to recruit the prestigious young poet. As a measure of good faith and as an indication of the party's new-found latitudinarianism, Pollitt offered the pages of the *Daily Worker* to Spender for an article critical of the Communist Party. The deal was struck, Spender joined, the Hammersmith cell of the party was delegated to contact him, and the article was published. But Spender was never contacted, and as he later wrote in explanation, "I heard that several influential Communists had been indignant at my article and also the terms on which I had been admitted into the Party" (Spender, 1951, p. 192). Just as casually as he had joined, he left.

Spender's experience was hardly the greatest political event of that decade. It lacked the drama and implications for British society that the later revelations about Guy Burgess, Donald Maclean, and Kim Philby provided. But, in a way, it was symbolic of the intellectual's absorption in politics in the 1930s. Against the background of the murderous assumption of power by the Nazis and the fratricidal bloodletting in the Soviet Union during the forced collectivization of agriculture and the Moscow Trials, hundreds of thousands of people were to seek political solutions in various movements of the Left and Right. After all, it was reasoned, there had to be a political solution to these horrors that were pushing the world into another great war, culminating in the most depraved attempted genocide that humanity had ever experienced. The correct "line," the correct analysis, could be the remedy for the insanity that the world was experiencing. (Or in the turgid vernacular of the Left: "Comrades, we cannot go forward until we have reached ideological clarity on this question.")

Consequently, workers, middle-class youth, and intellectuals joined or associated themselves with various political tendencies. It is easy to overestimate the influence of those who did so; their power, at least in the United States, was always minimal, but they gave a special character to the age. Thousands joined and dropped out of the Communist Party and its various fronts. The Socialist Party (SP) and the smaller Trotskyist groups and those intellectuals associated with *The Partisan Review* all exerted extraordinary influence on an entire generation of Americans. From the 1920s to the 1950s, hardly any intellectual or literary figures remained untouched by the radical movement.

Spender, too, like thousands of self-mobilized European and American youths, went to Spain either to fight or to see for themselves the defense of the republic. It was part wanderlust, part ideology that sent them, just as, a few years earlier, two sons of a socialist German immigrant, Walter and Victor Reuther, had made their pilgrimage to Europe and the Soviet Union.

The Reuthers left in 1933 for nearly three years of travel in Germany, France, Italy, Austria and England and worked for about eighteen months in the Soviet Union. During that time, unemployment in the United States was estimated to be about twenty-five to thirty-three percent; through open windows in summer, Fr. Coughlin's radio speeches were heard on most Detroit streets; General Motors paid, in an eighteen-month period, a total of nearly a million dollars for spying on their own employees; the National Labor Relations Board (NLRB) later estimated that a minimum of $80 million a year was spent by all of industry for the same purpose. In 1936, the Socialist Party and the Communists failed to work out a common platform, and Nat Ganley, a leading Communist unionist, was "colonized" from New York to Detroit to work in the auto industry. Europe was in the midst of the agony that preceded World War II. The Reuthers arrived in Germany soon after the Reichstag fire and took a Nazi-conducted tour of the site. They heard Benito Mussolini speak in Rome, and they worked in a Russian auto shop. Here one of the major indiscretions of their careers was committed: Victor wrote a letter.

There are about six versions of this letter to Melvin and Gladys Bishop, their Socialist comrades in Detroit. In some of these versions the expression "Carry on the fight for a Soviet America!" appears; in others, it does not. Despite the variety of renderings of this letter, in the main it is a paean to the Soviet Union and a denigration of the Socialists in Germany and England (the attack on the Socialists is not included in all versions). With variation, "Mel and Glad" were informed that "we are more than just sympathetic toward our country ['our country' in one version is rendered 'the Soviet Union'], we are ready to fight for it and its ideals." Subsequent "editors" of the letter showed little understanding of the auto shops: One used the expression "lath kells," which makes no sense until another one is read that speaks of "lathes and kellers," both of which are machines typically found in automobile manufacturing. Victor Reuther admitted to having written a letter to the two friends, including some of the enthusiastic parts about the Soviet Union, but denies that any expression calling for the establishment of a Soviet America was ever written.

The letter appeared in hotly contested UAW local elections for years and was put to rest in the public mind only in the Congressional elections of 1958. Hubert Humphrey, in an effort to head off the reappearance of the letter, asked Senator John McClellan to investigate the matter. McClellan did and concluded that the "unreliability" of Melvin Bishop warranted closing the subject. Reuther's opponents had made a mistake of altering the letter for their immediate political purposes, an act undoubtedly done by different people in differing circumstances. While the dissimilar copies of the letter revealed at least parts of it to be fraudulent, certainly the Reuthers shared with many radicals of the 1930s a tendency to view the Soviet Union as a bastion of socialism and a major hope for the resolution of world problems (Cormier and Eaton, 1970, chap. 10).

In a critique of a fellow Communist's manuscript, Nat Ganley wrote in May 1952:

Propose to eliminate reference to Reuther joining the Communist Party. Although it's true he was a member-at-large and I collected his dues. Reason: we can't prove his membership, Reuther would deny it and possibly sue for libel—We take no particular pride in his membership in our Party and should avoid the charge of inverted redbaiting that Reuther would make against us. . . . Reuther agreed to remain in the Socialist Party and bore from within in agreement with us (course we were foolish to do this). (Ganley Collection, box 6; folder: 1929, UA,WSU).[1]

At the UAW 1941 convention, John Anderson, Local 155, one of the leading Communists in the UAW, complained that some UAW leaders "had taken applause for policies that were worked out in my house with Walter Reuther present" (UAW Convention Proceedings, 1941, p. 702). One Socialist, in 1938, insisted that despite their membership in the Socialist Party the Reuthers used this as a "mere blind for their Stalinoid activities." The author added that Walter Reuther's "outlook on life and labor is thoroughly middle class and his 'radicalism' is largely verbal and very naive" (Stolberg, 1938, p. 165).

Certainly, after April 1938, the split between Reuther and the Communist Party was real and irrevocable. Following a period of some distrust, the division came, not as a result of a principled objection but over the mundane political question of whether the Communist Party was going to support Victor Reuther for office in the Michigan State CIO. The Communist Party reneged on a promise of support, and the past queasiness was solidified into opposition.

Reuther's alleged membership in the Communist Party is of little interest beyond a biographical concern. But it does help to reconstruct a time in which the Communist Party enjoyed an acceptance, with some suspicion or uneasiness, as a legitimate part of the union movement.

Even the usually conservative Association of Catholic Trade Unionists responded to the emotionally charged political atmosphere of the times. At least in its early history, ACTU perceived a need for the discipline and tight organization of the radical groups. In late 1938 or early 1939, Paul Weber, chairperson of the Detroit section, wrote a challenging "Memorandum to ACTU–NY re Intra-Union Organization." Weber's first sentence establishes the nexus of the problem: "It is my opinion that the 'cell' or 'chapter' type of intra-union activity is necessary in some form if we are to be a vital and effective force toward Christian unionism" (ACTU Collection, box 2; folder: ACTU NY—1939–1943, UA,WSU). The critics of ACTU would have felt confirmed in their suspicions about ACTU because of the cell form of organization, but most political tendencies organized in this way.

The Homer Martin split in the UAW precipitated this change of tactics. ACTU members were caught on both sides of the dispute between Martin and the Unity caucus, which eventually included all the political elements, all the radical groups, and the major union figures. Martin finally left the UAW, taking a small minority of members into the American Federation of Labor (AFL). Because of the activities of the Lovestoneites (a dissident Communist Party split-off) and the Communist Party, the Martin split impressed on ACTU leadership the vitality of self-conscious minorities within the union movement. Weber concluded: "I think it is time we recognized that unions, however much we may deplore the fact, are run by minorities, and the best hope of any existing union is to be run by an enlightened, honest, Christian minority" (ACTU Collection, box 2; folder: ACTU NY—1939–43, UA,WSU).

Weber became eloquent about the necessity of dedication to a doctrine that transcended mundane unionism and inspired a vision of a new society. Continuing his philippic on cells, he said that what was needed was

a minority passionately devoted to something *positive,* something which has the qualities connoted by the words "revolutionary" and "utopian." . . . Men sense the fact that there is something not superficially but *fundamentally* wrong with the existing system. . . . They sense the need of a revolution, . . . the passing of an outworn order. . . .

The power of the Marxist groups lies in the fact that they, alone, utilize this hunger for justice. . . . Consequently, many thousands . . . follow Marxist leaders . . . for want of any other leadership. . . .

That other leadership, I believe, is for us to supply. The green flag of Christian hope must supplant the red flag of Marxism. (Emphases in original) (ACTU Collection, box 2; folder: ACTU NY, 1939–1943, UA,WSU)

The millenarian tone of this statement gave way to a more sober judgment in 1947 after the Communist-backed slate won in the election in Local 600 of the UAW.

Actually, there is no mystery about it at all.

The simple fact is that workers do not elect their leaders upon ideological grounds. They make their decisions upon very practical economic considerations. . . . A corrupt political machine that gets Uncle Billy out of jail when the cops pinch him, that fixes the streets in front of the right houses, and that passes out jobs where they are needed, will triumph time and again over a reform ticket which merely appeals to the conscience of the voters on high civic grounds. (Weber, 1947, p. 6)

Weber had figuratively moved from Karl Marx to John Commons.

Several favorable factors worked for the Communists in the early UAW days. In the first place, the political context had changed. The New Deal, despite its length on promise and shortness on performance, had created a new mood of optimism in the country. In the past, the strikes called by the AFL and the Communist Party (such as the one in Gastonia, North Carolina, for example) were desperation efforts, with small hope of success. Now there was a sense of buoyancy. John L. Lewis was rumbling in the councils of the AFL. It was obvious that significant change was possible, even in Detroit and Pittsburgh, those bastions of industrial antiunionism.

In addition, the Communists had developed considerable skills during their radical permutations, particularly in the attempts to organize the Auto Workers Union (AWU). The knowledge they had obtained through these heroic years prior to the CIO were invaluable as the AFL faltered in its halfhearted attempt to organize the auto shops. It had experienced cadres in place, men such as William Weinstone, Nat Ganley, Max Salzman, Billy Allan, Walter Moore, Bud Simon, Joe Devitt, Wyndham Mortimer, Bob Travis, John Anderson, Bill McKie, and hundreds of lesser known, not openly identified party members. John L. Lewis, recognizing the skills and selflessness of the Communists, deliberately sought out party members for staff jobs as the CIO embarked on organizing the industrial unions, on the theory that it was the hunter and not the dog who got the bird.

Still, the disadvantages that the Communist Party suffered were many. The major one was the political conservatism of the country. Despite the yeasty new radicalism of the 1930s and the success of the New Deal, a sizable section of the population was extremely (often violently) anti-Communist and very conservative. Nativism was rampant and openly racist; pro-Fascist groups flourished. In addition, the workers had an ideology of their own. It was, as Brendan Sexton noted in an interview, a kind of left-wing New Dealism, with an extraordinary devotion to Franklin D. Roosevelt (Sexton, 1986). But they were not revolutionary; otherwise, radicals would not have hidden their political affiliations.

Despite their individual, personal popularity, radicals did conceal their ideological positions. Thomas E. Linton notes that it was not the absence of a political philosophy that deterred an expression of an integrated criticism of the social system. But "since the bulk of the union members did not share their views, the left groups did not openly emphasize their political values" (Linton, 1965, p. 3). Ideology did motivate many radicals to extraordinary efforts of self-sacrifice and devotion. This devotion is what compelled the support of the rank and file, not the belief system itself. For the radicals, the Socialist heaven may have been ahead, but strait was the way and narrow the gate.

But not all the difficulties encountered by the Communists were those inherent in the political and social fabric of the United States. Some were of their own making. The Communist Party could not enter the American union movement with clean hands because there were too many radicals and liberals around who were aware of the horrors of the Moscow Trials, the Moscow-Berlin Pact, and the forced collectivization of agriculture in the Soviet Union, which led to millions of deaths by a deliberate policy of starvation and other "excesses" (as some apologists for the Soviet Union now call them) of the Stalin period.

There was also the astonishing record of their gyrating political line. The Soviet Union's perception of world affairs, created by isolation, even intervention by foreign troops in their country, determined the actions of the American party. After the successful Bolshevik revolution, the Communists had a euphoric belief in the "revolutionary offensives" of the great working-class parties of Europe. This was the "First Period."

By 1924, after the failure of several European uprisings, the Soviet Union developed a new position of the "Stabilization of Capitalism," the Second Period. After the Communist International announced the Second Period, the Communist Party had a consistent line of "boring from within" the existing unions and, following Lenin's dictum in *Left Wing Communism: An Infantile Disorder,* was opposed to creating "Red" unions outside of the existing union structure.

Then, in 1928, came the dramatic "Third Period," presaging, according to Communist theoreticians, the "death agony of capitalism." The world, the Sixth Congress of the Comintern maintained, was in a prerevolutionary situation: The collapse of capitalism was not only inevitable but imminent. This analysis called for radical changes in strategy, particularly in unions. The new union vehicle in the United States was the Trade Union Unity League (TUUL). In Orwellian language, this "Unity League" was really divisive of the union movement. The old aversion to working within the conservative AFL unions held by some Communists now had full sway.

By 1935, it was apparent to everyone, even the Communist Party, that capitalism was not going to disappear to be followed by a Socialist millennium. In fact, the Nazis seemed more likely to succeed. In response to these new conditions, the Seventh Congress of the Comintern inaugurated the "Popular Front" period. "Communism is Twentieth Century Americanism," Earl Browder later intoned. In one of their most extraordinary about-faces, the Communist Party sought acceptance, not as a vanguard party but as just one of the boys. The anticipated European war ceased to be an "imperialist war" and became a peoples' war against fascism. Traditional bourgeois parties were sought as political allies, eventually Roosevelt was supported for president,[2] monarchs were solicited for support, a leading French cardinal of the Catholic church was committed to cooperation with the Communists, and the Socialists (theretofore "social Fascists") became desired comrades.

The Popular Front permitted them to exercise their skills and stringent discipline to good advantage in the organizing drive of the new CIO. The Socialist Party was in almost total disarray. It was undisciplined and held to only one major tenet, support of the party's electoral activity. It offered small opposition to the Communist Party. The other radical political sects were minuscule, and Catholic liberals had neither political strength nor even an organization until the late 1930s. Thus, there was little competition from a highly ideological, devoted radical group. The Communist Party emerged with an acceptance in the union movement that was in violent contrast to its position in 1950.

Joseph Stalin brought this love feast to an abrupt close on August 24, 1939. Apparently without even notifying the Comintern member parties, he signed a nonaggression pact with Germany, permitting the latter to invade Poland from the west while the Soviet Union invaded from the east. England and France declared war on Germany, and another dazzling shift took place. The war again became an imperialist war, and England was proclaimed the "chief enemy of the international working class." Front groups that had been for a Popular Front now had to be scrapped and others created. The consternation within the party soon settled down. The Communist Party unionist experienced a twice-born leftism. The intransigent John L. Lewis became a hero once more. Sidney Hillman, the Socialist trade unionist who was prointervention, became the bête noire of the Communist Party, along with Franklin D. Roosevelt, whose administration initiated a series of harassing legal actions against the Communist Party, including jailing Earl Browder, the Communist Party leader. The defections from the party at this time were enormous, for many anti-Fascist radicals were appalled at the Moscow-Berlin Pact.

Two events solved this uncomfortable position for the Communists, neither, for a change, of their own doing: On June 22, 1941, Germany invaded the Soviet Union, and on December 7, 1941, the Japanese bombed Pearl Harbor. Again the Communist Party was caught by surprise. Anti-Communist leaders in the UAW had dozens of stories to tell about how the obligatory change in Communist Party line was affected. Local 174, Reuther's home local, issued a three-page flyer, "The Line Has Changed Again," consisting of two resolutions submitted by Local 51, UAW, a Communist Party stronghold, to the Wayne County (Detroit) CIO Council. The first was received June 23, 1941, calling on the CIO to convene an antiwar congress "drawing together all the forces and allies of Labor in a concerted struggle to get America out and keep America out of the war." Local 174 pointed out that Adolf Hitler declared war on the Soviet Union the day after the resolution was mailed. Undaunted, Local 51 promptly sent a second resolution calling for support of the Soviet Union, "the only Socialist nation in the world," and condemning Hitler for trying "to extend Fascism and its barbarous practices." To UAW activists, the abrupt shift provided one more example of the CP's cynicism (UAW Local 174 Collection, box 21; folder: Factionalism, UA,WSU).

The new prowar line extended even to race matters. After the German invasion, A. Philip Randolph was excoriated by the *Daily Worker* for threatening a march on Washington to ensure that African-American workers would not be discriminated against in the high-paying defense jobs. Roosevelt reluctantly acceded to Randolph's pressure, promulgating Executive Order 8802 forbidding hiring discrimination for those companies with government contracts (Cochran, 1977, p. 227).

The Communists lost ground with some radicals and part of the population at this time, but the war period was one of the most successful times they had experienced. They recruited more members during the war than at any other period, and their influence in the unions expanded. "Everything for Victory" became the rallying cry. They were the most ardent antistrike element in the country. Even the conservatives were amazed at their restraint.

The brooding presence of World War II that had created the intense radicalization of social groups also affected the internal life of the UAW. Many of the participants on both sides had been members of various of the Left parties. Even those such as R. J. Thomas and George Addes who were not members had been marked by the debates and the quality of Left critical thought. The war's close brought an end to the radical identification of most of the activists, but the ambiance remained. The idealism, the imagination, and even some of the horrors of the Left experience pervaded the actions of the caucuses, imparting a special character to the contests.

EARLY ORGANIZING HISTORY

At the completion of World War I, Detroit, City of the Straits, stood poised for a decade of frantic growth. Formerly the city of lumber, furs, and missionaries, it now made cars and, in pursuit of that end, fought unions. The antiunion "American Plan" had as many and as powerful adherents in auto as it did in the steel industry. The Palmer raids, led by the attorney general of the United States—A. Mitchell Palmer—who gave them their name, had destroyed the Industrial Workers of the World (IWW), severely damaged the Socialist Party, and by several terribly anticivil libertarian trials, successfully kept the Communist Party underground for a long period.

The American Plan was touted as the embodiment of American ideals of freedom. In action, it was sheer corporate terrorism. Despite stiffening business attitudes, unions felt some strength as a result of the government's efforts to woo them during the war to ensure uninterrupted production.

The steel industry, the bastion of the open shop, became the first battle-ground. The AFL union in steel was ineffective and bound to the craft union approach. However, there was some optimism among unionists. John Fitzpatrick, head of the Chicago AFL, had successfully organized the butcher workmen on an industrial base in Chicago. He got the National AFL to establish a committee to organize the steel industry, of which he became chairman. William Z. Foster, ex-Wobbly, ex-syndicalist, became the secretary.

Foster, one of the greatest labor organizers of the time, enjoyed the confidence of the AFL leadership despite his known radicalism. He had created the Trade Union Educational League (TUEL), dedicated to working within the existing union structure, educating to radicalize American workers. Later, the Communist Party, in an amazing coup, secretly recruited Foster, with the promise that the TUEL would become the trade union agency of the Communist Party.

The structure of the work force in the steel industry was a forbidding obstacle to organizing. There were dozens of nationality groups employed in the unskilled sectors of the industry, most of them largely without knowledge of English. The skilled sector was dominated by English-Scottish workers who enjoyed a wage above what the government claimed was necessary to sustain a minimum level of comfort. That comparative affluence, however, did not dampen their support for the strike. The overall wages for the industry were below the government standards for a minimum level of comfort in seventy-two percent of the cases. The unskilled had wages below the government budget for minimum *subsistence*. The workday was twelve hours.

Thinking to take advantage of the high profits in the industry, Fitzpatrick and Foster created a council of twenty-four craft unions that might have some jurisdictional claim on steelworkers. The strategy was to attack the perimeter of the industry, Youngstown, Cleveland, and Buffalo, rather than a direct attack on Pittsburgh, the center, even though there was considerable pressure to strike there also. Throughout this preparation, the company refused to meet. The federal government vacillated, and President Woodrow Wilson refused Samuel Gompers's request to help arrange a conference with U.S. Steel until just before the strike, when he asked for a delay. By that time, the pressure for action was too great, and the strike began.

It followed the path of many pre-CIO strikes: Pennsylvania became a police state. Beatings, shootings, and denial of civil liberties were commonplace, the police and the courts openly sided with the company, Foster was attacked for a syndicalist pamphlet he had long since repudiated, red-baiting was rampant, African-Americans were used as strike breakers, ethnic differences were exploited, and the whole panoply of native reaction was employed. The terror, beatings, and jailings, plus the enormous financial resources of the company, were the major reasons for defeating the 370,000 strikers, but the AFL did not offer much help (only $6,322 in contributions, although other national unions gave generously), and the friction between the craft-oriented, twenty-four-member committee hampered decisive action. In January 1920, the strike was canceled. It took nearly two decades, under entirely different circumstances, for steel to be finally organized.

The defeat of the 1919 steel strike was the last major effort of the AFL to break out of its craft orientation and to organize the industrial worker. In 1921, the bane of union activity, a depression, struck the economy. Only long-established unions managed to survive this economic setback and extend their gains. The Amalgamated Clothing Workers (ACW), the International Ladies' Garment Workers' Union (ILGWU), and the printing trades unions succeeded as others failed. By 1924, unions had fallen to seventy percent of their 1920 levels.

Farm prices broke in 1921. While agricultural products went down, the cost of manufactured goods stayed up, catching farmers in the recurrent battle between the cost of goods they sold and those they purchased. As farmers suffered, the courts continued their assault on unions. Labor had rejoiced when the Clayton Antitrust Act had passed that specifically exempted unions from antitrust provisions of the Sherman Act. Injunctions against picketing and strikes were to be used only in cases where irreparable damage to property could be established. However, injunctions continued despite the clear intent of the law. In the *American Steel Foundries v. Tri-City Trades Council* (1921), all picketing was declared illegal except where it was limited to one person, picketing peacefully.

These new times created two antiunion responses from industrialists: the "American Plan" and welfare capitalism. The latter used newly created industrial relations departments to introduce profit sharing, stock distribution, life and disability insurance, and pensions. All provisions of these plans were, of course, securely in the hands of management; pensions could be discontinued without any control by workers, for example. But given the depressed circumstances of the times, welfare capitalism was largely successful as a device to keep an already frightened working class in line.

The American Plan was the diabolical side of the relatively benign, paternalistic welfare system. The American Plan meant open shop, no unions under any circumstances, regardless of the financial cost (manufacturers spent millions of dollars to fight unions), cost in workers' lives, lynchings, murderous assaults on women and children, or cost of corrupting the judicial system in America. After the war, the companies started to use the Hitchman Coal case (*Hitchman,* 1917, p. 229), rendered by the Supreme Court in 1917, that validated the yellow-dog contract. New employees were forced to sign a contract that they did not belong to a union and that they would not join one or seek to get their fellow workers to join during their period of employment. Under these contracts, in effect, all strikes became illegal. Thirty or forty years later, even after the great organizing days of the CIO, old-time unionists recalled the days of the yellow-dog contracts with loathing. When the courts could not control, industry contrived other means. Strikebreaking became a large-scale, non–cottage industry. Millions were spent for espionage and the recruiting of scabs.

In 1922, the Communists (now called the Workers Party [WP]) stepped into this arena by taking a major step of joining the Auto Workers Union, led by William Logan, a Socialist Party member. The auto industry in 1924 had a work force that was eighty-five percent unskilled, ten percent skilled, and five percent inspectors. This fact was almost an insurmountable obstacle to the AFL, with its craft orientation. Although the AWU was an industrial union, it had nowhere near the resources necessary to successfully organize the autoworkers. But the CP did make effective use of shop newspapers, such as the *Ford Worker*. They were short, punchy messages about shop conditions that had a great reception among the rank and file. The CP supported the establishment of a Labor Party, and was supportive of the Soviet Union and Nicola Sacco and Bartolomeo Vanzetti.

The Communists were more activist than was Logan, the SPer. The latter had a position of organizing first and then striking. The Communist Party wanted to use strikes to educate the autoworkers and, consequently, was for strike activity first, hoping to organize members out of the conflict. This was not the only difference between Logan and the Communist Party. Radicals had for years debated the establishment of a Labor Party that would stand to the left of the Democrats and the Republicans, but not necessarily making a primary issue of a Socialist program. The Labor Party was to be reformist rather than revolutionary; it was to appeal to all sections of the society, not primarily to the industrial working class.

The Socialist Party was on doctrinal grounds opposed to a Labor Party. The Communist Party held different positions, depending on the times. The AFL was opposed to aligning its self to any party. In 1924, the situation changed. In the face of union-organizing failures, American labor often turned to political action for possible remedy. When employer resistance defeated efforts to organize, there was always the possibility that a political party and legislative action might produce results not obtainable through collective bargaining.

The Teapot Dome affair had severely damaged the Republican Party, and William McAdoo, the presumed likely Democrat to be nominated, had not himself escaped being tainted by the scandal. Into this breach, in 1924, stepped Robert La Follette, the leading Progressive in America. The radical unionists in the Conference for Progressive Political Action; independent radical unionists, like John Fitzpatrick in Chicago and William Mahoney in Minnesota; the Farmer-Labor types; and even the AFL and the Socialist Party began to believe a labor progressive alliance could field an independent party with La Follette as the candidate.

The AFL threw over its studied neutrality in politics, and the Socialist Party, contrary to its usual position, supported the candidacy of La Follette. The Communist Party, after some bizarre maneuvering that managed to alienate everyone, came out against this coalition and ran its own ticket. It got 33,000 votes and La Follette got nearly 5 million, an excellent start for a third-party candidate. But the expectations of American politics and the system of patronage distribution make it almost obligatory for a third party to jump immediately to become the second party. The AFL immediately went back to its nonpartisan stance, and radicals reverted to working within the established parties. The Communist Party failed to support La Follette, fielded its own ticket, and savagely attacked La Follette in very personal terms. After several years of operating in a context that recognized the value of a Progressive ticket, this decision had nothing to do with the American political scene. Again, the Comintern's shadow was felt over the American Communists. The Communist Party had several different factions, divided, as it often was, over the battle between the politicals and the trade unionists. This was a common split in all radical groups. The sanctity of the political line was often challenged by the more pragmatic union activists. The latter had considerable political power and, at a later date, were often heads of unions with millions of members; the former were the keepers of the holy writ with a limited number of party members.

Incapable of resolving the matter internally, the various factions repaired to Moscow for guidance. The political situation in the Soviet Union determined the outcome of the American dispute, as it often did. Stalin, Grigory Zinoviev, and Lev Borisovich Kamenev were in earnest battle with Leon Trotsky, who viewed this effort of the Americans to support a "bourgeois" candidate as right-wing capitulation. Stalin and company decided to support the smallest of the American factions that was opposed to support for non-Socialist third parties. Trotsky won a Pyrrhic victory, and the American Communist Party suffered a disastrous defeat that delayed its entrance into American politics (Howe and Coser, 1957, pp. 136–137).

In Detroit, the failure of the Communist Party to support the Progressives did not have much significance. The head of the Auto Workers Union, as a Socialist Party member, supported La Follette. The Communist Party in the union did not. But the consequences were minuscule. Logan was no match for the skill and numbers of the Communist Party, and it eventually took over the union completely.

The major loss for the Communist Party in the 1924 campaign was the opportunity to strike an independent role for an American Labor Party based on American conditions. Along the way, it totally alienated its staunchest allies in the union movement, Fitzpatrick and Mahoney, and created considerable distrust about its reliability as a political partner. But the damage was not irreparable. While the Socialist Party did not clothe itself in the chiliastic mantle as did the Communist Party, it, too, was caught in troubles of its own making: the sanctity of the Socialist Party's electoral activity. Dogma, doctrine, even analysis, went out of the window as long as the members supported the Socialist Party ticket in campaigns. By 1936 and 1940, the most vital and active of the party members were involved in the union movement where the political line was to support Franklin Delano Roosevelt and the New Deal. As a consequence, most SPers quietly dropped out of the party, resulting in a political cachexia from which the party never recovered.

Political purity versus tough-minded pragmatism of the union party faithful has plagued most political movements in the Industrial Age. Daniel De Leon, leader of the Socialist Labor Party (SLP) (dubbed an "impossibilist" by Eugene Debs), hovered like a vestal virgin over the sacred flame of Marxian socialism in the latter part of the nineteenth century. He forbade any party member from holding office in a non-Socialist union. The result was that members had little influence if they did not belong to one of the short-lived SLP unions. The 1948 presidential election re-created this problem for the Communist Party. The political leadership of the party was for all-out support of Henry Wallace's third-party candidacy for president. The Communist Party trade unionists recognized that such activity would lead to a major split with the CIO, a situation that they wanted to avoid. The battle was particularly devastating for the United Electrical Workers with its predominantly top Communist leadership.

The advent of the "Third Period" of intense radical activity had little impact on the Communist Party's performance in the auto industry. While unions were created under the umbrella of the TUUL (none very successful), the Auto Workers Union was simply folded into the TUUL. Since there was no other union active in auto, it meant that there was no serious rival in the industry that might cause conflict. The center of activity was in several convulsive strikes, marked by great courage, principally in Gastonia, North Carolina.

The logic of the Communists was simple: If U.S. capitalism is in a state of impending collapse, then ordinary trade union objectives are not adequate to the situation. Strikes must have a political purpose beyond wages, hours, and working conditions; they must be harbingers of the coming revolution.

While the Gastonia strike was a failure, probably no union could have succeeded in this brutal southern mill town in 1929. But there was the lingering suspicion that the political activity of the Communist Party, based on furthering the fortunes of its party, was the real motivation for the strike—not the immediate welfare of those terribly exploited mill hands.

There was a horrifying innocence about the Communist Party's activities during the Third Period. Capitalism is doomed, the line went, and the time for action is now. It was to be a time of "the electrification of the masses," one of the worst examples of volitionism in Marxism. The model was Lenin's successful revolution, not the vacillating Mensheviks and other radicals. In fact, the Socialists now became the principal enemy—they became "social Fascists." Rather than a united front against fascism, the Communists propagated the slogan "After Hitler, us." The united front proposed was from "below," not a coalition of separate and differing parties but an attempt to recruit the members of rival parties into the Communist Party—hardly a prescription that would lead to confidence in later Popular Front attempts. A series of national efforts were initiated: African-Americans in the United States were defined as an "oppressed *nation,*" not a minority group, and a Black republic was proposed; unemployed councils were started; the defense of the Scottsboro "boys" became a prime party effort; and the Socialists were constantly vilified.

In Detroit, radical and union activity proceeded on several fronts: organizing the unemployed and union organizing among those working in the shops. The most striking achievement of the Communist Party was the Ford Hunger March in 1932. The struggling AWU and the Detroit Unemployed Council called for a march on Ford's leviathan Rouge Plant in Dearborn, Michigan. The Dearborn police and the Ford servicemen acted predictably. In the course of an otherwise peaceful march, the police opened fire and four young Communist leaders were killed and scores were wounded in the indiscriminate shooting. Of course, no police were killed or even wounded. Thousands of Detroiters joined or lined Woodward Avenue down the center of Detroit for the funeral march. The AFL paper, the *Detroit Labor News*, fittingly remarked, "The outrageous murdering of workers at the Ford Motor Plant in Dearborn on Monday has cast a stain on this community that will remain as a disgrace for many years" (Sugar, 1980, p. 71).

Unemployed councils created a problem for radicals, Socialist, Communist, or other. It was possible to invigorate the unemployed for short mobilizations but difficult to create a sustained movement capable of continuing activity. (Some radicals argued: Comrades, workers can only be organized at the point of production.) Union organizing did not fare much better. There were dramatic successes in 1934: Auto-Lite in Toledo (led by the followers of A. J. Muste), Maritime on the West Coast (led by Harry Bridges and the Communist Party), and Minneapolis (led by the Trotskyists in the Teamsters). These strikes were unmitigated class warfare and led to the formation of a strong union movement in these areas, but they did not lead to the formation of national unions capable of organizing the giants of auto or steel.

The results of the Communist Party's activities in Detroit were also mixed. The party was dominated by the various nationality groups, most of whom left the Socialist Party after the split following the Russian Revolution. While they provided a base in the auto shops, they also tended to isolate the party. There were some dramatic strikes in the 1930s that reflected the frustration of autoworkers and were harbingers of the organizing that was to follow the formation of the CIO, but these efforts did little more than create cadres and educate rank and filers to union activity.

The Communists led strikes at Fisher Body in 1930 (lost) and at Briggs in 1933 (partially successful). However, they began to trip over their own dogma of the Third Period. Other radical groups were very active in these strikes—the Socialist Party, IWW, Musteites, and the Proletarian Party—but the Communist Party called meetings at which only party members spoke, ignoring the contributions of other involved groups. Typical of the Third Period, Norman Thomas of the Socialist Party was reviled as a "Social Fascist."[3] Eventually, the Communist Party was purged from the strike committee in response to genuine dissatisfaction with its sectarianism and the ground swell of red-baiting that occurred in the general community, fanned, naturally, by Detroit's newspapers.

The activity was intense in Detroit, Toledo, and Cleveland. The Mechanics Educational Society of America (MESA), initially a tool and die union, was formed and worked, uneasily, with the Communist Party. The latter, among other criticisms, accused Matt Smith, MESA Socialist leader, of relying too heavily on the National Labor Relations Board, which was part of the Third Period litany. In the frenzy of this period, the Communist Party lashed out at the New Deal for its alleged "fascist tendencies" and attacked all New Deal legislation, the Wagner Act, the NLRB, and so on. This permitted William Green at the first convention of the UAW, then in the AFL, to say of the Communists in his address: "Who spoke for workers at the time of the Wagner Act hearings? Was it the uplifters . . . who speak with the persuasive, soft voice of Jacob, but extend to you the hand of Esau?" (UAW Convention Proceedings, 1935, p. 18).

In the mid-1930s, there was a happy coincidence of political developments for the Communists and others attempting to organize auto: John L. Lewis left the AFL and formed the CIO with other sympathetic AFL unionists, and the draconian Third Period gave way to the Popular Front for the Communist Party itself. All the rage and heroism of the rank and file, plus the skills and dedication of the radicals, had not been sufficient to crack the auto industry. Now the feeble efforts of the AFL gave way to the energy of Lewis's dedication to industrial unionism.

But the political problems of the Communist Party were not over. Radicals in the union movement, particularly the various orders of Socialists, had lain like an indigestible lump in the conservative stomachs of the union officialdom. Even John L. Lewis, who would consciously use the Communists as organizers in the early days of the CIO, showed no such tolerance in his own United Mine Workers (UMW) union. At the 1926 convention of the UMW, Lewis, from the chair, launched an attack on William Z. Foster, Communist Party union leader, who was sitting in the balcony, and in 1927, the union barred Communists from union membership. This precedent affected the UAW from its beginning. The first convention of the UAW, convened by the AFL in Detroit, August 1935, passed a resolution in the waning moments of the final day that was reported in the Convention Proceedings in this manner:

Delegate Distefano, (Local) 19382, offered a motion that the convention go on record condemning the communistic centers of the world in meddling with the internal affairs of this country and commending Secretary of State Hull in sending the note to Russia, condemning the activities of the Communists in this country. The motion was seconded and carried. (p. 116)

There is no record of a debate. It appeared to be a perfunctory AFL political gesture, almost an afterthought of a convention minutes from adjourning.

At the Second Convention, a special convention called to create an autonomous UAW, Francis J. Dillon, a William Green appointee, resigned as president, and Homer Martin was elected. A resolution was introduced stating that "communism is contrary to the laws of the United States government" and "that the International notify all its affiliated locals to immediately expel from membership all known Communists." The Resolutions Committee recommended nonconcurrence. A substitute motion was made "that no known Communist be permitted to hold office." It was amended to read "proven" Communist, debated extensively, and referred back to the committee where it died (UAW, Convention, 2nd [Special] Convention, 1936, UA,WSU).

Rose Pesotta, an ILGWU organizer who had been active in the Akron sit-downs, was a guest speaker, and she had a few words about political dissent:

I say while we work for a living whether IWW, or anarchist, or Socialist or Fascist, or what-not, once an employer knows he can exploit us he will, and we in the Labor Movement should not create artificial divisions in our own ranks. A trade union is an economic organization, and anyone who earns a living by working for wages has a place within his own organization. (p. 146)

She went on to attack the Italian Fascists in the ILGWU as being more destructive than the Communists. Another delegate made a motion some time later that the UAW members "express our unalterable opposition to Fascism, Nazism and Communism and all other movements intended to distract the attention of the membership of the Labor Movement from the primary objectives of unionism" (p. 232). It carried unanimously. But the convention was not through with the Communists. Homer Martin, the newly elected president, revealed that a letter signed "The Communist Party" had been circulated, endorsing Martin and Wyndham Mortimer for the two top positions in the union. The letter also said, "With these two men there can be but one thing happen, that is, a close knit organization that will enforce the demands of workers through the only medium the bosses know—STRIKE" (pp. 72–73). There was also introduced a letter from Earl Browder, head of the Communist Party, branding it as a fake (p. 74). The purpose of the forgery was to reinforce the belief of the rank and file that the Communist Party was strike happy, a designation it neither wanted nor deserved, and to alienate George Addes who would have been running against Mortimer.

The two resolutions that were introduced in 1935 and 1936 represent the two extremes of anti–Communist Party sentiments in the UAW, and the consequences for civil liberties were extensive. The draconian one that would expel all Communist members was the greatest threat to the membership. The one that was adopted expressing opposition to fascism, Nazism, and communism was a legitimate expression of the political sentiment of a union. The substitute motion barring known Communists from holding office completed the spectrum of actions against the Communist Party. The first one, which would expel communists from the union, was the greatest threat to the civil liberties of workers, representing an attitude that holding a job was dependent on political orthodoxy. The substitute motion prohibiting dissidents from holding office was illogical. If a worker can be a Fascist, Nazi, or Communist and still hold a job, why should the choice of representation be limited? Both of these positions perpetuated the myth that unions were only interested in wages, hours, and working conditions, and they pandered to the fear of outside groups, including ACTU and the Socialist Party, that some autoworkers held.

It is a difficult educational process to insist, in the face of the suspicions of the membership, that workers have a right to hold dissenting political positions, to propagate them, and to elect officers on the basis of their programs. It was never clearly asserted, in a union Bill of Rights, for example, that any party or religious group can legitimately advance political programs in the union. If churches take political positions, they are within their constitutional rights, but they endanger, in the process, the immunity that society accords to the clergy. Without a specific recognition in the union movement of the right of dissent, the alternative was demagogy that located an "outside" group within the opposition caucus and exposed them, rather than debating a program on its merits.

The 1937 UAW convention was the "unity" convention. Having just split from the AFL, the delegates were apprehensive about another such schism. Greetings were read from two unionists in prison, Tom Parry, UAW organizer, in a Canadian jail for strike activity, and "Thirty One Nine Twenty-one, San Quentin Prison" (Tom Mooney) expressing hope for a harmonious convention. The unity theme was so pervasive that a resolution was made to abolish national caucuses in the union. Walter Reuther spoke on the proposal: "There is no need in an organization as democratic as ours for the formation of cliques prior to the Convention, to further their own selfish political purposes—and that goes for both sides. . . . they [caucus members] would assume sole responsibility for any split which might occur in our organization" (UAW Convention Proceedings, 1937, p. 130). Dubinsky, that old "red-baiter," reflected the fear of a split in his remarks when he defended the Communists, a somewhat unusual role for him. They had the right, Dubinsky maintained, to union membership and participation in union activities "as long as they place the interests of their fellow workers above the interests of a political party" (p. 202). Dubinsky closed his speech pleading for "unanimous approval, unanimous decisions, unanimous actions, and unanimous spirit at this convention" (p. 203).

Even with all of the pressure from the officers, an anti-Communist resolution was submitted, stating that the UAW is opposed to the "aims and principles of the Communist Party and to the Communist Party itself" (Appendix III, p. 38). There were also resolutions calling for an embargo on arms to Germany and Italy because of the Spanish Civil War. Reuther's Local 174 had four resolutions adopted, one denouncing fascism and three separate ones in support of the

Scottsboro defendants, an ambulance for the Spanish Loyalists, and the need for more African-American organizers. Again an anti–Communist Party resolution surfaced:

Contrary to the Strumpet Press theory that Communism is the dominating influence in the CIO . . . we . . . are opposed to Communism and to any other of the so-called "isms" except real, true Americanism, and that we believe in the Capitalistic Profits System, if and when it will allow the laborers to receive their just share of profits. (p. 69)

It did not pass. The rank and file, politically innocent for the most part, were resentful of the attacks on the union for being "red" dominated. Since they had no influence over the press, they attempted to prove their virtue by passing such motions.

The advent of the Popular Front, initiated by the Seventh Congress of the Communist International in 1935, meant a break with the tiresome Stalinist version of Marxism and the extreme sectarianism of the now-retired Third Period. A succession of front groups were established: the American League for Peace and Democracy, the National Negro Congress, American Student Union, and the American Youth Congress—all of which enjoyed wide popular support in political, academic, and union circles that ordinarily would have no truck with Communists. The Spanish Civil War and the fear of Nazism felt by radicals, liberals, and workers helped catapult the Communist Party into a new-found popularity. It was a heady experience, and it meant respectability, increased recruiting, and the sweet taste of success. All of this coincided with the beginnings of the great drives of the UAW, particularly the Flint sit-downs.

These were the salad days of the Communist Party's activities in the unions. The problems they encountered grew out of a solid conservative American resistance to radical ideas and to their own, all too frequent, idiotic behavior. There is little likelihood that without a solid mass base in the American working class the CPUSA (Communist Party—United States of America) could evolve a course independent of the Soviet Union. It was not in the anatomical perspective of the Third International that tails wag dogs. Given the small probability of an independent course of action, it still does not explain the "inflexibility" of the American Communists, as they later, overgenerously, described their activity. If there was slippage in applying the party line to every aspect of union life, there was no lack of enthusiasm for adherence to the Communist International's main positions.

After the second International Convention, the UAW soon joined the CIO. But it faced enormous battles, both external and internal. Despite the ineffectiveness of the Wagner Act, which was constantly facing court battles, workers believed that President Roosevelt wanted them to organize. Accurately or not, it was the first time that workers felt that government was, for a change, on their side. In addition, the figure of John L. Lewis loomed like a benign presence over organizing efforts, instilling confidence and militancy. As a leavening in this dough stood the radicals with the Communists, the largest group. For at least a short while, the Socialists, Communists, Proletarian Party members, Trotskyists, and independents put aside their doctrinal differences and applied themselves to organizing.

In Midland Steel, John Anderson, early Communist Party union leader, had won a dazzling victory. Walter Reuther, president of Local 174, with less than 100 members, called a sit-down in Kelsey Hayes, producer of dies for Ford Motor Company, who tried to take the dies from the plant. Barricades were established, and the effort was defeated. The victory pushed 174's membership from less than 100 to 35,000 within a year. In the fever that gripped Detroit, sit-downs occurred in dime stores, restaurants, parts suppliers, bakeries, large plants, and small plants. A new labor technique was rediscovered that found its greatest expression against General Motors in Flint.

This was drama of the highest order, starting at the end of December 1936; the strike was over February 11, 1937. There were plots and counterplots, deceit, threats of massive violence, judicial and police perfidy, involvement of women and children, and the insouciant workers that expropriated (at least temporarily) the expropriators and howled in disbelief when GM threatened to shut off the water and electricity. The weapons were the Flint police, well armed, the National Guard, car hinges, machine guns, bolts, tear gas, espionage, a women's brigade, picketing children, injunctions, and all levels of government. GM was granted injunctive relief, and the courts ordered the strikers out. Lee Pressman, CIO counsel, discovered that the issuing judge owned a quarter of a million dollars of GM stock, and the injunction was voided.

The company created a front group, the Flint Alliance, and after tentatively agreeing to negotiate with the UAW and not with the Alliance, GM reneged and said that it would negotiate with both of them. The UAW discovered GM's alteration, and the strike was back on. There were so many company spies that the union made use of them. The UAW leadership let it be known that they were going to march on Chevy Plant 9, confident that the stoolies would report that to the company. They immediately reinforced that plant while the main UAW march was against Chevy 4, which they took, stopping all Chevrolet production. Women, wearing red berets, battled cops, carried food, and broke windows in the plants so that the tear gas fired inside by the police could escape.

The politicking was incredible. Frank Murphy, a liberal democrat, had recently been elected governor and was not disposed to fire on strikers. The new UAW president, Homer Martin, was driving everyone crazy by his erratic behavior. Lewis and John Brophy joined the fray. President Franklin Roosevelt and the secretary of labor, Frances Perkins, were in constant contact with the situation. No one knew what to do. When Murphy threatened finally to use the National Guard to vacate the plants, Lewis threw open his shirt and said that the first bullet would hit him. GM signed. Chrysler soon followed.

Two facts were clear from the effort to organize the CIO. First, despite the heroism of the various radical sects, the drive to organize the major industries would not have succeeded without the effort of John L. Lewis and other major unions firmly dedicated to industrial unionism. The resources of the radicals were too meager in money and manpower to effectively organize these industries in the face of the extraordinary resistance of the companies. For decades, American business had fought unions with a severity unknown in the capitalist countries of western Europe. Nowhere were strikes as violent or the loss of life and property as high as they were in the United States (Sexton, 1991, chaps. 2 and 3).

Second, the role of the government had to be at least neutralized. No union movement had faced the ferocious attacks of the military, police, and courts as had the American movement. Federal troops and the National Guard had to be contained if the organizing drive was to succeed. The courts had to be constrained in order to allow picketing and mass meetings. The impact of the New Deal was to provide at least a sense of that protection for the new unionists.

HOMER MARTIN AND JAY LOVESTONE

The organization of GM and Chrysler provided the setting for one of the most dramatic intraunion fights since John Lewis punched William Hutcheson, Carpenter's president, at the AFL convention. Creating a viable union against the most antiunion employers in the country, the automakers, was an overwhelming task. It required administrative and organizing abilities beyond the capacity of Martin, who was endowed with little beyond a mellifluous voice. The problems soon became more than Martin could handle. The autoworkers, who had chaffed for years under the most brutal conditions, soon began to wildcat in an exuberant display of their new-found strength. Martin, in an attempt to stop the wildcats, tried to centralize more power in the hands of the president. This was not popular with the membership, who had experienced the same treatment under the AFL. The other officers, recognizing Martin's lack of ability, began to get restive, looking for a way to get rid of or reduce Martin's influence.

The beleaguered and ineffective Martin decided that the presence of the considerable power of the Communist Party was responsible for his troubles.[4] This made it possible for the second actor in the melodrama, Jay Lovestone, to enter the action. Lovestone had been the head of the Communist Party in 1929 and a practiced infighter in its chronic and interminable factional disputes. With about eighty percent of the party behind him on a doctrinal question of whether America represented a possible "exception" to the crude Marxist notion that history was marching inexorably to the Communist future (and soon, too), Lovestone was summoned to Moscow to settle the dispute. Caught in the battles within the Soviet Union, over which he had no control, Lovestone was divested of his position. If there was ever any doubt as to who was going to control the CPUSA, the American Communists or the Kremlin, it was now settled. Lovestone returned to the United States and started a party, the CPUSA (Majority Group). The name was as grandiloquent as his pretentions. Later, in a succession of name changes, Lovestone's party became known as the Communist Party Opposition and, at the time of the troubles in the UAW, the Independent Communist Labor League.

Martin, casting about for allies, seized on Lovestone with his demonstrated political skills as his political guide. Some of Lovestone's followers showed up in staff positions surrounding Martin. The problem was that the Lovestoneites, so named because of that horrid radical practice of naming their political tendencies after their leaders, had no significant following in the shops or the cadres that the Communists or even the Socialists had. There was considerable movement on the part of all the factions regarding Martin. Richard Frankensteen and R. J. Thomas had been closely associated with Martin. Reuther and his small Socialist group, uneasy about the power of the Communists in the anti-Martin faction, nonetheless knew that Martin was not capable of handling the job of president of the union. In hindsight, it is apparent that Martin could not continue in the top office if the UAW were to grow. At the time, the picture was not as clear. The UAW had suffered a recent traumatic split with the AFL, and no one wanted a repetition of that fight. Martin forced the issue by suspending Addes, Mortimer, Frankensteen, and two other officers in June 1938.

The five officers appeared at a trial by the executive board of the union, but, frightened off by the presence of 150 to 200 burly autoworkers, they left. Fear had been so high that when, in September 1937, a group of rank and filers did get to Martin's hotel room, he greeted them with a drawn pistol. Martin was not the only one eventually to arm himself. As late as September 1939, Reuther was issued a gun permit, signed by Judge Patrick H. O'Brien and witnessed by R. J. Thomas (Walter Reuther Collection, box 5; folder 8, UA,WSU; collection not fully processed when examined). The five accused officers released a document, in newspaper form, called the *Bulletin*, which was to have only one issue (R. J. Thomas Collection, box 4; folder 5, UA,WSU). It caused such a shock wave throughout the union that it eventually resulted in Martin's downfall. The lead article said: "In these pages will be found absolute proof of a tremendous conspiracy on the part of Homer Martin and Jay Lovestone to hand over control of the UAW to Lovestone's so-called Independent Communist Labor League." This conspiracy allegedly gave Lovestone, "an irresponsible disruptive political adventurer and intermeddler," the power to fire and advise on negotiations and even had one Lovestoneite employed by "one of the great automobile manufacturers . . . and being at the same time a confidential agent and operative of Jay Lovestone" (Sugar Collection, box 45; folder 15, UA,WSU).

The versions of this series of charges in affidavit form are contained in the Maurice Sugar files deposited in the Reuther Archives at Wayne State

University. The pagination slightly changes, and the numbering of the charges varies from version to version. All, however, contain the same basic material, the changes indicating minor revisions as it was being prepared. It is hard not to conclude that Sugar, the UAW counsel and longtime associate of the Communist bloc in the UAW, was one of the major writers. Fourteen people were named as members of the National Council of the Lovestone group. Seven of those were also identified by their aliases, which were, following the old Bolshevik practice they learned in the Communist Party, their party names. One of those listed said that he was in the UAW headquarters on the day the document was discussed at the board meeting. As the meeting broke up, a board member walked out, grinned at the person, and called him by his party name. These names were carefully guarded secrets, and that anyone outside of the group could know them was an indication of a mole fairly high in the Lovestone organization (Strachan, 1982). Fifteen others were named as sympathizers "who occupy positions of control and influence in the International Union." Three of those were identified as "Trotskyites" (Sugar Collection, box 45; folder 15, UA,WSU).

There is in Sugar's papers, along with the three different versions of the basic document, a list in Sugar's handwriting of thirty-eight letters between Martin and Lovestone. The letters were quoted to prove that

Jay Lovestone gives and Homer Martin takes orders in relation to the most minute detail of the functioning of our International Union, we shall show . . . that the approval of Jay Lovestone was required before Homer Martin undertook to send a communication to the President of the United States. (Sugar Collection, box 42; folder 15, UA,WSU)

They quoted letters from Lovestone to one of Martin's chief lieutenants on how to run the union, how to hold board meetings, how to remove enemies from the staff, much of which Martin did, whether or not on the advice of Lovestone. They also submitted evidence purporting to show that Lovestone and Martin conspired to defeat the peacemaking efforts of Frankensteen, John Brophy, Adolph Germer, and John L. Lewis; to show Lovestone's participation in the GM negotiations and his influence in staff appointments and selection of insurance agents; and to reveal the identification of the Martin follower in a responsible GM position (Sugar Collection, box 32; folder 5, UA,WSU).

Some of the letters revealed matters of a financial nature about the Lovestone group. Addes and company charged:

We shall show that persons in responsible positions in the International Union by appointment of Homer Martin and whose positions were procured at the solicitation of Jay Lovestone, have appropriated moneys of the International Union in order to furnish financial support for the machinations of Lovestone. (Sugar Collection, box 42; folder 15, UA,WSU)

This refers to Francis Henson's letter to Lovestone (December 29, 1937, in the first version of the statement, changed by pencil in the second statement to

"November 29, 1937"), complaining about how he needed to be reimbursed for some of his phone calls and asking that the cost be offset against his financial pledge made to the organization. He added: "This is in addition to more than $10.00 per week which I added to my expense account." The illegal use of UAW funds by padding an expense account did little to endear the Lovestoneites with the rank and file (Sugar Collection, box 42; folder 15, UA,WSU).

The Addes group even printed a letter allegedly written by Martin's assistant to Lovestone in November 1937 complaining about Martin.

Homer has been everywhere and nowhere. The Executive Board meeting here was sick and disgusted with him for his chronic lack of interest. He attended for about an hour after keeping the Board waiting for 5 hours while he did everything else but appear before them. It got so bad a number of them are coming in to talk to Homer threatening a break unless he mends his ways. (Sugar Collection, box 42; folder 5, UA,WSU)

John L. Lewis was also mentioned in the correspondence: "Jay should write Lewis demanding they stop further publication or else he will print correspondence of Lewis and Lovestone" (Sugar Collection, box 42; folder 5, UA,WSU).

Workers Age, the Lovestone paper, had a front-page story headed: "Lovestone Home Is Burglarized by G.P.U.; Documents Missing." The story added, "The home of Jay Lovestone was broken into and burglarized on July 17 [just two weeks before the Addes group made public the letters], it was revealed this week" as was "the use of some of these stolen documents by Attorney Maurice Sugar in the suspension trial in the United Automobile Workers Union" ("Lovestone Home Is Burglarized," 1938, p. 1). Since a watch and other valuables were also taken, it apparently did not occur to Lovestone that it was anything more than a normal burglary. It was only when the missing documents, not detected as having been stolen, surfaced in the trial that Lovestone knew more was at stake than a simple theft. He maintained that some of the materials used were faked and some were outright forgeries but provided no specifics on these charges.

The *Daily Worker* carried stories on the revelations on August 4, 5, and 6, 1938. Some observers noted that since the documents had only been released on August 3 in the afternoon that the *Worker* seemed to have an advantage of prior knowledge over the other papers. In the first story, the *Worker*, on a front-page story, headed: "Martin Puppet of Lovestone in Drive to Disrupt C.I.O." Lovestone, in the body of the story, was labeled the "American Leon Trotsky" ("Martin Puppet," 1938, p. 1). This writing and subsequent stories were essentially repeats of the original charges.

Given the fact that correspondence had been stolen that was highly incriminating and there was obviously a Communist Party spy in their organization, it should have occurred to the Lovestoneites that their telephones might also be suspect. Evidently, it did not, because in the Browder file of the Daniel Bell Collection the following transcript appears:

Aug 3rd, 4:20 P.M.
Conversation between Bill Munger and G. J. Thorton Lovestone
M stands for Munger
L stands for Lovestone
M — Hello J. . . . They really got the dope on us. That explains the raid on your confidential archives. . . .
L — Well, you know we can repudiate it.
M — They've got too many original letters. I was wondering whether we could press the criminal offense for theft of the letters. . . .
L — Well we can say they stole them and manipilated [*sic*] them. (Daniel Bell Collection, box MB3, Wagner Library, NYU)

This was not the only tapped phone conversation between Lovestone and his associates in the UAW headquarters. The Browder file contains the summary or transcript of thirty seven conversations between Lovestone and his confederates at the UAW headquarters between August 2 and 6, 1938. This file also contains some of Browder's personal correspondence on the UAW fight (letter: "They [Addes group] decided not to go to trial . . . weakens evidence against the Martin Lovestone clique"), reports from an informant on closed Lovestoneite meetings, reports on closed and public meetings of the Socialist Party and the Socialist Workers Party, and a copy of Browder's report to the subsequent Communist Party Plenum in 1942. The tap was obviously placed at the UAW headquarters because calls were recorded between Lovestone's supporters at the UAW to other than Lovestone, but no calls were recorded between Lovestone and any parties other than the UAW people. On August 5, 1938, William Munger, Martin's assistant, named as a Lovestone supporter by the document of Addes and the others, at 11:50 P.M. called Lawrence Davidow, Martin's attorney, and said, "After the trial we ought to try debar [*sic*] Sugar." Some of the material in the Browder file was simply a chronicle of calls, for example:

Thursday, August 4, 1938.
10 PM   Eve Stone to unidentified individual
9:05   Eve Stone to unidentified individual
6:05   Eve Stone call to Munger

Sometimes there was a note: "Francis Watson was here til approximately 10:15 taking dictation and typing. Bill Taylor called in the morning. Norma took the phone and asked Eve if she had Klein's address in Lansing. About 10:30 Irving Brown came in. Eve called NY, Bryant 9–0127 [Lovestone's number] twice could get no answer." On this date, 5:40 P.M., Eve Stone called Lovestone, and he is reported as saying, "For 1½ years my life has been in danger. The International G.P.U., who have worked with terror in Spain and Europe generally, are now in America" (Daniel Bell Collection, box MB3, Wagner Library, NYU).

It should not be supposed that only the Communists were guilty of tapping phones. James Carey, past president of the UE, bragged to Daniel Bell that he had bugged the hotel room of Joe Curran, president of the National Maritime Union. According to Carey, a conversation between Roy Hudson, Communist Party trade union functionary, and Lee Pressman revealed that the former scolded the highly placed Pressman like a child. This was not the end of Carey's activities. He also claimed to have tapped the hotel room of the Federal Bureau of Investigation (FBI)! (Bell Collection, box MB4, Wagner Library, NYU).

These charges against the Lovestoneites plus Martin's inept politicking led to the eventual split, with Martin taking a small minority into the AFL. Coupled with the mild xenophobia of UAW members against "outside" groups trying to run the union, it made Martin's loss certain. The incident of Lovestone's activities in the UAW illustrates how a minuscule political sect can exert an influence far beyond its numerical strength. It also demonstrates how the Communist Party, also small in numbers, could exert an even greater power. It is obvious from the evidence of a spy within the Lovestone group (the knowledge of their party names), the records of telephone taps in Browder's file, and the different versions of the affidavits on Lovestone's group in the Sugar papers that the Communist Party was responsible for these illegal acts of espionage.

This was no matter of sending an observer to an open meeting of a rival caucus, a common union practice; these acts of burglary and telephone tapping were daring and skilled, indicating an apparatus far beyond that available to George Addes. The phone taps and the theft of the letters were done by the same party. The telephone taps were made just at the time the Addes group released the stolen letters. Keeran (1980) reports that, according to Lee Pressman, CIO counsel and an admitted Communist, the Communist Party was "quite aware of Lovestone's machinations, because one of their number managed to tap Lovestone's phone conversations with Martin" (p. 188).

There never was a trial on the theft of the letters, but the internal evidence points to the Communists as the culprits. An ally with the ability to provide such material in a critical factional fight is not one to be treated lightly or easily discarded. The exposure of Lovestone's role in the UAW helped to change the course of the union. and it also helped to define the role of the Communist Party in the union.

NOTES

1.   Martin Glaberman was the first to have written about this Ganley quote. Glaberman reported on it in *Radical America* (Glaberman, 1973, p. 114).

2.   As an indication of the internal democracy in the Communist parties of the world, one sympathetic writer notes that the Seventh Congress of the Comintern decided that the dispute over whether the U.S. party should support Roosevelt or run its own candidate should be left "to the decision of the American comrades." A strange democracy, why

could not the CPUSA have made this decision without permission from the Comintern (Keeran, 1980, p. 4)?

3.   The catechism of the Third Period often faltered. What precisely was the distinction between "Fascist," "social Fascist," and "Left social Fascist" in the Communist lexicon? Seeking clarity on this and other matters, Max Bedacht went to Moscow in 1930 and wired to his waiting comrades: "AFL Plainly Fascist Muste Social Fascist Not Social and Left Social Fascist Respectively." Clarity at last (Klehr, 1983, p. 16).

4.   Klehr maintains that the Communist Party was responsible for much of the wildcatting, pointing out that the *Daily Worker* had supported the Chrysler wildcats and a subsequent GM strike in Pontiac. In fact, William Weinstone, head of the Michigan Communist Party operation, was removed by the party for his support of the wildcats. The consensus is that the Communist Party acted in a very responsible trade union manner. Klehr even quotes the Politburo minutes. "People suspect us of merely biding out time until we can make a coup and stab them in the back." Some people certainly felt that, but the spirit of the Popular Front prevailed (Klehr, 1984, p. 409).

2

EARLY HISTORY OF THE ASSOCIATION OF CATHOLIC TRADE UNIONISTS

ORIGINS

Until the late 1930s, the different voices in the UAW had been political ones, reflecting ideological differences between the Right and Left. Sectarian differences, especially on a confessional level, had been nonexistent. But as the doctrinal differences became more marked, there was an uneasiness among Catholic trade unionists that their position was unrepresented, and they felt they had a distinctive point of view. But there existed an obstacle to the realization of a formal organization representing a Catholic position: the Catholic hierarchy. The history of the relationship between the Catholic hierarchy and ACTU is a mixed one. Under Archbishop Michael Gallagher, a staunch Fr. Coughlin supporter and confirmed ultraconservative,[1] it is unlikely that ACTU would have received the imprimatur of the Church. Even Gallagher's successor, the liberal Archbishop Edward Mooney, equivocated, citing what he considered the religious divisiveness of the Jewish War Veterans as a role model to be avoided. After John C. Cort and seven other laypersons formed ACTU in 1937, other chapters were started in various cities, mostly initiated by lay members (with the notable exception of the Pittsburgh chapter started by Fr. Charles Owen Rice), often having to overcome clerical resistance in the process. Bishop Francis J. Haas, liberal Bishop of Grand Rapids, Michigan, in a predominantly Dutch Reform community with a small Catholic minority, did not want an ACTU chapter there, fearing that it would exacerbate religious tensions (ACTU Collection, box 2; folder: ACTU 1939–1943, UA,WSU; Weber, 1982, interview).

However, lay pressure prevailed, and in July 1938, the Detroit chapter was started with seven members, one of whom was the chaplain. It espoused general prounion positions and carefully indicated that "the ACTU shall not be a labor union." This statement showed that ACTU was aware of the possible criticism of being a dual union from hostile observers. In addition, in order to establish its American credentials, it added that there was "consonance of Catholic Social

Doctrine and the Constitution of the United States and the Declaration of Independence" (ACTU Collection, box 1; folder: ACTU 1938, UA,WSU).

The various chapters, nationwide, in 1940, held a national organization meeting in Cleveland, Ohio. The *Articles of Federation* adopted there provide for a national director and a National Council composed of the chaplain and one member from each chapter, thus structurally ensuring clerical domination of the organization. Each chapter had one vote for each 100 members (dues-paying) or fraction thereof, with no delegate holding more than five votes. Also, "the Chaplain of each chapter shall be entitled to one additional vote." Dues were twenty-five cents a month.

Members pledged to abide by Catholic teachings, do their utmost "to oppose Fascists, Communists, Nazis, and racketeers and their philosophies," and "to be a faithful member of my union, to maintain my dues, and to attend meetings regularly." There are eight spiritual activities to be engaged in "so far as possible," such as holy hours, annual ACTU novenas, and daily prayers. Finally, "all members of the ACTU shall be Catholic and the Catholicity of members shall be determined by the Chaplain of the chapter of which he is a member." There is no record of the last provision being exercised even when there was a hot dispute about a member whose politics were highly suspect. In fact, the impression is that a quarter and a profession of being Catholic made anyone a member (ACTU Collection, box 2; folder: ACTU 1940, UA,WSU).

The elements of the archbishop's settling of disputes, the chaplain's certification of good standing in the Church, and the disproportionate voting influence of the chaplains seem to support the charges by the Left on "clerical domination" by the hierarchy. However, the relationship between the clergy and the laity in their actual behavior demonstrates a contrary position. For one, the clergy was hardly of a single mind about social and political questions. Paul Weber had no compunction about attacking priests of an antiunion bias, the most notable example of which was ACTU's assault on Fr. Charles E. Coughlin. Aside from that, in the early CIO organizing days, Fr. Louis A. Gales, editor of the Catholic paper *Facts*, published an article by Jacob Spolansky. Weber wrote to Fr. Gales:

It is a vicious weave of half-truths, untruths, and malicious innuendo. It will make the Communists in the CIO laugh and the Catholics in the CIO grieve that Catholic auspices should be lent to such unfair criticism. The entire brunt of the attack, ostensibly directed at the Communists, is actually delivered at the CIO. . . . I think that ACTU should be advised what to expect from "Facts"—attacks upon the unions, which we will have to defend; or effective Christian propaganda which we can whole-heartedly support.

Weber, in addition, protested to the New York chapter and asked them to investigate the Tarrytown, New York, situation where "a very thoroughly discredited rebel [*sic*] rouser and red baiter has gained the ear of Fr. Donoghue and as a result Fr. Donoghue is allowing the AFL unions to use the parish hall, while denying it to the CIO" (ACTU Collection, box 18; folder: ACTU NY 1939–43, UA,WSU).

There is little in ACTU's philosophical tenets to give comfort to the secular, materialistic contemporary. Like all intensely ideological movements, it was necessary to have historical antecedents—the further back, the better. A resolution was introduced at the 1941 convention of ACTU, stating:

Whereas: St. Joseph, the fire brand of Christ, is considered one of the great apostles of the Church, and

Whereas: St. Paul was especially effective in winning the souls of countless pagans to the Principles of the Christian faith,

Be it resolved: that this convention go on record as urging that St. Joseph be adopted as one of the special patrons of the special chapters of ACTU.

Then there was the laconic note: "St. Paul was defeated" (ACTU Collection, box 1; folder: ACTU, 1941, UA,WSU).

Despite this contest between the followers of these early saints to name the patron of ACTU, the genesis of ACTU was of a much later date: the papal encyclicals of Pope Leo XIII (*Rerum novarum* [On the Condition of Labor], 1891) and Pope Pius XI (*Quadragesimo Anno* [Forty Years After], 1931). Both popes wrote in periods of great social turmoil. The former saw the emergence of a militant socialist movement in the last decade of the nineteenth century, and Pius wrote at the beginning of the Great Depression. Both sought to reaffirm the social doctrine of the Catholic church to provide guidance for the largely Catholic working class of Europe that was faced with the threat of growing Socialist and eventually Communist and Fascist ideologies.

The archbishops and bishops of the Administrative Board of the National Catholic Welfare Conference in their 1940 statement on "The Church and the Social Order" gave the most concise interpretation of the Church's doctrine that guided ACTU at that time (ACTU Collection, box 2; folder: National Catholic Welfare Conference, UA,WSU). Noting Pius's injunction in *Summi Pontificatus* that "from the immense vortex of error and anti-Christian movements there has come forth a crop of such poignant disasters as to constitute a condemnation surpassing in its conclusiveness any merely theoretical refutation" (p. 2), the solution according to *The Church and the Social Order* was to "reaffirm the primacy of our Lord Jesus Christ" (p. 2). The primacy of Christ was to be achieved by bringing "God back into Government . . . into economic life . . . indeed into all life, private and public, individual and social" (p. 2). These aims must have occasioned considerable misgivings on the part of liberal Protestants who were wedded to the modern secular state and to Jews, given their particular vulnerability as a persecuted religious minority.

With the Church "as the teacher of the *entire* [emphasis added] moral law and more particularly as it applies to man's economic and social conduct in business, industry and trade" (p. 4), the bishops maintained that "the Church has always defended the right to own property and also to bequeath and to inherit it," but "no absolute or unlimited ownership . . . can be claimed by man as if he were free to follow his own self interests without regard to the necessity of others" (p. 5). In rebuke of nineteenth-century liberalism, the Church fathers insisted that labor cannot be treated as a commodity or workers treated as chattel.

The loss of faith by many Catholic workers and their alienation from the Church caused the bishops to ask, "Who can deny the close relationship between economic injustice and a long train of evils, physical, social and moral" (p. 9). They chronicle a list of these evils: unfair wages, excessive profits, undernourishment, bad housing, inadequate clothing, child delinquency, crime, impaired health, unsafe working conditions, break-up of the family, disease, and premature death (p. 8). This catalog of social ills attributed to unrestrained capitalism is reminiscent of the imprecations of liberals or radicals. The bishops characterized the two greatest dangers as "the concentration of wealth and the control of wealth" and the "anonymous character . . . of the existing business and corporation law." Given these dangers, the state (civil authority) has the obligation of "providing for the common good" and equitable distribution of wealth (p. 10).

The right of workers to bargain collectively was strongly asserted and also a right to a voice in "the regulation or the adjustment of these problems" growing from the concentration of wealth and power. The remedy for this situation was the adoption of the "right principles for the distribution of the income of industry" (p. 12). Adam Smith and other nineteenth-century economic liberals were criticized: "The principle that labor should be compensated to such an extent only that it remains physically efficient and capable of reproducing itself in a new generation of working men is a vicious principle, devoid of all respect for human dignity" (p. 12). Wages, according to the bishops, cannot be determined on the basis of supply and demand. While the main thrust of the statement is against the abuses of capitalism, workers are admonished that they "allow themselves at times to be misled by men of evil principles," engaging in the "criminal use of violence both against persons and property" (p. 13). Workers, in any case, "should be made secure against unemployment, sickness, accident, old age and death" (pp. 15–16). In short, the bishops posit a modern welfare state under ecclesiastical guidance, based on Catholic moral teachings.

In their final section, "The Establishment of Social Order," the fathers determined that two equally pernicious social doctrines were at work, "the extreme individualists or the so-called school of economic liberalism" and the tenets of communism and socialism. The former calls their system "free enterprise but the freedom is for those who possess great resources and dominating strength rather than for the weak or those who depend simply on their own labor for their well being." The latter, the Communists and Socialists, "rush to the opposite extreme" where "persecution is the logical and inevitable result of such economic dictatorship" (pp. 25–26).

Solution? "Between these two extremes there is a 'via media' completely consistent with Christian morality and sound economic principles" (p. 27). This middle way is not the Swedish welfare state but a return to "some form of guild or vocational groups which will bind men together in society according to their respective occupations, thus creating a moral unity" (p. 27). Finally, there must be a moral regeneration along Christian lines *preceding* the social reconstruction.

The polarity of the dual threats to human society, unregenerate capitalism and collectivism, is ahistorical and anti–social science; the bishops' statement arrests socialism at the time of the *Communist Manifesto* and capitalism at the publication of the *Wealth of Nations*. It does not do justice to the capitalist reformers, nor does it show recognition of the great split in social democracy between the Second and Third International. However, this was the model and officially sanctioned social philosophy of the Catholic church, causing constant efforts on the part of Catholic radicals to defend against the charges by left-wing critics that the Church was proposing a corporate state that was analogous to the Italian Fascists' social doctrine.

These guidelines were reflected in the September 27, 1940, issue of the *Michigan Labor Leader*, the ACTU newspaper, which carried a story headed "The Other Party," stating:

In all the hue and cry about the Communist Party, let no one forget that the ACTU and all Catholic workers stand unalterably and fundamentally opposed to the Socialist Party.... "No one" said Pope Pius XI "can be at the same time a good Catholic and a good Socialist." This statement holds all the force of a dictate of Christ, Himself. There is no such thing as a "Catholic Socialist" unless one or the other words is misused. ("The Other Party," 1940, p. 5)

In final denigration of socialism, they added that its emphasis on material wants makes it "identical with Capitalism. The Socialist is merely an advanced Capitalist" (p. 5).

For the most part, the Catholic church and the Communist Party exchanged invectives, although occasionally there were grudging signs of respect for their opposite numbers, most often for the wrong reasons. Max Badacht, one of the early leading Communists, wrote:

The Catholic Church is and has been one of the strongest and most consistent counter-revolutionary forces in society.... The reason for this is its ideological unity and its organizational centralization. If we revolutionists have not already learned these lessons in our experience, we could learn the value of ideological unity and organizational centralization from the Catholic Church. (Howe and Coser, 1957, p. 160)

Occasionally, there was a note of agonizing envy. An unsigned letter was sent to the *Michigan Labor Leader* (predecessor to the *Wage Earner*), plaintively complaining about the resources of the Communist Party:

The attached exhibit [a Communist Party news service] is a typical example of the way the Communist Party is able to do things, as contrasted with our puny little volunteer efforts.

This sheet is sent out to all labor papers, and the papers are invited to ask for free mats of the pictures, [but] the New York Labor Leader was unable to afford enough to print a single picture, and the *Michigan Labor Leader* is forced to depend for most of its pictures on the cheap mat service of Federated Press, a Service operated by Communists. (ACTU Collection, box 2; folder: Communist Party, 1939–1945, UA,WSU)

Perhaps envy is the sincerest form of flattery, but ACTU was no paragon of centralization, and the resources of the Communist Party were not as great as imagined by ACTU.

The clergy associated with or sympathetic to ACTU often spoke like old-time soapboxers. Father Raymond Clancy, Detroit ACTU chaplain, said the "oppression of the workingman, injustice toward the weak, cheating the powerless, wringing money from the tears or bent backs of others transcend the crimes against the individual men concerned. They are crimes that cry to God for vengeance. They are crimes against the Son of God Himself" (Clancy Collection, box 1; folder 21, UA,WSU).

After the Detroit ACTU was started and Archbishop Mooney was convinced that the organization would not create divisiveness in the religious or labor community, he was enormously helpful. In 1939, Mooney pleaded "for a lively interest on the part of priests and Catholic workers in the ACTU program." Excerpts from this message were used in an ACTU handbill. Part of the purpose of ACTU was to provide a bulwark against the "inroads of communist agitation," according to the same statement (ACTU Collection, box 3; folder: ACTU handbills— 1939, UA,WSU). Later that year, he added that the union movement was not simply acceptable to the Church; "it is something which she wholeheartedly approves . . . something for which her Popes have been crying for generations like a voice of a prophet in the wilderness of 'laissez faire.'" Workers were obliged to have an active interest in their unions, and if priests did not actively encourage such interest, "they are derelict in a duty which the highest authority of the Church misses no occasion to emphasize" (*Mooney,* 1939, p. 1). As helpful as these instructions may have been, Mooney's greatest contribution to the fledgling organization was in a labor dispute in which Fr. Charles E. Coughlin, an immensely popular Detroit priest, had sided with the company.

ACTIVITIES

Fr. Coughlin, a fiery and compelling orator, was created from the stuff that fed American populism and eventually made it so suspect to subsequent liberal social analysts. In the early 1930s, Coughlin was a champion of workers and unions. His attacks on the AFL's "class bigotry" for failing to organize industrial workers led to battles with the Detroit Labor Council, the AFL body. They, in turn, attacked him for building his church, the Shrine of the Little Flower, in suburban Ferndale, with nonunion labor and not using the union label (bug) on his parish paper. Coughlin answered that he had used unemployed parishioners for the construction of the church, had paid over union scale, and had offered to help organize them. As for the paper, Coughlin maintained that it was all donated, material and labor, but that he would change to a union shop. Francis X. Martel, head of the Detroit AFL and later critic of ACTU, called Coughlin "one of the principle racketeers in the United States." This was contradicted by William Green, then-president of the National AFL, who said Coughlin was "most sympathetic and friendly to the labor movement" (Brown Collection, box 7; folder: Rev. Charles E. Coughlin, UA,WSU).

Fortune magazine in February 1934, in an article on Coughlin, stated that he was "no iconoclast"; he had been against: "Communism, fascism, inflation, prohibition, big bankers, and the uneven distribution of wealth. No sign of iconoclasm here. And these are the things Fr. Coughlin has been for: 'Christian Capitalism,' President Roosevelt and all his works, silver money, and the soldiers bonus" ("Father Coughlin," 1934, p. 34). This list was to change dramatically in a few years. Coughlin developed a deliberately inflationary monetary policy, dropped most of the liberal aspects of his program, and evolved into an admirer of fascism. George Morris, writing in the Communist *Political Affairs* (1950), saw Coughlin's National Union for Social Justice as the precursor of ACTU. According to Morris, when Coughlin was silenced as "Hitler's victory began to look doubtful" (p. 53), the Church, casting about for a new standard bearer, shifted toward Wall Street, and ACTU was the carrier of the refurbished Coughlinite line. This is not serious political argumentation, and it debases historical and intellectual inquiry.

Typical of many liberal priests, Coughlin supported the mild social reforms of the New Deal. Bettan (1976) even maintains that Upton Sinclair tried to get Coughlin's support when he ran for the governor of California. Coughlin was obviously as much guided in these days by the Church's teaching on the excesses of capitalism as he was by the current liberalism and even gave support originally to the Automotive Industrial Workers Association (AIWA), an independent union organized largely in Chrysler. Richard Frankensteen was later associated with this union and helped take it into the UAW. His oral history of the time tried to downplay both the help and influence Coughlin exerted in the AIWA (Bettan, 1976, p. 120; Frankensteen, 1961, OH, UA,WSU).

From 1934 on, Coughlin drifted to the Right and attacked labor and the Democratic governor of Michigan, Frank Murphy, in the famous 1936 strikes. The National Union for Social Justice was started in 1934 by Coughlin with a strong dictatorial cast. His proposal for a new representation scheme replacing the two-house Congress reflected a strong rightist leaning. Instead of congressional elections, each industry would have delegates in Congress with equal representation from owners, management, and labor, thus giving a two-to-one advantage to owners. After 1938, Coughlin became an outright Fascist sympathizer, blatantly anti-Semitic, and publisher of the infamous forgeries the *Protocols of the Elders of Zion*. At one point, he asked Mussolini to write an article for *Social Justice*, his newspaper. Coughlin had that strange quality of combined native rebellion and reaction that originally marked so many American Populists. He lacked the radicalism that Tom Watson originally showed, but he shared in abundance Watson's later racism. With William Jennings Bryan, he shared a belief in a weak-minded monetary theory.

During the 1939 UAW strike against Chrysler, Coughlin, in his radio broadcast, exhorted the Chrysler workers to return to work. The strike was in bad enough shape without this appeal from the popular priest, and the newly formed ACTU realized that some response was necessary from the Church. They went directly to Mooney with an appeal for help. The *Michigan Catholic* ran an editorial supporting the strike and attacking the corporation (Fardela, 1981, p. 45). On November 16, 1939, the *Detroit News* carried a news story on Rt. Rev. John S. Mies's assault on Coughlin, quoting ACTU as saying that Coughlin had distorted Church teachings in his broadcast (Robinson, 1939, p. 10). Resolutions were received from Pittsburgh ACTU and Local 7 of the UAW, lambasting Coughlin. The latter protest showed the hand of ACTU in its reference to Coughlin's misinterpretation of Church doctrine (ACTU Collection, box 2; folder: ACTU, Pittsburgh, 1939–1940, UA,WSU).

Fr. Raymond Clancy, then executive secretary of the Archdiocesan Labor Institute, later chaplain of ACTU, made a painstaking rebuttal of Coughlin's previous speech. Reading the transcript, it seems that it must have been one of the dullest programs aired since the invention of radio. Point by point, Clancy demolished Coughlin's surprising ignorance of the then-current labor legislation. Coughlin had not only distorted the UAW position, but he also misrepresented the powers of the National Labor Relations Board and falsified the papal encyclicals. Coughlin had asserted that a strike was unnecessary because the NLRB and the courts had sufficient powers to adjudicate the matter. This was not true, and Clancy so demonstrated. The greatest error that Coughlin made was in the way he misquoted Pope Pius XI. Coughlin said that Pius's teaching was that "the state alone can represent respectively working men and employers, and the state alone can conclude labor contracts and labor agreements." Clancy pointed out that the quote, ostensibly Pius's position, was really Pius's criticism of fascism. Clancy ended by urging "the strikers to remain steadfast until they had a contract" (Clancy Collection, box 4; folder 2: Taft, UA,WSU).

Boring or not, the Clancy rebuttal gave the ACTU paper their headline for the next issue: "'Back to Work' Move is Smashed." They continued the story: "An attempt, aided by Father Coughlin to start a 'back to work' movement and stampede the Chrysler workers into surrender, was smashed this week by the resistance of the ACTU and other Catholic agencies" ("'Back to Work' Move is

Smashed," 1939, p. 1). In a page-one, boxed, two-column spread headed "Fr. Coughlin Errs," the paper pointed out that Coughlin, as a result of misquoting Pius XI, had "ended by advocating what would amount to a fascist dictatorship over labor and industry in America" ("Fr. Coughlin Errs," 1939, p. 1). Richard Rovere, writing a somewhat unsympathetic article in *The Nation* on ACTU, said that "there was little doubt in the minds of most observers that the credit for reversing the trend [of the Chrysler strike] belonged to the Catholic unionists" (Rovere, 1941, p. 13).

In addition to the trade union work, Detroit ACTU's other major accomplishment was its educational activities. These two efforts were aspects of the same problem, educating for union involvement. In Detroit, ACTU had only eight schools being conducted between February and May of 1939, according to their own account, which was a signal achievement in its own right. There followed a period of intense activity that boosted the total to thirty-four in 1940, twenty-seven of which were in Metropolitan Detroit. A penciled note in 1940 gave a revised statement of the 1939 attendance. There were twenty-seven Labor Institutes in Detroit parishes with an enrollment of 965 (912 men; 53 women). August was their biggest month, with 406 students (384 men; 22 women). In addition, there were fourteen parishes that ran schools outside of Detroit with a total enrollment of 160 (159 men; 1 woman). The August figures for those areas outside Detroit indicate that nearly sixty percent of their enrollment occurred in this month, a total of 95 (only 1 woman). The total for the year, all parishes, was an astonishing 1,125 enrollees (1,071 men; 54 women). In August alone, all parishes, the attendance was 501 (478 men; 23 women). Only the major unions could claim such educational activities among their members and, even then, probably not for 1939 (Clancy Collection, box 1; folder 18: UA,WSU).

If the course outlines and the lecture notes of 1943, 1945, and 1946 are any indications of what transpired in the 1939 classes, it must have been a dreary experience for those workers. These outlines and notes suffer from the turgidity of both academic and clerical life, a combination hard to equal for obfuscating a problem. Nonetheless, these offerings were well received if we are to give credence to the evaluation of one 1939 class. Evaluations, perhaps in all of education, are self-serving because students generally tend to be supportive. The occasional response to an open-ended question is often the most revealing one. For example, the students were asked: "Have the classes helped you to be a better unionist? How?" One student answered in the affirmative and explained: "Taught me to be less radical" (Clancy Collection, box 1; folder 16, UA,WSU).

This same 1939 class in answer to the question, "What part of the course did you find most helpful?" responded: encyclicals on the Communist Party, 17; parliamentary procedure, 12; down to 1 vote a piece for unions and economics. In a report on the evaluation, the evaluators noted that the most beneficial result was "the pleasure and appreciation of the workers for the interest which the Church is taking in their problems. . . . A new regard for their responsibilities to their employers [!] and to their fellow workers. 'Catholic mindedness.' " One worker wrote: "The priest of our parish should learn more of labor's problems. And to show him positive leadership in every day life. Instead of being a Sunday morning well wisher" (Clancy Collection, box 1; folders 18 and 16, UA,WSU).

The ACTU leadership went through the soul-crushing routine of the organizational work with as much patience as the situation allowed. In the early days, there were never enough prayer cards available to fill the requests of other chapters. And they wrote letters to everyone. During the war, they informed the editors of *Parish Publications* that the Communist Party Association was supporting five candidates and asked that ads not be accepted from them, adding, "We have further advised the *Michigan Catholic* that in our opinion the Catholic press should not publish the ads for Edward A. Carey . . . because of anti-Semitic propaganda put out over his name when he was a candidate for Mayor" (ACTU Collection, box 15; folder: Communist Party, 1939–1945, UA,WSU).

They passed innumerable resolutions against Communist penetration of the union movement, and St. Gregory Parish ACTU decided that "Gerald [L. K.] Smith was disqualified as a union man and pronounced an industrial stooge." Poor attendance (six members) at the St. Gregory ACTU meeting was explained by the priest as probably due to the Bingo game occurring at the same time. Spiritual advice was dispensed: It was explained to applicants for membership that their first obligation was to save their own souls and "then bring Christianity into the factory" (ACTU Collection, box 3; folder: Parish Captains Minutes, 1939–1941, UA,WSU).

The Catholic hierarchy may have remained implacable in their opposition to Marxists, particularly the Communists, but some of the Actists, as they called themselves, showed markedly ambivalent attitudes toward their enemy. Involved in the same struggles in the unions, frustrated, driven by a sense of urgency, respecting discipline, and above all, devotion to a cause, Actists gave grudging respect to their foes. The *Labor Leader*, New York's ACTU newspaper, conceded that despite their dislike of the Communists' objectives and tactics, "at the same time, we have been forced to respect and even admire the good work that many of them are doing" (Harrington, 1960, p. 241).

One reaction to this apparent ability of the communists to be disciplined, hardworking, dedicated, and successful was an exhortation by a member of the secondary leadership of the ACTU. For those who believe that "muscular Christianity" was confined to Protestants, witness the following call to arms for a "strong, active, virile" ACTU that was circulated among the chapters:

It is, indeed a very sad thing to see some Catholics who are active in the labor movement living in union environments, as is too often the case, where drunkenness is considered necessary to be regarded as a regular person, where running around with other's husbands or wives is fashionable, where a little bit of misuse of union funds gradually grows into a whole lot of racketeering, where a desire for political advantage and considerations of a political nature stop individuals from answering sneering remarks against religion in general and the Catholic religion in particular, where the prevalence of these remarks and the exposure of the weak Catholics to them cause them to become weaker Catholics and eventually fallen away Catholics, where these same political considerations cause so-called Catholics to be part and parcel of movements that are essentially or practically anti-religious in nature, where political considerations can even cause alliances with out and out Communists, where Sunday Mass at week-end out-of-town conventions is attended by a much smaller than proper number of delegates (ACTU Collection, box 1; folder: ACTU undated, UA,WSU).

This "Rake's Progress" of Catholic unionists from a drink with the boys to drunkenness to adultery to racketeering and loss of faith, culminating in the most heinous of sins, popular fronts with the Communists, and missing Mass at conventions was an object lesson in progressive degeneracy.

In 1939, they admonished the faithful: "Remember! It takes a few Finns to lick the Reds in Russia. It will take a few workers here to lick the Reds—if you will work" (ACTU Collection, box 3; folder: Parish Captains Minutes, 1939–1941). They advised, "The invitation of Fr. Clare Murphy to participate in the peace meeting at Belle Isle be declined because of the fact that a labor baiter . . . and a police cossack are on the program." They commended the *Michigan Catholic* for having the union bug in their paper and "for their recent liberal attitude" (ACTU Collection, box 3; folder: General Meetings Minutes, 1937–1940, UA,WSU). Paul Weber, as a Newspaper Guild member, wrote to the chief of Detroit Police to get a press card for Billy Allan, the *Daily Worker* reporter, who had previously been denied one. It was a busy life, and the rewards were few. The activity itself was probably one of the main motives for continuing. The adversaries derived great pleasure in small victories, particularly Tom Doherty, labor writer for the ACTU press, over George Morris, the *Daily Worker* writer. Occasionally, major victories occurred. Doherty sent a telegram to the *Wage Earner* recounting the events of the 1946 UAW convention. The last two sentences read: "Reuther majority one twenty four. Pleasure to watch George Morris face" (ACTU Collection, box 25; folder: UAW Convention—1946, UA,WSU).

NOTE

1. Gallagher (on Flint sit-downs): "We're fearful that it's Soviet planning behind it. The Communists advocate these strikes—often followed by riots—as a smoke screen for revolution and civil war" (Cormier and Eaton, 1970, p. 87).

3

THE WAR YEARS, 1940–1946

NORTH AMERICAN STRIKE

Homer Martin had been decisively defeated by the time of the Special Convention in 1939. Philip Murray and Sidney Hillman were at the convention to represent the wishes of John L. Lewis. They successfully stopped the candidacy of either George Addes or Wyndham Mortimer, probably on the grounds that both were too close to the Communist Party. Mortimer, a leading, if not self-avowed, Communist, had no office in the new organizational setup, and John Anderson, an acknowledged party member and candidate for governor on the Communist Party ticket, was defeated for the International Executive Board (IEB). Thus, the Communists were at an all-time low in terms of representation among the leadership in the UAW.

On August 24, 1939, the world was stunned by the announcement of the Moscow-Berlin Pact. Finland and Poland were invaded by the Soviet Union, and Great Britain and France went to war with Germany when Poland was invaded by the Nazis. CPUSA suffered considerably by this move on the part of the Soviet Union. The Communists had garnered considerable support on the basis of their seemingly intransigent opposition to Nazism, and the about-face traumatized their nonparty followers. Even more than the Moscow Trials and the enormous death toll during the forced collectivization in the Soviet Union, this joining of the Communists with the barbarism of the Fascists spelled political disaster for the party.

If the ten-year period of the 1930s was "a low, dishonest decade," its reputation certainly was not enhanced by the Communists.

The 1940 convention of the CIO saw an outbreak of anti–Communist Party attitudes. John L. Lewis, who had supported Wendell Willkie in the presidential election of 1940, stepped down from the presidency of the CIO, as he promised he would in the event that Roosevelt was elected. Murray, having lived for so many years in Lewis's shadow, was reluctant to assume the vacated president's position. Lewis was too strong a figure to follow, and Murray saw the

Communist Party as an annoyance in the CIO. Lewis finally prevailed on Murray to accept, but according to Bernstein (1970), Murray

imposed one condition that he would not compromise: the convention must adopt a resolution against Communism. Ironically, it was introduced by Pressman, reading, "The Congress of Industrial Organizations condemns the dictatorship and totalitarianism of Nazism, Communism and Fascism as inimical to the welfare of labor, and destructive of our form of government." All the delegates, including the Communists, voted for it. (p. 276)

This passivity on the part of the Communists was reflected later in the 1941 convention of the UAW. It should be pointed out that the CIO resolution did not preclude any Nazi, Communist, or Fascist from holding office or propose any penalty for their beliefs; it only stated political condemnation of these ideologies.

The process of condemnation of dictatorships continued in the 1940 UAW convention. The resolution said that the UAW should "vigorously condemn the brutal dictatorships, and wars of aggression of the totalitarian governments of Germany, Italy, Russia and Japan." Speaking in support, one delegate announced that he thought "the time has come when we have got to stop hiding behind windows" (UAW Convention Proceedings, 1940, pp. 292–293). (How does one hide behind a window?)

Another delegate, not hiding behind windows, who was a member of the Constitution Committee, wrote to Paul Weber, chair of ACTU, that the committee had a majority to bar Nazis, Fascists, and Communists from holding office. He also indicated that Reuther was willing to support the proposal, which he was not prepared to do the previous year. The delegate was writing to Weber for guidance on how to avoid the pitfalls of having to bar all political parties, proving someone is a Communist, and avoiding a witch hunt. This was a preview of the arguments that arose during subsequent conventions. The delegate proposed to Weber that the Communist Party be joined with the Nazis in that neither permit legitimate unions; thus, it is proper to bar them from office. He added that "Socialists (according to Reuther) more or less controlled Norway & Sweden & Denmark governments and Unions flourished there. Rep or Dem or ACTU do not belong to organizations who will eliminate unions" (All punctuation in original). Weber's response was a knowledgeable history of the Communist parties and their relationship with the Comintern, the Lovestone split, the Foster-Ruthenberg fight in 1925, and a quotation from Georgi Dimitrov on the unity of the Communist International. The respondent concluded by saying, "A strong reason why we should not permit members of foreign government agencies to become officers of our union, lies in their capacity for reversal of policies upon demand of other controlling foreign governments." All of this came to nothing until the 1941 convention when Reuther found an ally stronger than ACTU (ACTU Collection, box 14; folder: Communism, UA,WSU).

At the 1941 convention, Reuther and Richard Frankensteen, who had suffered a verbal attack when he was sent to get the workers back in the shops during a strike at North American Aircraft in California, became allies. Local 683 had called the strike in June 1941 without the authorization of the International Executive Board. Sidney Hillman, president of the Amalgamated Clothing Workers (CIO), was the codirector of the Office of Production Management (OPM), a body designated by President Roosevelt to oversee defense production. William S. Knudsen, codirector of OPM, and Secretary of the Navy Frank Knox ordered the strikers back to work, as did Philip Murray and R. J. Thomas. On the other side, those that supported the strike were Lewis Michener, regional director of the UAW on the West Coast, and Wyndham Mortimer, an International representative of the UAW; both had been associated with the politics of the Communist Party in the UAW. On June 6, 1941, Frankensteen apparently had Michener's and Mortimer's agreement to have the strikers return to work.

The following day they reversed themselves and refused to give Frankensteen permission to speak to fifty leaders in the local. At a subsequent localwide meeting in a beanfield, Frankensteen tried to speak in order to get the local back to work. He was booed so badly and heckled by a small group that it was impossible for him to continue. All the leadership of the International UAW was opposed to the strike, because it was tying up a major defense industry. Finally, the army was sent in, and the strikers returned to work. It was charged that the strike was inspired by the Communist Party, which was undoubtedly so. It was further charged that the strike was political in origin, in that the Communist Party was against the war now raging in Europe and was deliberately sabotaging the defense preparation. (The general expression of horror by many American commentators about "political" strikes does not extend to the refusal of East Coast longshoremen to carry some Soviet cargo.) It may be true that the Communist Party deliberately made a decision to disrupt the defense effort, as several ex-Communists have testified; however, the wages and working conditions at North American were bad,[1] and without any reason to support the government, they felt no compunction about striking a defense industry.

The record of the Communist Party in this period is mixed. Anti-Communist writers have long maintained that the Communist Party conducted political strikes against defense industries during the Moscow-Berlin Pact ("The Yanks aren't coming"), and following the German invasion of the Soviet Union, they became the most quiescent of unionists. Army intelligence informers were more specific, asserting that during the period of the pact the Communists "are not so very much concerned with the results of negotiations as long as they can cripple and paralyze production" (Goode Collection, U.S. Army Intelligence, p. 10, UA,WSU). According to these critics, the Communist Party's trade union positions, in substance, were products of the international needs of the Soviet Union and not the needs of American workers. This belief about political strikes in defense conducted by the Communist Party has been challenged by two authors highly critical of the Communists' overall performance in the union movement.

In fact, the strike activities of the Communist Party–dominated unions, as these writers have demonstrated, did not follow the pattern ascribed to them. Some struck during the period of the Moscow-Berlin Pact, and others did not. For those that struck, the duration of the strikes seemed to be a response to the local union situation and not some dictate from Moscow to disrupt defense production. While it is incontestable that the political positions of the American Communist Party were dominated by the needs of the Soviet Union, their union behavior could not always follow their political line (Cochran, 1977, ch. 7, and Levenstein, 1981, pp. 145–150).

In June 1941, the Communist Party line changed again. Germany invaded the Soviet Union, and the Communist Party became stalwart defenders of the war effort. So in August 1941, at the UAW convention, the Communist Party was defending itself against a policy that had now changed.

The commotion about the North American strike began on the first day of the convention. Frankensteen rose to protest the presence on the table of the California delegation a collection of toy tanks, airplanes, and troops, accompanied by a sign "Frankensteen's Local 0.0.0." He rose to say, "Although I disapprove of troops, I would rather symbolize the American army than the Red Flag of Moscow" (UAW Convention Proceedings, 1941, p. 78). The rest of the discussion barely got above that level. The IEB had referred the problem of the North American strike to the Grievance Committee of the convention. The Majority Report, a preliminary one, recounted the events of the strike, not much in dispute by anyone, and asked that the convention fully support the action of Frankensteen to bar Michener from holding office for one year and to place Region 6 (California) under an administrator.

The Minority Report supported the role of the International in the strike and called for the expulsion of Michener from the union, proposed that the five International representatives be fired for their activities in the strike and be prohibited from holding office for five years, recommended an administratorship for the region, and ordered the International Executive Board to get the fired workers back to work. The Super Minority Report was the least punitive, recommending that the fired workers be returned to their jobs, that Michener not be allowed to run for regional director at this convention, and that the case of the fired representatives be sent to the board for consideration. In the discussion, the Communist Party came in for a few knocks, but the violation of union discipline was the main charge against the local. One delegate noted that the strike was "a planned program because Joe Stalin and Adolf Hitler had not gone to war yet, they were still sleeping in the same bed. . . . Tomorrow morning if Adolf Hitler pushes another hundred miles into the Soviet Union you will find the leaders of the Communist Party urging workers to walk through picket lines" (pp. 401–407). A prescient remark.

James Lindahl, Local 190, a Communist Party supporter, in the first discussion diverted the argument to assault Sidney Hillman and the OPM, associating Reuther and Hillman. Reuther spoke in favor of the Majority Report on constitutional grounds, making one short allusion to outside "interests." Melvin Bishop of Local 157 stated that "Brother Victor Reuther is the only person in this union who has ever tried to influence me concerning the Communist situation in Russia" (p. 410), and again the famous letter written by Victor Reuther from the Soviet Union was brought before a UAW convention. Michener asked that the convention put its finger on those responsible for the North American situation, the corporation, and the OPM: "so that we may make our position clear, we refer specifically to Sidney Hillman and his red-headed stooge in this convention, Walter Reuther" (p. 440).

The Super Minority Report was accepted by the convention, providing for the least severe punishment for those involved. The debate had a strange character: The Communist Party got little mention, all of the delegates admitted that Michener had made "mistakes," and the Communist Party leadership in the union did not take the floor. It seems as if the Communist Party did not want to battle on this issue since its position regarding the war had changed, and tactically, it had more important issues facing its members at the convention. Michener's culpability was so obvious that it was hard to broach a defense in the political climate of the convention.

Frankensteen was so infuriated by the Communist Party's stand on the strike that Reuther and he decided to assault the Communists through a resolution, not only on the North American strike but on their right to hold office in the union. The Majority Report of the Constitution Committee, after noting the resolution of the previous convention against Nazism, fascism, and communism, proposed adding to the Constitution.

No member or supporter of any organization whose loyalty to a foreign government or who supports organizations which approve of totalitarian forms of government, shall be eligible to hold elective or appointive office in the International Union or any subdivision thereof. (p. 688)

No parties or philosophies were named, and the regular trial procedure was provided for. The minority report was substantially the same as the majority proposal except that it named the Communists, Fascists, and Nazis and added the Socialist Party, "which seeks to impose upon the UAW-CIO a trade union policy . . . in opposition to the policies of the Congress of Industrial Organizations" (p. 692).

Lindahl, Local 190, who made the minority report, assailed the Socialist Party, noting that if the truth were known, "it would be shown that all our difficulties have been introduced by outside organizations." Quoting at length from the Socialist Party conventions or their newspaper the *Socialist Call*, he attacked them for being revolutionary, to the Left of the Communist Party. He attacked

them for being "center-of-the-roaders" and for being so far right that "they are
ready to betray the union movement" (p. 692). Once he attacked them with an
old, familiar Communist charge: "If Fascism come tomorrow, the Socialists, as
they did in Germany, will kiss the foot of the Fascists" (p. 694). This is an echo
of the Communist Party position on the German Social Democrats that held that
they were indistinguishable from the Fascists and were labeled "social fascists"
(p. 694). Len De Caux, a longtime fellow traveler, dismissed this Socialist baiting as "opportunists on the left, reluctant to defend communists as such, thought
it smart to retort to communist-ban proposals: 'Okay let's also include socialists
then; they interfere in the union as much as the communists' " (De Caux, 1970,
p. 472).

The Constitutional Committee offered even another report, the Super-
Minority Report, that did not mention the Socialist Party, differing only slightly
from the Majority Report in that it named the Nazis, Fascists, and Communists.
It was a hot debate, Hillman was pilloried, the Socialist mayor of Milwaukee was
lauded, political innocence was claimed, and dark motives were imputed.
Frankensteen and Thomas supported the Majority Report. Addes seemed to be in
favor of the Minority report without directly saying so. He maintained: "I am for
eliminating from this union once and for all any minority political party" (p.
696). John Anderson, a known Communist from Local 155, announced: "I rise
at this point, as men of courage have always risen—the name is John Anderson,
the local is 155" (p. 700). He defended the Communists as good trade unionists
and then attacked Reuther for being a draft dodger: "He hid behind the skirts of
his wife" (p. 702).[2] Anderson continued:

> The "royal family" [the Reuthers] came into the first convention as left wingers, the
> last convention as middle-of-the-roaders, and this convention as right wingers, and if they
> follow the policy of the Socialists in Germany as pronounced at the last meeting of the
> Reichstag they will come into a future convention of full-blooded Fascists. (p. 703)

There was a lot of tattling going on. One delegate, a supporter of the minority report, revealed that the Majority Report supporters had, in their sessions,
been singing Italian, German, and Russian songs. Addes said that Reuther's con-
version to anticommunism was rather recent, that in 1936, 1937, and 1938, "he
told me the opposite in his convincing manner" (p. 705). Tracy Doll, speaking
for the Super Minority report, told of the Communist Party's changing earlier in
the year from a resolution seeking to have the CIO sponsor a peace conference
to, four days later, another resolution on "Bundles for Britain" (p. 705). Another
speaker, a supporter of the minority report, wanted to add draft dodgers to the list
of proscribed parties (p. 713).

The Super Minority Report was adopted. Several things are apparent from
the proceedings of the convention. The minority report that proposed to add the
Socialist Party to the list prompted some of the most reactionary positions taken
during the debate—for example, the story that the Majority Report advocates had

been singing German, Italian, and Russian songs or the argument that the Minority Report would "do away with all parties." Most notable about the debate was the complicity of the Communists in the Minority Report and their ambivalent position throughout the debate. Addes and Lindahl, the maker of the Minority Report, were the two speakers closest to the Communist Party, outside of the known party members, and they had similar positions against all minority parties being active in the union. The remarks of Lindahl, who had employed the old Communist allegation that the Socialists (Social Fascists) were lackeys of the Nazis, indicate that a conscious tactical decision was made regarding the anti–Communist Party resolution at the convention. Apparently, it was decided by Communist Party members not to make an issue of the attacks and to weather the storm. They made no effort to mount a civil libertarian position, and the draft dodger charges against Reuther did little to enhance the reputation of the Communist Party in their new-found patriotism.

The change from condemnation of the totalitarian political philosophies and barring them from holding union office, introduced by Reuther and Frankensteen, to barring Nazis, Fascists, and Communists from holding office was a step back from a civil libertarian stance, even though there was no question that it was never intended to be used. According to the FBI report on Nat Ganley, he made a statement at a *Daily Worker* press conference in December 1944 that "there was a clause in the UAW Constitution to the effect that no Communist could hold an office in the union." He pointed out that he was on the Referendum Committee (for the No-Strike Pledge) and was known as a Communist (Goode Collection, FBI File, Nat Ganley, p. 66, UA,WSU). Disregarding the credibility of FBI informants, whether Ganley made the statement or not, the facts were true. There was no effort to remove Ganley from this committee or anyone from any position in the union for their political beliefs. Nevertheless, the majority position, barring Nazis, Fascists, and Communists from holding office, did get Reuther into trouble after he was elected president of the UAW in 1946, when he was challenged about a trial procedure. Reuther had no intention of enforcing the constitutional provision, but it was perfectly legitimate to force him to state how he intended to implement the provision since he had supported it.

He maintained that an acknowledged CPer, one about whom there was no doubt, did not have to be tried in a formal situation and could be removed by membership action. Hence, Reuther was put in the position of depriving members of their constitutional rights in the UAW by denying the dissidents a fair trial. There was little danger that this punitive change in the UAW constitution was ever going to be enforced, which may account for the Communists' lack of resistance to the resolution. For one, it would have been impossible to get a local trial board at that time to remove John Anderson or Nat Ganley, so well entrenched were they in their local. What is onerous about the constitutional change is its threat to the rights of UAW members. It was a surrender to political expediency. The Communist Party was vulnerable because of its role in the North American strike and its dramatic shift in line about the war; consequently, this antilibertarian stratagem was used to punish it (Walter Reuther Collection, box 108; folder: Factional Statements on Convention Issues, Press Release, October 3, 1946, p. 4, UA,WSU).

The final embarrassment for the UAW in regard to this provision did not come until the 1980 convention. The committee moved that it be removed in its entirety. Pat Geathouse, UAW vice-president, was in the chair at the time and said:

We have been told there isn't much sense of having philosophical argument about this. The Sixth Circuit Court of Appeals has ruled that this is illegal. The Labor Department said to us it should be taken out and the Public Review Board has recommended that it be taken out, that you cannot really police this kind of an operation. As we know, these political parties have been made legal in both the United States and Canada, and it's based upon those recommendations that we're proposing the change.

There was unexpected resistance to what was considered a routine matter. There was debate on both sides, and those for the change were forceful and accurate. Those against eliminating the provision may not have been as cogent in their arguments, but they were forceful. The speech that may have defeated the resolution to rescind was made by a woman delegate. Her complete speech is as follows: "I am opposed. I lost a brother in Korea. That's all I have to say." The motion was defeated, and the 1941 provision of the constitution remains operative but unenforceable (UAW Convention Proceedings, 1980, pp. 153–158, UA,WSU).

In addition to the protracted debate on the North American strike and the resolution on the Communist Party, the 1941 convention, one of the longest and most inflammatory of the many feisty UAW conventions, had another conflict: the report of the Credentials Committee on the seating of the controversial Local 248 delegates, representing workers at the Allis-Chalmers Company in Wisconsin. The convention began with a speech by the president, R. J. Thomas, that indicated the strain over the Communist Party and the international politics that dominated the meeting. He announced that he was in favor of aid to Great Britain, Russia, and China, adding that this did not imply "an endorsement of the Communist Party." He continued, "A few months ago when I went out and made statements that I was for material aid to Great Britain, by certain people I was called a war-monger" (UAW Convention Proceedings, 1941, p. 12). These same people, according to Thomas, now wanted to go further than he was prepared to go. The reference to the change of position on the part of the Communist Party was not lost on the delegates. In a tempering statement, Thomas also warned against charging all opponents with being Communists, as Homer Martin had done. The chaplain of the Steel Workers Organizing Committee, Fr. Charles A. Maxwell, gave a rousing union speech in which he touched on an issue that was to plague the convention. He said, "Don't be frightened because they say 'they went out on strike to sabotage this defense program.' Don't be frightened if they call you radicals. You know anyone today who is not a radical is nobody. I am a radical. Christ Himself was a radical" (p. 27).

The Majority Report of the Credentials Committee was opposed to seating the Local 248 delegation, containing a letter signed by seventeen members of the local protesting the seating of the delegation on several bases: the illegal Election Committee, failure to notify the membership in the time required by the constitution, and failure to keep the polls open the required time. As a consequence of these violations, the top vote-getter received only 220 votes out of a membership of about 4,000. The local leadership admitted that they had conducted elections in this illegal manner for three years (pp. 53, 54, 82–83).

Tom Doherty, secretary of the Credentials Committee and an ACTU activist, made an explicit statement of some of the politics underlying the difference of opinion, stating, "We are opposed to Adolph Hitler and Stalin and their Godless Fascist and Communist machines." Hitler and Stalin, he continued, "believe that constitutions are only made to be broken, and the majority of this committee believe that the ruling officers of Local 248 believe the same thing" (p. 83). Doherty also said that Harold Christoffel, president of the local, had been warned by Thomas that delegates must be nominated and elected a week apart, and if the credentials were received past the deadline because of the requirement, Thomas would fight to seat them despite the lateness.

The Minority Report was for seating the delegation, maintaining that the lateness of the vote and the subsequent violations of the constitution were caused by the International Executive Board. If the credentials were to be timely, the violations were necessary. They pointed out that the convention was the highest body in the union and the delegates had the right to accept the Minority Report despite the violations, and that conventions had made exceptions in the past (p. 84).

The debate that followed was furious. One speaker contended that the 17 signers of the protest against seating the delegation had walked through a picket line with about 500 other local union members after the government ordered the local to return to work. Richard Leonard branded that "a damnable lie" (p. 115). Further, Leonard charged that the strike vote contained 2,200 fraudulent ballots, as attested to by handwriting experts hired by the State Mediation Board and confirmed by a handwriting expert hired by the local, at a fee of $100 a day. His revelations on the manner in which the Election Committee was selected revealed a curious procedure: Rather than elect them, it was done by lottery; 19 people were nominated and drew numbers from a hat, and those drawing the lowest number, one through five, constituted the committee. It is an interesting coincidence that the same person had drawn number one for three successive elections. On the strike itself, Leonard pointed out that subsequent to the return to work of approximately 500 members after the federal government had requested their return, all

members of the local were required to sign a statement that they had not complied with the government's request. Those that failed or refused to sign such a
statement were fined and denied the right to vote. This left only 1,500 out of
4,000 eligible to vote.

Walter Reuther took the floor to give an account of the Executive Board's
actions on the Allis-Chalmers Local's vote, quoting one board member sympathetic to the local that "there is no need of taking steps insuring these fellows
have the right to vote. . . . If they get the right to vote they will be afraid to go
near the hall because Christoffel's goon squad will kick hell out of them" (p. 95).

Those speakers in favor of seating the Local 248 delegation did not enter the
constitutional debate. They frankly admitted that the election violated the UAW
constitution, claiming that because of the UAW Executive Board's action, a violation was inevitable: Either transgress against the rules for electing or get the
credentials in late. They, too, had a political ax to grind. Sidney Hillman had
ordered the striking workers to return to work because Allis-Chalmers was vital
to the defense effort. Hillman, identified as a Socialist in later debate, became the
goat of the Minority Report position, and John L. Lewis, who had threatened to
strike at the same time despite government pressure not to, became their hero.
One delegate read a letter from Lewis praising Christoffel for his militancy.
(Lewis was not long to remain a hero; his continued strike activity during the war
brought down on him some of the harshest criticism that this caucus could
muster.) They also supported the delegation on the basis that they had gone
through a vicious strike against one of the most reactionary employers in the
country (an opinion agreed to by all parties) and that a negative vote would
enhance the charges brought by the conservative elements in the state. On the
matter of the fraudulent ballots, a speaker claimed that in 1939 "all the General
Motor's locals padded the ballots to go on strike" (p. 91). This was certainly the
strangest and most indiscreet defense raised by the Local 248 supporter even
though it may have been true.

The minority position to seat the delegation lost, and a compromise resolution was passed to send a three-man committee to the local to conduct another
election. They soon returned from Wisconsin, unable to reach agreement with
Christoffel as to how the election was to be conducted. They reported in some
detail the reaction of Christoffel on their suggestions, pointing out that he had
called Thomas, Frankensteen, Reuther, Leonard and Nordstrom "a bunch of
phonies, rats, and Hillmanites" (p. 303) and described the convention as a bunch
of "bastards" (p. 303). The committee of three also reported on the attitude of
Christoffel on how the local was to run the election. Owing to the time con-
straints and the demands of the UAW constitution, the committee proposed to set
up some hurried meeting to make nominations and decided on questions of eligibility to vote by notifying the membership by handbills of the meetings.
Christoffel, according to the committee, undisputed by him, said that "this would
not be allowed and that anyone trying to do this would be taken care of," and fur-

ther, that "only Finks, rats, stooges and Hillmanities pass out or accept literature at the gates. That is the way we have our people educated" (p. 304). The negotiations broke down on the questions of eligibility to vote, the number of days for the election, and who was to chair the meeting determining eligibility. The committee report loosened a torrent of abuse on Christoffel from the delegates, but in the democratic tradition of the UAW, he was given the floor.

To all appearances, Christoffel's speech apparently was one of the most masterful delivered at the convention. If he had been contentious with the committee, he was now a model of reasoned demeanor, denying that the differences between the local and the committee were very great: "In fact," he said, "to this day, to this moment, I don't know why the committee did not proceed to hold the election as they had agreed" (p. 308). He indicated that they were not far apart; there was little dispute on the facts as presented; and—with an attitude of "Was it something I said, fellows?"—all was well. He recounted his version of the encounter, the agreements that had been reached, and his surprise at the termination of the discussions. But he had some "ideas on the subject" of why the committee left town. As he warmed to his subject, he dramatically produced an opposition leaflet asking delegates to support the anti-Christoffel slate, passed out, according to Christoffel, by "paid agents" of the regional director, Nordstrom. Then he held up copies of the leaflet, stencils of the mimeographed leaflet, and copies of a press release from Nordstrom—all having been discarded because of errors and all procured from the regional offices. The reason for the departure of the committee was now obvious, according to Christoffel: It was a political move on the part of the regional director, who was hostile to the local. Christoffel also noted that because one of the secretaries was president of the Office Workers Union and a Christoffel supporter, the regional officers had asked her not to come in on those days, and they also asked her to turn in her key. "Oh, they are so clever," he said dramatically, "but they forgot to empty their wastebasket" (p. 312). Someone sympathetic to the local had gone in the office, emptied the wastebaskets, and gave the contents to Christoffel. He followed with a narration of his personal history and the local's fight against Allis-Chalmers, the AFL, and Homer Martin and the local's defiance of Knox and Knudsen when ordered back to work, ending with a rousing finale on militant unionism. The record indicated "Prolonged applause" (p. 315).

One member of the committee, in rebuttal, tried to dispel the impression that sweetness and light prevailed by quoting Christoffel as saying: "We don't need an election, we have our ten delegates. Any man who accepts nomination against these delegates will be a traitor to the labor movement and will never live it down" (p. 316). Another Executive Board member of the local was quoted as making a statement: "We were asked to take these fellows that signed protest against seating of the delegates out into the alley and punch their noses off of them. . . . I am advising them to get out quietly unless they want to be carried out. Everyone of these men will be taken care of" (p. 316).

Nordstrom, the regional director, asserted that one of his staff and wife had been beaten in front of the local. He added that the secretary referred to by Christoffel who had obviously secured the mimeographed material from the wastebaskets was his personal secretary and a "Communist stooge." However, in support of Christoffel, one of the three-person committee insisted that a fair election could have been held and that the committee should not have left so soon. A delegate from Local 190 took the floor to announce: "I am just as good an American as Dick Leonard . . . but I don't have to wake up every morning with a Bible in this hand and the American Flag in that hand to prove it to myself" (p. 327). After interminable debate, the three-man committee was enlarged to seven and sent back to the local to conduct an election. On the afternoon of the tenth day of the convention, the committee returned and reported that an election had been held; all conditions of the constitution had been met; and the same ten delegates were elected, with 1,488 ballots cast rather than the several hundred cast in the first election (p. 574).

Despite the irregularities of the election procedure, the vote firmly established the popularity of Christoffel's leadership, not that it had been in dispute. The UAW was a beleaguered union in 1941, and aggressive leadership provided the cement for Local 248 that faced a bellicose and reactionary employer. According to Cochran (1977, p. 167), Harold Christoffel was a committed radical, having joined the Socialist Party by 1933. In that year, he was tried by the Socialist Party for being a Communist Party infiltrator, acquitted, and then expelled at a later date. In 1947, the House Committee on Education and Labor indicted him for perjury, and he was convicted and jailed in 1950.

His victimization at the hands of the House Committee apart, one question remains: How did this Communist Party–dominated local conduct itself in terms of internal working-class democracy? The evidence strongly indicates that, in addition to Christoffel's high level of personal popularity, the local suffered under a constant implicit and explicit threat of violence. The evidence comes from undisputed testimony of the opponents of the local leadership, from sympathizers, and from the words of the leadership. Christoffel was half militant Wobbly, half Stalinist functionary with little regard for the niceties of internal democracy. There was considerable activity and involvement of the membership in educational programs and flying squadron and other local activities, but even if the endemic threat of violence is ignored, there was still no mechanism for opposition expression. The traditional avenue for an opposition group in the UAW was the mimeographed broadside; however, the membership had been "educated" to abstain from factional leafletting or to ignore the efforts if an opposition had the courage to do it.

The local's 1940 membership pledge card contains the following statement, in part:

If for any reason I should drop my membership in Local No. 248 UAWA-CIO, without being exonerated or being granted a withdrawal card or if I should be suspended or expelled under said Local's By-laws, or rules, I will immediately be liable for liquidated damages in the sum of fifty ($50.00) and shall pay to the order of Local 248 UAWA-CIO, the said sum of fifty ($50.00). Such sum may become due by reason of the occurrence of any of the foregoing facts or circumstances and or at such time when Local 248 UAWA-CIO, has determined that such facts or circumstances have occurred and such sum has become due. (UAW Research Department Collection, box 4; folder 4, UA,WSU)

This kind of provision was unheard of in the UAW, and it represented part of a pattern of intimidation of the membership. The logic of it is unclear. That Christoffel and his group had the allegiance of a large majority in the local is indisputable. Why, then, did they feel it necessary to use coercive tactics with them? One of Nordstrom's staff and wife were beaten up according to the testimony of Nordstrom at the convention. A pall hung over the local regarding dissidents. An ACTU member of Local 248 sent a letter to the *Michigan Labor Leader* outlining his version of the Allis-Chalmers strike, adding "P.S. *Don't* use my name. The flying squadron here is quite active" (ACTU Collection, box 8; folder: AC-1941, UA,WSU). The right of dissent has little meaning if it cannot be exercised without fear of retribution.

Undemocratic procedures, while not usual in UAW locals, were not unheard of, but in those locals where the Communist Party had undisputed control, these procedures were raised to a philosophy more reminiscent of a military group than a free association of workers. The leadership of Local 248 was an assortment of self-confessed radicals, ostensibly dedicated to democracy in the fullest sense, but that dedication evidently did not extend to "bourgeois" rights.

One aspect of the Local 248 dispute that was soon forgotten in the fury of the debate was George Addes's apparently unprovoked attack on ACTU. He was the first speaker to take the floor on the seating of the delegates, stating that this decision not to seat the delegates was not made on its merits but was the result of a caucus action because it was reputed that Local 248 represented the "philosophies of Stalin." Then he launched an attack that reverberated throughout the UAW for years, charging that the secretary of the Credentials Committee (Thomas Doherty)

represents an outside movement—remember that. He represents what is known as the A.C.T.U.—and let me inform you that organization does not represent Catholicism. I happen to be one—I happen to be one, but I cannot tolerate the policies of that organization, because many of the decisions that are made in the union, wherever we have members of the ACTU, are made on the outside of the organization. (UAW Convention Proceedings, 1941, p. 85)

Given the number of Catholic members of the UAW, this would seem to be an unpolitical foray against a powerful opponent. It was carefully couched to appeal to the xenophobic impulses at the convention; "outsiders" were the source of the UAW's problems, not the Catholic church itself.

Addes's attack was really a counterattack. ACTU, sensing the vulnerability of the Communist Party because of the North American strike and the recent change of party line, sent a telegram to Addes on July 25, just eleven days before the 1941 convention, asking Addes, "as a Catholic," whether he would repudiate Communist Party support as had R. J. Thomas. Addes did not respond and instead attacked Doherty at the convention. The *Michigan Labor Leader*, August 15, 1941, in a straight news story reported Addes's words. However, in a boxed statement in the same issue on page one, the paper quoted Archbishop Mooney as saying that ACTU "definitely presents the Catholic doctrine on labor and labor unions" (Boxed statement, 1941, p. 1).

Fr. Clancy (Detroit ACTU chaplain), in a strange mea culpa column, accepted part of the responsibility for Addes's alleged confusion about whether ACTU represented the Church, because he had not sent a copy of the encyclicals that Addes had requested. It is doubtful that even the most studious perusal of the encyclicals would have changed Addes's mind. Clancy continued, expressing his "disappointment" that Addes had not repudiated Communist Party endorsement, but ended, "Loyal to George as a friend, I am hurt to see him in a position where anyone might dare raise the slightest question about his Catholicism, his Americanism or his unionism" ("The Chaplain's Corner," 1941, p. 1).

Two weeks later, with what might be interpreted as a sigh of relief, the *Michigan Labor Leader* headed a story on page one, "Communist Threats to 'Blast' ACTU Flop Hard" (1941, p. 1). On September 26, 1941, the *Michigan Labor Leader* picked up a story on Addes from the Packard Local 190, which had strong Communist Party influence, utilizing their own head: " 'I Will Never Witch Hunt' by George Addes" (1941, p. 4). The statement was evidently prepared for the convention but was not delivered. He pointed out that he had "no position on union problems, AS A CATHOLIC" and stated that he did not believe in "Communist philosophy or doctrines." Addes would have done well to have left the argument at that; it was a sounder argument than that which followed. He added that the idea that there is a separate Catholic position "is what breeds bigotry. That is what breeds anti-Semitism. That is what breeds prejudice against Catholics. Yes, that is what breeds fascism." That is a monumental jump from a separate Catholic position on social issues (which no civil libertarian could complain about) to the breeding of fascism. The *Michigan Labor Leader* did not respond to the story; they simply printed it without comment.

Addes was undoubtedly sincere in his abjurations against red-baiting but was ambiguous about principled criticism of the Communist Party on a sound union basis. Even that was red-baiting, according to Addes. If the Communist Party in its later self-criticism admitted to major mistakes in policy, why was it red-baiting to criticize those same policies at the time they were formulated? Army Intelligence had a cute designation for Communists at one time, calling them "premature anti-fascists." The Communist Party should have developed a similar designation for their opposition, perhaps "premature anti-Browderite." Another aspect of Addes's retort to critics of the Communist Party was his constant reference to the Socialist Party. The *Michigan Labor Leader* quoted him as saying, "You know that no Communist Party can tell me what to do. And so, that the matter may be crystal clear, let me add that no Socialist Party can tell me what to do either" (p. 4). The Socialist Party had no particular line in the UAW; it was in a state of dissolution, for one thing. And if they had a party position, the Reuthers, having left the party some time before, were well beyond any Socialist Party discipline, as meager as it was. This posturing on Addes's part smacks of the Communist Party disposition to attack the Socialist Party as if they were back in Germany during the 1930s once again, replaying a chronic battle of the sects that was beyond Addes's limited political purview and irrelevant to the UAW situation.

The Communists at this point were in a very ambiguous position. They had recently experienced a dazzling change in their political line toward the war. This shift from "Imperialist War" to the "War against Fascism" caused the CP considerable embarrassment not only on the political front. The CP position on UAW union matters was also compromised. The North American strike and the following convention fell astride this policy change. Instead of being against the war, the invasion of the Soviet Union caused a change in attitude on the part of the CP regarding strikes, particularly in defense industries that might soon be providing arms for the Soviet Union. The party was shackled in its defense of the striking North American workers.

Since the Communists never had had a decent perspective on civil liberties, their machinations on the principled question of the rights of union members to hold dissident political views should not have been surprising. Rather than make a principled position, their fellow travelers offered a hokey substitute motion that worsened the situation. But, again, there is little evidence that these devices caused much damage to the position of the CP. It took the Communists' activities during the war years to irreparably harm their status in the union.

POLITICS DURING THE WAR

World War II produced in America a sense of solidarity not always seen at times of armed conflict. There were no "draft riots" as there were in the Civil War. There was no Eugene Victor Debs imprisoned for antiwar activities or a large pacifist movement, as there was in World War I. Perhaps the attack on Pearl Harbor created this unity among the American people. In any case, except for splinter radical activity, there was a strong consensus in support of the war aims. The disputes in the UAW revolved around how best to conduct the war. Once the Germans invaded the Soviet Union and the Japanese attacked Pearl

Harbor, antiwar sentiment disappeared. However, conflict in the UAW did not. But the 1942 convention of the UAW was mostly love and light.

Richard Leonard nominated Reuther for vice-president, and Addes seconded the nomination and Reuther reciprocated. Later in the convention, on the debate about a proposed Supreme Economic Council (labor, management, and government), Reuther reported on some of the absurdities of wartime planning. Eighty thousand needle trades workers were unemployed in New York City, where ninety percent of all needle trades workers lived. To meet the new demand for uniforms and to save three cents a pair, economic planners had allocated most of this work to the South. But they had to build new factories while New York factories remained idle. This new construction of machines and buildings tied up the machine tool industry needed in war production. In a brilliant domino effect, the expanding clothing industry absorbed southern agricultural workers, which was to be corrected by bringing in 50,000 Mexicans at eighteen cents an hour. Reuther's planning instincts were whetted by the ineptitude of government planners (UAW Convention Proceedings, 1942, pp. 394–396, UA,WSU).

The rank and file were guarded in their response to administration efforts to have conventions on a two-year basis, rather than yearly, during the war, to increase dues and to have a $20 spread in staff wages ($70 to $90 a week), instead of a flat rate for all reps. The equalitarian rank and file defeated all three. The African-American delegates made a symbolic move by having Hodges Mason nominate Oscar Noble for vice-president. Shelton Tappes seconded the nomination, and Noble declined with a brief speech. A unanimous resolution was passed to oppose the deportation of Harry Bridges, the Australian-born leader of the West Coast longshoremen, long associated with the Communist Party. In a final unity action, R. J. Thomas was presented with a small hatchet signifying that "political hatchet jobs in the UAW . . . be a matter of the past." Thomas thanked the delegate and noted that he was "perfectly willing to bury the hatchet." A delegate shouted: "In whose head?" Thomas shot back: "In Hitler's back" (p. 317).

Despite this sanguine sentiment, hatchet jobs were hardly over in the UAW. Many people were maligned in the factional disputes; however, few suffered the treatment of Richard L-G Deverall, onetime educational director of the UAW and an activist in ACTU. He was appointed educational director by R. J. Thomas in March 1939. This was the period following Martin's defeat and extended to just after America's entry into the war. Linton's history of the UAW Education Department maintains that "under Deverall the educational work was greatly enlarged" (Linton, 1965, p. 91). Linton's account of Deverall's achievements is an impressive one, but his politics, not his performance, was the basis of the attacks on him. In January 1942, a statewide educational conference was held in Detroit at which Sam Sweet and Sam Levine, of Communist-dominated Local 51, offered a resolution to set up a statewide UAW education body. Deverall argued that it was out of order because the conference in session had no legislative function and the resolution bypassed the authority of the UAW Executive Board. Later conversations between Thomas and Deverall confirmed Deverall's position. The resolution was passed anyway and Frank Marquart of Local 600 was elected chairperson (Deverall, 1942, p. 1).

Marquart checked with Thomas who declared that the new statewide body contravened the UAW's constitution. Marquart promptly wrote to the participants, telling them of Thomas's ruling. Sam Sweet, a longtime associate of the CP, called a meeting despite this. Marquart did not attend, and Sweet, from the chair, according to Deverall's statement, denounced Deverall as "a fascist, a fifth columnist, a saboteur, a man hiding behind the Catholic Church and a man who knows nothing about education" (p. 2).[3]

Deverall, in his report of this incident to Thomas, quoted a pamphlet written by Sweet just prior to the German invasion of the Soviet Union that "the present war raging over four continents is not a war for a 'new social order,' or for democracy. It is a war for profits, for new conquests. It is an imperialist war" (p. 2). This was the crux of the matter: Both the Communist Party and Deverall, a Catholic radical and opponent of British imperialism, were opposed to the war. The Communist Party changed its position after the invasion of the Soviet Union: Deverall changed his mind after the attack on Pearl Harbor. The Communist Party, recognizing the importance of the education director as a purveyor of propaganda, wanted this "unreliable" Deverall out and someone more attuned to their position appointed.

Deverall, defending himself against accusations of Fascist sympathies, noted that he was the editor of *Christian Social Action*, a liberal, prounion Catholic magazine for whom John L. Lewis and Frank Murphy, governor of Michigan and later Supreme Court Justice, had written articles (p. 3). In September 1939, Deverall in his magazine had castigated Coughlin's Christian Front as an anti-Semitic Catholic group and said that the Brooklyn *Tablet*, an influential Catholic paper, "gives it implicit support and encouragement" (ACTU Collection, box 22; folder: Jews, UA,WSU). "Catholic opinion of me is divided," wrote Deverall. "The reactionary elements of the Church think I am a member of the Communist Party. A Philadelphia Cardinal so advised me. The liberal elements of the Church have always supported my work" (Deverall, 1942, p. 4).

At the UAW convention in August 1942, a resolution was introduced on Deverall saying that, as editor of *Christian Social Action*, he had "printed editorials and signed articles directly and indirectly praising Hitler, Franco, Mussolini and Petain" and as editor of the UAW *Distributor* had reviewed books "by known fascist and anti-Semites." The resolutions committee felt "that there is undoubtedly justification in the charges and validity to the complaints"; nonetheless, they recommended referring it to the Executive Board because there was not enough time to investigate the charges (UAW Convention Proceedings, 1942, Resolution 18, UA,WSU). The board, the following month, decided not to reappoint Deverall but "dismissed as unfounded the charges that Deverall was

Fascist-minded, but found out that he had failed to carry out the educational policies of the board" ("Education Department," 1942, p. 6). No evidence was produced for the latter statement. Deverall's crime was that he was a liberal
Catholic, and he was excoriated in this manner because he became a pawn in the
Communist Party's desire for an individual of more pliable politics.

INTELLIGENCE GATHERING

One activity that kept all factions of the UAW occupied was the effort to
collect information about the opposition. Nobody provided score cards, and since
much of the political effort was covert, intelligence gathering occupied considerable time. ACTU's attempts in 1937 through 1941 were sporadic, a casual part
of other activities. During the war, intelligence gathering seemed to cease, sur-
facing again after the war in the intensified battle with the Communist Party. The
early targets were not always the Communists; the Socialists and the Ku Klux
Klan (KKK) also came under surveillance. Thomas Doherty, secretary of Detroit
ACTU, wrote to the chair of the Pontiac, Michigan, branch in 1939, asking, "If
you can send me any information as to the political hook ups in your area, I shall
be glad to use them. I understand that the Socialist Party is quite strong in that
area, and I have often wondered where McAuley [UAW regional director] stacks
up" (ACTU Collection, box 2; folder: ACTU Pontiac, 1939–1949, UA,WSU).
Later in the year, Doherty wrote again on organizational matters but touched on
the KKK, showing apprehension about their small but apparently growing
strength in the Detroit UAW. There were also exchanges on an interunion basis.
A letter to Paul Weber in 1940 noted that R. J. Thomas, president of the UAW,
was supporting Joe Curran, president of the National Maritime Union (NMU-
CIO), for Congress. The writer stated:

Curran is one of the most important Communist Party whips in New York. Curran is not
his right name; he is a Pole, and changed his name just before becoming head of the NMU.
      At present Curran is trying to pull Irish Catholic votes . . . by posing as one of them.
But he is not Irish, as for being Catholic, he is divorced and remarried. . . .
      Tell Thomas there is no honest American labor leader in the East behind Curran.
(ACTU Collection, box 2; folder: ACTU, New York, 1939–1943, UA,WSU)

Intelligence gathering extended to utilizing other organizations, sometimes
Catholic. A functionary of the Workers Alliance, a Socialist-led unemployed
group who joined in 1936 with the Communist Party group, wrote in 1939 to
Paul Weber, asking for help in a project. Weber was suspicious and had Richard
Deverall write to the Detroit Council 305 of the Knights of Columbus. They
replied with a one-page dossier on the person in question, giving not only his real
name not used in the correspondence with Weber but a summary of his history
in the Communist Party (ACTU Collection, box 15; series 2, folder: CP,

1939–1945, UA,WSU).[4] The Communist front groups also occupied some time. Rank and file members of ACTU, perhaps politicized for the first time, wrote in March 1940 to Detroit ACTU for information about the "Civil Liberties Commission [*sic*]" or the Civil Rights Federation. The enquirer had determined on his own that the group had aided those who had enlisted in the Spanish Loyalist Army. Deverall replied that the group was the League for Civil Rights, a Communist Party front group. He cautioned about the tactics for exposing it. In a May 8, 1940, letter about the league to another member from Pontiac, he pointed out that John L. Lewis was "emphatically against any affiliation" with them and that a direct attack "would be suicidal because you'd be just making a martyr" (ACTU Collection, box 2; folder: ACTU Pontiac, 1939–1941, UA,WSU).

This cautious approach was also demonstrated when outside groups attempted to get information from ACTU. Paul Weber, in response to a Florida editor's request in 1946 for enlightenment of the Food, Tobacco, Agricultural and Allied Workers (CIO), replied that he regretted that he had no information on the union. This was untrue: The political character of this union was well known, but it was organizing cannery workers in Florida, and Weber was not interested in an anti-union drive by a conservative Florida editor. The editor's letter illustrates the currency given to the *Wage Earner*. He quoted an Executive News Letter to the effect that the union in question was Communist dominated, based on ACTU reports (ACTU Collection, box 19; folder: Food, Tobacco, Agricultural and Allied Workers (CIO), UA,WSU).

But front groups and political alliances of workers were not the only concern of activists in the political cauldron of the UAW. Tom Doherty wrote to a fellow unionist in 1940 about a woman who was attempting to get a job at Local 7, UAW, Doherty's home local. "Now," he wrote, "I wonder if you could give me a line on the little girl because if she isn't on the up-and-up, she doesn't get any job." The response was that she was "100% American and anti–Communist Party. Long association in paid jobs made her reluctant to announce her stand" (ACTU Collection, box 1; folder: ACTU—Chicago, 1943, UA,WSU).

Late in 1940, Fr. Clancy wrote to Vincent Sweeney of the Steel Workers, on the advice of Richard Deverall, that "there seems to be a definite campaign to discredit [on the part of the Communist Party] Murray and Hillman and to brand the former and you as 'red baiters.' . . . Hessler [*sic*] contends that John L. wanted Eddie Levinson fired but that you who are, according to Carl Hessler [*sic*] 'a &$%! and Redbaiter and a %&*$%! Hillman stooge,' went to Murray, whom he has similarly described, and got him to block the discharge." Levinson was a close friend of Walter Reuther's and an anti-Communist. Why he was to be discharged is unclear. By 1945, inquiries were again being directed to Detroit ACTU about Haessler. W. A. Copeland, Memphis director of the CIO, wrote to a newspaper guild member for information that was forwarded to Weber. He wrote back, telling about Haessler's activities in the UAW, his wife's role in the guild auxiliary, and Haessler's then-position at the Federated Press. Weber said that Haessler had signed American Newspaper Guild contracts with Federated Press as the employer and consequently had "no right to membership in the Detroit Guild," although no effort was made to deprive him of his union standing (ACTU Collection, box 20; folder: Carl Haessler, 1942–1945). These bits of information were typical of everyone's efforts in the hectic Detroit scene to assess their opposition's background and actions.

The FBI and Army Intelligence managed to reach a new high (or low) in untrustworthy intelligence gathering. It is generally known that their files contain unevaluated, sometimes downright idiotic material, but few would be prepared to encounter the photocopy of a postcard, unsigned, containing the announcement that Walter Reuther "IS A GERMAN, & COMMUNIST" (Goode Collection, Army Intelligence, Walter Reuther, p. 2, UA,WSU). A lot of capital letters seem to be a mark of the radical Right. Occasionally, a feeling develops that the FBI does not use the same nomenclature employed by the rest of society. One entry is entitled "REUTHER, WALTER PHILLIP with the alias REUTHER, WALTER P." (Goode Collection, FBI Reuther file, p. 64). There is a long list of absurdities: Victor is described as a "Cunning C.I.O. Communist" in 1941 (p. 62). Walter Reuther's "wife's maiden name is reportedly MAY WOLF but in fact was MAY WOLFMAN" (p. 109).[5] Walter Reuther is described as a "well known Communist, . . . probably not a member of the Communist Party (1939), . . . suspected Communist (1942) . . . leaning at the present time toward the Socialist ideals rather than Communism (1943)" (pp. 115–117).

It is perhaps comforting to derive some pleasure from these absurdities, but decisions of great importance flowed from them. In April 1941, Walter Reuther was recommended for "custodial detention in the event of a national emergency," signed "J. E. Hoover, Director" (p. 46). It might have been of some interest to Nat Ganley, Communist Party auto leader in Detroit, that he was given the same "recommendation" four months later than his arch foe Reuther (Goode Collection, FBI, Ganley file, p. 10, UA,WSU). The custodial detention card for Reuther was lifted on November 1, 1941. His brother Roy was finally removed from the "Security Index" in 1947 (Goode Collection, FBI Reuther file, pp. 75, 123, UA,WSU). (See the Appendix.)

The FBI reports, except when the conclusions of informants are quoted, are generally without analysis, just straight cataloging of information, however silly. But Army G-2 (Intelligence) showed curiosity about their subjects and had a disposition to conjecture about the motives of those reported on. In 1941, Reuther proposed that a tripartite board be established, composed of government, labor, and industry, "to organize and supervise the mass production of airplanes in the automobile and automotive parts industry." This was the famous "500 Planes a Day" proposal that asserted that military airplanes could be built in existing and unused auto plants. This was a puzzle to Army Intelligence. The Communist

Party was in the "Yanks Aren't Coming" period, when the war was still an "Imperialist" war, and since Reuther, according to G-2, was a known Communist, why was he so interested in war production? The *Daily Worker*, rather than wanting to produce war material, was complaining: "Warplanes to Cost Average Family $100 Annually. Analysis Made at West Coast Plane Center Shows that American People Will Pay Building Cost Through the Nose" ("Warplanes to Cost . . . ," 1941, p. 3). Apparently, G-2 was not aware of the well-known fact that Reuther, from an uneasy alliance with the Communist Party, had gone into open warfare with them. This apparent discrepancy had to be resolved, and they managed it. A memorandum, January 24, 1941, from one G-2 officer to another, noted:

Inasmuch as the Communist Party in this country is presently engaged in efforts to nullify our national defense efforts, Reuther's announced desire to increase our plane output is not consistent with the Communist Party policy and it may be safely assumed that there is some ulterior motive behind the proposal. Two possible motives appear on the surface: one—profit accruing to labor through the expansion of the automotive industry; two—transfer of a large percentage of our plane production from the airplane industry, in which the Communist Party is experiencing organizational difficulties, to the automotive industry which is largely dominated and influenced by the UAWA in which the Communist Party has a strong voice.

If this proposal should receive official recognition and the transfer be effected, an important phase of our plane production would pass under possible Communist control with the ever-present threat of a general strike within that industry at any time. (Goode Collection, Army Intelligence, p. 24, UA,WSU)

The FBI, Army Intelligence, and the Communist Party demonstrated the extent to which extralegal devices and faulty political judgments abounded during the 1930s and 1940s. Political detention, burglary, and wiretapping, all clearly illegal, were part of the political landscape. These threats to civil liberties and privacy were perpetuated largely by government agencies, culminating in the use of the Smith Act against both the Trotskyists and the Communists. The 1950s were to produce even greater abuses of government power against political dissidents, mainly the CP. At a later time, the civil rights movement became the target of inquisitorial government activity.

1943 TO THE END OF THE WAR

The 1943 convention of the UAW brought several significant changes in the politics of the UAW. The clergy still managed to strike the most radical note. The invocation by Dr. Herman J. Hahn thanked the Almighty for providing

a working man, the Gallilean [*sic*] Carpenter who was nailed to the Cross by forces of reaction because he sought to break the chains of the working class . . . and gathered them into a great solidarity, in a movement that would put down the mighty . . . to establish a sane social order where only those who serve with brain and brawn . . . shall be considered Worthy. (UAW Convention Proceedings, 1943, p. 4)

The Communist Party entered into a period of hyperthyroid activity that was the basis for much "self-criticism" after the fact. Like most self-criticism, it was more self-serving than corrective. The issues were two: incentive pay plans and the no-strike pledge. The entire union movement adopted a no-strike pledge for the duration of the war, and the Communist Party joined in this agreement with an enthusiasm that would make the most conservative manufacturer blush. The problem for the political future of the Communist Party was that their eagerness was not shared entirely by the workers. In particular, autoworkers had a legitimate detestation for incentive pay plans. In the past, they were used to speed up production by the simple device of raising the base rate, usually by making a small improvement in procedure. Once the base rate was established, say, 100 pieces a day, a bonus was paid for any production over that base rate. However, the autoworkers had experienced the situation where the base pay, determined as 100 pieces a day with a bonus for anything over that figure, had been changed to 110 pieces in order to get base pay, with a bonus for any production over that. It was an unending treadmill. Workers would increase their productivity, only to find the production rate raised to a new level. The incentive pay proposal, first advanced by the War Production Board, according to one author, "openly split the UAW's top leadership for the first time in the war and provided the vehicle for a reemergence of unionwide factionalism" (Lichtenstein, 1974, p. 392).

Now that the war had become metamorphosed into a war against fascism and not an imperialist war, the Communist Party adopted a position of everything for victory, and they pursued it to a degree that made it possible for the Reuther caucus to score heavy political points. The *New Masses*, a Communist theoretical organ, ran an article in 1943 entitled "Detroit: Muscle Bound Giant, How Incentive Pay Would Help the Workers and Production" (Magil, 1943, p. 14). No analysis of a situation would be complete without the usual denunciation of the real or imagined enemies: "A glance at the background of the incentive pay proposal will explain why it has been possible for the ragtag and bobtail of Trotskyites, Socialists, leaders of the Association of Catholic Trade Unionists and assorted disrupters to have muddied this issue" (p. 14). At the 1943 convention the proponents of incentive pay, aware of the unpopularity of their cause, had two techniques for carrying their arguments: (1) They surrounded the proposal with so many conditions that no company could possibly accept them, hoping only to get the principle passed. (2) They also claimed the real issue was local autonomy; any strategy was preferable to directly supporting this hated gimmick.

The resolution on incentive pay came to the floor recommending that incentive plans be adopted. The majority of the committee was opposed. Victor Reuther, for the majority, said, "The International Union of the UAW-CIO reiterates emphatically its traditional opposition to . . . incentive plans." Further, "we believe that piece work will neither bring our Nation maximum war production nor provide workers with an adequate annual wage" (UAW Convention Proceedings, 1943, p. 172). The minority report favoring the resolution hedged their support, with the following provisions supplied by David Miller: (1) Membership of the local must approve and have the right to eliminate "at any time." (2) If there is a change to incentive systems, the hourly base rates "shall be no less than the previous hourly day rate in all classifications." (3) "Incentive payments . . . shall be in direct proportion to the increase in production." (4) "Base rates and production standards shall remain unchanged." (5) "Non-production workers must participate." (6) Employers must guarantee full employment and "a guaranteed weekly wage equal to forty times the basic hourly rate" (p. 184).

Charles Kerrigan, a regional director who usually supported the Addes positions, noted that "there are damned few corporations in this country that are going to accept those conditions, so therefore we need not worry about the incentive plan too much" (p. 203).

The officers were polled. George Addes voted for the Minority Report supporting incentive pay, "because I am interested in preserving the democracy of our local unions" (p. 177). R. J. Thomas voted against, citing the possibility of speedup if the proposal was adopted. This year was the time of Thomas's greatest alienation from the CP. The *Detroit Times*, May 13, 1943, in a story on Thomas, reported: "Rolling up his sleeves and whacking a cud of tobacco into the spittoon in his office today, Thomas said: 'I'm getting sick and tired of the Communists butting into other people's business and I'm going to do something about it' " (Crellin, 1943, p. 9).

Even though the Communist Party had made a big issue out of incentive pay, the first mention of its involvement was made by Richard Frankensteen, a supporter of the proposal. He quoted Philip Murray, head of the CIO, on the Steel Workers' exploration of incentive plans. "Are his policies those of Eddie Rickenbacker [a reactionary World War I hero who supported piecework], or does anyone want to say that Phil Murray is now a Communist?" (UAW Convention Proceedings, 1943, p. 184, UA,WSU). Melvin Bishop, also a supporter, noted that Reuther's Local 174 had incentive pay in 1937, and it was signed by Reuther. He added, "It has been referred to by some that because Browder had something to say about incentive pay, that therefore the Executive Board did, too" (p. 193).[6] During this debate, one delegate protested to the chair that "someone over here . . . is dropping stink bombs down here and a certain amount of the delegates are getting sick at the stomach" (p. 190). Thomas warned the offenders to stop.

The opponents of incentive pay directly attacked the plan on the basis that it would forestall the much-needed industrywide wage in auto and would lead to cutthroat competition among workers and a greater speedup. Addes pointed out that a GM plant had an incentive work plan, and Reuther responded that the union tried to argue the local out of it, to no avail. There were shouts of "Why did you sign it?" Reuther answered, "My name is not on it. It was approved by the International Union" (p. 181). This was not a high point of the anti-Reuther polemical skills. When Reuther posited the goal for the UAW to be an industry-wide wage like they had in coal, the opposition rejoinder was a monumental non sequitur: "I wonder if we want to have democratic principles as set up by the Mine Workers. I wonder if we want to have our officers appointed; I wonder if we want our delegates appointed" (p. 182). Or, if Reuther was so determined to have industrywide wages, why hasn't he achieved it in GM yet? (p. 184). On the question of a local's right to institute such a plan if they desired, Reuther said, "Supposing a local union wanted to sign a wage agreement working twelve hours a day without an overtime. Would you say that was interfering with local autonomy if they could do it?" (p. 198).

The same bitterness was reflected in the campaign literature passed out at the convention. The Reuther propaganda, a six-page printed pamphlet entitled "A Union Program to Win the War at Home and Abroad," stated, "We oppose: Piece Work [incentive payment plans] whether sponsored by reactionary Rickenbacker, Communist Earl Browder or other antiunion forces" (Walter Reuther Collection, box 3; folder 5, UA,WSU). The proincentive caucus also put out a six-page printed document, "Incentive Pay—A Phoney Convention Issue," asserting:

Every honest Unionist can readily recognize the fact that Leonard and Reuther are using the Incentive Pay Issue as a smoke screen for their real purpose: to break down Local Union Autonomy. Hitler and Mussolini both misled their people into granting the power to govern them to a small political group. We all know the results: DICTATORSHIP. (Walter Reuther Collection, box 3; folder 6, UA,WSU)

A resolution was passed, reaffirming the UAW's opposition to incentive pay, and quietly dropped, only to be raised again as a political issue in the 1946 and 1947 UAW elections. Brendan Sexton, president of Local 50 in the 1946 convention and later education director of the UAW, said in a 1987 interview that Reuther was elected by the stupidity of the Communist Party: "In a city of missing fingers, they proposed to auto workers that they should have incentive pay" (Sexton interview, 1986).

The no-strike pledge did not disappear so easily. Labor was caught in an inflationary spiral with their wages frozen. The "Little Steel" formula was devised to provide for wage increases only if they did not exceed price increases. Unions protested that the government data on price increases were inadequate, a generally accepted proposition. The War Labor Board was in charge of all defense-related labor relations, and it faced its greatest battle when John L. Lewis threatened to strike the coalfields, war or no war. The response of the *Daily Worker* was instantaneous. It called on the government to "Take Any

Steps" to halt the strike ("Communists Call on Government . . . ," 1943, p. 1). Browder later propounded: "Advocates of strike threats or strike action in America in 1945 are SCABS against our armed forces, they are SCABS against the labor movement" (Browder, 1945, p. 8). The necessary analysis of the political alignment had been previously provided: "No one can deny that the Ku Kluxers, Coughlinites, supporters of John L. Lewis [are] opponents of the no-strike policy. Trotskyites and Norman Thomas socialists and other brands of anti-war elements have participated in the Reuther caucus" Going further than the obligatory denunciation, the *Worker* applauded the action of R. J. Thomas and Frankensteen, asking the House Labor Committee to "ferret out and bring to light America's Industrial Fifth Column" ("UAW Leader Asks U.S. . . . ," 1943, p. 5). Leo La Motte charged in a story carried by the *Detroit Times*, the Hearst paper, that a UAW strike in a Chrysler plant was "fomented by the followers of Walter P. Reuther, UAW, Vice-President" ("28,000 Still Idle . . . ," 1943, p. 1). The Communist press was like a group of sharks in a feeding frenzy. There was no recognition that some of the strikes were eminently justified by management actions, and most of them were started on rank and file initiatives, not the diabolical plotting of their traditional enemies, all of whom had been joined by the *Worker* in one indistinguishable morass.

Only Emil Mazey was for outright revocation. He noted that the majority resolution called for government takeover of plants where management refused to bargain in good faith and that this was an illusion. "We do not have collective bargaining in our plants at the present time" (UAW Convention Proceedings, 1943, p. 409). Addressing John Anderson, Local 155 Communist Party leader, Mazey said, "Brother Anderson, the class question has not been stopped by the war—it has been intensified" (p. 409).[7] In *Labor Action*, journal of the Workers Party, a Trotskyist splinter group, there appeared a headline that presaged the charges to be used against the Communist Party because of its stand on the no-strike pledge: "Detroit Proves It—Fink is the Name for Stalinists" (1943, p. 8). They continued, castigating Reuther for not leading the militants' fight against the pledge.

There were two other matters that came before the convention, both involving minority issues. The first dealt with the establishment of a Minorities Department. The Majority Report, supported by the Reuther caucus, called for the creation of a Minority Department, the chair to be appointed by the president of the union, subject to the approval of the Executive Board. The Minority Report, supported by the Communist Party, among others, stated that the director be elected by the convention as a whole and that the director be a member of the Executive Board.

Nat Ganley said that it was not mandatory that a Negro be elected, but "I am confident" that a Negro would be elected. He also noted that it had been said that women, Italians, and welders would want representation. But, he said forcefully, "women and welders are not lynched in America just because they are women and welders, but Negroes are lynched just because they are Negroes" (UAW Convention Proceedings, 1943, pp. 371-372).

Both the Majority and Minority reports lost. The Resolutions Committee then had the right to redraft the resolution and resubmit it to the convention. It elected instead to recommend that the constitution stay as it was. Passed. Nobody looked very good in this exchange, but certainly Nat Ganley shone better than the rest.

The second matter involving minority rights was a straightforward, nonpolitical resolution stating that the UAW was opposed to discrimination and will fight for "negro" representation in all departments of the UAW and that an educational program be established in the UAW for ridding the UAW of discrimination. The caucuses did not split on this motion, and it is hard to explain the ugly reaction to the proposal. Perhaps because it was the second of the two minority resolutions and "hate" strikes[8] had appeared in Detroit plants regarding the hiring and upgrading of Blacks, some of the racist members decided to fight, causing the ugliest exchanges of the convention. One delegate from Local 174 flatly stated, "I would never go to any union function and take my wife and daughter when they were supposed to mingle with the negro race" (p. 417). At the conclusion of his speech, the proceedings said: "(There were boos and shouts of 'Sit down,' 'Sit down')" (p. 417).

Stuart Strachan and Victor Reuther of Local 174 took strong exception to the racist remarks, as did Harold Christoffel of Local 248. The resolution passed.

Only Charlie, the bartender from the Mayflower Bar, was happy with the activities of this convention. He thanked the delegates by telegram for the business they had given him (p. 288).

The 1944 convention brought the no-strike pledge to a climax. One resolution supported by Addes and the Communist Party was for retention, the rank and file caucus supported repeal, and in the center, was Reuther calling for retention only if those plants were engaged in war production. None of the three positions could garner a majority, and it was submitted to a referendum of the membership, with thirty-five percent voting to discard the pledge. The vote did not reflect the future difficulties that this question was to cause in the later politics of the UAW.

John C. Cort, New York ACTU leader, following the 1944 UAW convention, wrote:

There is undoubtedly a tremendous rank and file sentiment against the no-strike pledge, although the convention renewed it. Of course, in line with present Communist policy, what Communist leadership there is in this union is committed to the no-strike pledge and even is probably committed to a no-strike pledge after the war is over. No leadership, however, could possibly hold in check the rank and file mood of resentment to the extent of making a post-war no-strike commitment. (Cort, 1944, p. 557)

The violent and indiscriminate accusations against all strikers during the war were not just a case of misguided lack of restraint or overzealousness. These charges were often false and were used to finger opponents. Not only was logic violated, but basic union rules of behavior were transgressed. Latter-day apologists for the Communist Party often attributed these "excesses" to Browder and his policies during that time. The difficulty is that the tenor and character of these assaults preceded Browder and certainly succeeded him.

As the war in Europe drew to a close, the "class collaborationist" period of the Communist Party also came to an end. No more would Earl Browder proclaim: "Labor will remedy its grievances by assuming responsibility for the war . . . by cooperating whole-heartedly with the Roosevelt administration, and by developing more serious cooperation with management in production" ("The Mine Strike . . . ," 1943, p. 19). The change occurred not because of some radical insurgency within the party, or the simple trade union knowledge that strikes always followed a major war. The shift happened because Jacques Duclos, leading French Communist, told them to change. In April 1945, he wrote an article accusing Browder of "revisionism" and "liquidationism," charges that in the argot of the Communist Party meant a serious shift in policy (Howe and Coser, 1957, p. 442). This shift to the "Left" by the Communist Party caused the *Wage Earner* to remark February 1, 1946, that the Communists were now saying that "all employers were thieves and fascist. . . . This comes from the same people who two years ago were advocating the Bedeaux speed-up system and insisting the Capitalists would raise pay voluntarily if labor would extend its no-strike pledge into time of peace!" ("GM Strikers Won . . . ," 1946, p. 2).

NOTES

1. At the 1942 convention, an Executive Board member rose to say that "North American Aircraft is forcing its Negro employees to sign a statement that they will not talk to any white production workers in the plant" (UAW Convention Proceedings, 1942, p. 345). One Black worker was discharged because he had "the effrontery to talk to a white woman in the plant" (p. 345).

2. The next day, a delegate asked if Reuther was deferred at the "instigation" of the UAW. Anderson said that his understanding was that Thomas and Murray had asked for a deferment but that Reuther was deferred on his personal plea that his wife was dependent on him. Thus, Reuther had lied, according to Anderson, because the UAW would not get rid of the wife of a soldier. Thomas: "I told the Governor that if Walter Reuther was drafted I would fire his wife, due to the fact . . . I would have no use for her" (UAW Convention Proceedings, 1941, p. 706). Reuther maintained that he had never asked for any kind of deferment. Murray and Thomas asked him to be a guinea pig to see if unionists could get deferred for occupational reasons, since most of the CIO officials were of draft age, and it might weaken the union. The draft board gave a dependency deferment because it was compelled to give the deferment that gave the lowest protection against being drafted, according to Reuther (p. 713).

3.   Several years later, Sweet was to be subjected to an even more vicious attack than he visited on Deverall. He had become the education director of Local 742 when the opposition in the local put out a printed leaflet with Sweet as its target. It read, in part:

SZLOMA SWIECZNIK, alias Sam Sweet, was born April 15, 1911, in Poland of Hebrew parentage[!]. [His] petition [for naturalization] was denied . . . for failure to prove attachment to the Constitution of the U.S. San Sweet is a high ranking member of the COMMUNIST PARTY of Michigan. The COMMUNIST PARTY has insinuated him into several locals as Education Director. (ACTU Collection, box 25; folder: Briggs Forge 742, n.d., UA,WSU)

4.   The FBI also quotes the same source on Walter Reuther on January 8, 1941, as reporting that "Reuther is a recognized Communist Party member and that he ran for Common Council in Detroit in the 1937 election on the Communist Party ticket" (Goode Collection, FBI, Walter Reuther, p. 10, UA,WSU). Since Detroit elections are nonpartisan, there could not have been a Communist Party ticket. Reuther did run for that office on a union-endorsed ticket that failed to elect even one of its candidates.

5.   There is a modicum of truth to this assertion. Some of May Reuther's siblings have the last name Wolf; others, Wolfman. When the father was asked about this discrepancy by an in-law, he shrugged his shoulders and replied, "Wolf, Wolfman, it's really Shapiro" (Wolf, 1987).

6.   While criticism of the Communist Party on the convention floor was circumspect, it was different in the lobbies of the hotel. Some Reuther supporters wrote a parody of "Reuben, Reuben" that swept the convention. In part it went: "Who are the boys who take their orders/straight from the office of Joe Staleen?/No one else but the gruesome twosome/George F. Addes and Frankensteen" (Keeran, 1980, p. 247). This certainly ranks close to the Communist Party song in the ILGWU: "The cloak makers union is a no good union/It's a no good union by the bosses." Bosses and Norman Thomases were rhymed, and the Socialists were damned.

7.   The following handwritten note in Nat Ganley's Collection is reported here in its entirety:

Worker, Mar. 3, 1968 "Strategy and Tactics for a growing strike wave" By Geo Meyers and James West. "The history of American labor is replete with proof that when the strike weapon is taken away or *given up* [emphasis in original], trade unions are at the mercy of Big Business." (That's what Emil Mazey, Trotskyists said during WW2 when we were supporting the no-strike pledge). (Ganley Collection, box 5; folder 20, UA,WSU)

8.   See Meier and Rudwick (1981, pp. 162–174) and Bernard (1983, p. 86). Walter Reuther, in April 1943, was the only International officer to appear at a Cadillac Square rally against discrimination, stating that any worker who refused to work with "Colored" workers could leave the shops.

REUTHER'S ASCENDANCY

GM STRIKE

The Left shift by the Communist Party probably came too late to help it at the 1946 convention. By that time, Reuther had the political momentum on his side, largely because of the 1946 General Motors strike. It is impossible to ascribe to any single event the cause for historical change, but certainly this strike, led by Reuther, was one of the major reasons for his assumption of the presidency of the UAW in 1946. All the elements were there for a major strike. The autoworkers, restrained by the "Little Steel" formula and restive after four years of war, were ready to strike. Union membership had increased by about forty percent to nearly 15 million members. Some 300,000 Michigan war workers had already lost their jobs.

Fortune magazine, December 1945, recognizing the volatility of the situation wrote of Reuther: "Moreover, management sees him not as an *enfant terrible*, but as something quite serious—even a menace"; and quoting George Romney: "Walter Reuther is the most dangerous man in Detroit because no one is more skillful in bringing about revolution without seeming to disturb the existing form of society" ("Reuther: FOB Detroit," 1945, pp. 149, 288).

Management saw the period as a possible major confrontation for power and were not disposed to settle easily. The government under Truman wanted a peaceful transition out of the war economy regardless of who paid the price for it. One writer felt that all the strikes in the postwar period were political, the GM strike particularly, in the sense that labor was attempting to maintain Truman's wage price policies of permitting wage increases as long as prices did not rise (Lichtenstein, 1974, p. 701). Truman soon discarded this position in the face of industry's resistance. The GM strike was the last opportunity to salvage this position. Reuther entered the strike with a demand of a thirty percent increase in the hourly wage with no price increase and, if GM asserted its inability to pay, it would have to open its books to public scrutiny. The *Detroit News,* on November 12, 1945, editorialized:

The UAW claims that wages, far from being fixed by a labor market, must be regarded as entitled to a share, much like the stockholders' share, in the employing corporations earnings. Hence, not merely wage rates themselves but also profits are asserted to be a subject of collective bargaining. . . . That is quite a step. Employers naturally will oppose it, not only on grounds of the ancient concept of property rights, but also because including profits in wage-bargaining means disclosing business secrets. ("Up Comes a New Issue," 1945, p. 10)

The *Detroit Free Press* was even more critical. In an editorial on January 21, 1946, that was opposed to the strike, it quoted AFL charges that the "CIO's current wage demand is inspired by 'Communist policies' aimed toward creating industrial strife, chaos and unemployment" ("Hate, Greed, Stupidity . . . ," 1946, p. 6).

The GM response to the UAW demands was one of outrage. In a full-page ad in the *Detroit News*, it declaimed:

Here is the Issue, is American business to be based on free competition, or is it to become socialized, with all activities controlled and regimented?

America is at the crossroads! It must preserve the freedom of each unit of American business to determine its own destiny. Or it must transfer to some governmental bureaucracy or agency, or to a union, the responsibility of management that has been the very keystone of American business. Shall this responsibility be surrendered? That is the decision the American people face. America must choose. ("Here Is the Issue," 1945, p. 9)

The following month, GM again took out full-page ads in the *News*, asserting, "For Labor Unions to use the monopolistic power of their vast membership to extend the scope of wage negotiations to include more than wages, hours and working conditions is the first step toward handing the management of business over to the Union bosses" ("A 'Look at the Books' . . . ," 1946, p. 6). While GM was certainly hysterical about the implications of the UAW demands, the demands did have the impact of challenging in collective bargaining some of the most vaunted prerogatives of management. ACTU was quick to light on the implications of Reuther's demands. A *Wage Earner* story noted that it was a "historical struggle" by "insisting that wage increases come out of profits, and not from higher prices to consumers." They continued: "So this brings all parties squarely up against a showdown on the question: SHALL INDUSTRY BE FORCED TO REDISTRIBUTE THE FRUITS OF PRODUCTION BY GIVING MORE TO WAGES AND LESS TO PROFITS" (emphasis in original) ("GM Fight . . . ," 1945, p. 5).

The *Wage Earner* reported in a story headed "Clergy of Three Faiths Back Strikes for Wage-Price Balance" that the clergymen said:

The main issue in most of the present strikes is the attempt on the part of American wage earners not only to gain a more equitable share of our national income and a decent standard of living for themselves and their families, but to achieve such a balance of purchasing power, production, prices and profits as to benefit the entire nation with full employment and general prosperity. ("Clergy of Three Faiths . . . ," 1946, p. 5)

Reuther's conduct of the strike was obviously getting enormous attention, but the ATL caucus and the Communist Party were not in a position to criticize a strike in progress. Nat Ganley was reported in the *Wage Earner* as supporting a general strike of all the automobile industry. Ganley said, "Murray isn't going to shut down one company at a time. . . . He intends to shut down all the steel plants in the nation this week" ("Communist Leader Demands Strike," 1946, p. 4). This latter-day militancy on the part of the Communist Party flew directly in the face of the traditional UAW technique of "whipsawing" the major auto producers. Since 1937, the union had targeted one of the Big Three while the others produced and sold automobiles. Ganley was, in the vernacular of the Communist Party, trying to strengthen the "left-center" coalition of the pro–Communist Party elements in the CIO and Philip Murray, who had shown great reluctance about attacking the Communists. The *Wage Earner*, in an attempt to stop the appearance of an alignment between Murray and the Communist Party, wired Murray asking if he had taken a position on the one-at-a-time strategy. He answered, as he had to as head of the CIO, "Have not at any time discussed matters with officers of the United Auto Workers. Idea to me is simply preposterous" ("Commie 'Spread Strike' Line . . . ," 1946, p. 4).

The analogy with the steel industry is a faulty one. If they meet specifications, there is no difference between a ton of steel produced by Republic or U.S. Steel. There may be no difference, in fact, between a Ford, Chevrolet, or Plymouth, but as long as the public views them as different and buyer loyalty is threatened, then carmakers face the loss of a market if the buyer switches to another manufacturer at the time of a strike. Product differentiation is a fact of consumer preference, whether it is rational or not. That strike strategies vary from industry to industry is not always a choice between militancy and conservatism but may be dictated by certain factors within the industry itself.

Whatever political capital the Communist Party hoped to obtain from the plan to strike the entire auto industry was vitiated by a letter signed by Thomas, Addes, Frankensteen, Leonard, and Norman Matthews, dated November 23, 1945. They asserted that it was the GM policy "to divide the Union's strength by forcing other auto producers to close down." George Romney, head of the Automotive Manufacturers Association, had said that the GM strike would close down all the automakers. They added: "Romney and GM want that because it would at the same time divide up the fighting strength of the UAW and guarantee GM that competitors would not be free to turn out cars while its own plants are strike bound" (UAW Local 51 Collection, box 24; folder 11, UA,WSU). ACTU, always quick to report on the divisions in the ATL caucus, noted in a headline: "Addes Backs Reuther Against Communist Party Demands to Strike All Plants" (1946, p. 1).

The day the GM strike ended, just a week before the convention started that elected Reuther president, the *Daily Worker* labor writer George Morris had a full-blown critique of the Reuther strategy in which he blamed Reuther for "mismanagement and consequent prolongation of the General Motors strike to 113 days" (Morris, 1946, p. 7). His analysis included seven major points: (1) Reuther jumped the gun nine weeks before the steel strike deadline. *Daily Worker* headline, March 19, 1946: "Thomas Blames Reuther Jump the Gun Policy for Length of GM Strike" (1946. p. 5). This argument would have had some valence if, in fact, there was a CIO policy. However, none existed. Murray had no intention of striking if there were any alternative. It is conjectured that he expected Truman to establish the settlements, thus avoiding any strike. (2) For every dollar lost by GM in 1945 because of the strike, eighty-five and a half cents would have gone in taxe—hence, GM had little to lose. The Communist Party also argued that the enormous tax rebates that GM was to receive make the strike ill advised.[1] At times it appeared as if the Communist Party was arguing against any strike at all. The only point they missed was the old conservative saw that the strikers would never get the money back for the time they had been on strike. (3) Reuther had called for a general CIO strike but opposed a strike of all the Big Three in auto. A general CIO strike is a major strategic decision. In the absence of such a decision, the judgment to strike the Big Three one at a time was a tactical one, and, right or wrong, it was a rational choice, not evidence of conservatism. (4) Reuther opposed mass picketing. There was no reason to have mass picketing. There are two reasons to have large numbers at the plant gates: to stop scabs from entering and to build morale. Neither of these situations was a problem. GM had no intention of trying to run the plants; this was not 1936. (5) Reuther had failed to shut down the GM powerhouse and had not stopped the movement of GM tool and die work. There was no question that the dies were not being used in other GM plants, as they had been in 1936. All of the GM plants were closed. Dies may have been moved in and out, but they were not building cars anywhere. (6) Morris, in a continuing attempt to associate Reuther and Dubinsky asked why the latter did not argue with William Green when Green, the president of the AFL, ranted against the CIO strikes. This is a question better directed to Dubinsky. (7) Finally, Morris wanted to know why Reuther spent so much time in caucus activity rather than settling the GM strike. Accusations of this kind are traditional gambits of oppositionists used against every leader. In an editorial in the same issue, headed "Why It Took 113 Days," Morris said, "We communists have been pointing out that Reuther placed his factional ambitions above the interests of the strikers from the very start of the walk out" (Morris, 1946, p. 7). These arguments are all marked by their quality of pure and simple unionism rather than an incisive radical critique. Despite the possibility of a Left criticism, the Communists had no dramatic platform with which to counter Reuther's demands. In fact, the reporting in the *Daily Worker* had the tone of a middling local union newspaper, hackneyed, characterless, and devoid of political ideas.

Reuther had stolen the march on the entire union movement, moving with vigor and imagination in a troubled period.

The *Detroit News*, with a headline "Slight Rift in Solidarity Forever" and the appellation "Reuther the Opportunist," said:

There is not much to choose between Mr. Wallace howling for a purge of backward elements in the Democratic Party and Mr. Reuther Crying "Reds" at his union opposition. . . .

When Mr. Thomas opines openly that the strike with better handling could have been wound up in six weeks, he only says what many observers have thought was obvious in the light of the settlement finally made, but some might think was impolitic to spill in company. ("Slight Rift . . . ," 1946, p. 18)

Other *Worker* stories in the week of the convention repeated R. J. Thomas's allegation about the GM strike: " 'Master Strategy' Cost GM Strikers," the headline read, quoting Thomas that the "strike was ordered too early and lasted a month longer than necessary" (" 'Master Strategy' Cost GM Workers," 1946, p. 3). Both the *Worker* and Thomas hit hard on Reuther's press treatment. The former noted Reuther's favorable publicity in the Luce publications and added, "In view of Luce's connection with the DuPonts, the chief owners of GM, the story of Reuther as the target of big business is hardly plausible" (p. 4). But the press coverage of the GM strike was hardly all favorable. *Newsweek*, two weeks prior to the convention, said "Reuther's star is dim now because the General Motors strike . . . failed to win quick gains" ("Labor Trends," 1946, p. 7). *Business Week*, February 16, spoke of the "disintegrating position of Walter Reuther" ("Blow to UAW," 1946, p. 100). *Time,* February 25, was even more specific:

Walter Reuther, the CIO's cocky red head, had a noticeable wilt to his comb this week. Somehow his swagger towards fame had bogged down in the quicksands of the wage—price formula and union politics.

Reuther had planned the strategy of beating the auto industry by knocking off General Motors first. Now everything was topsy-turvy—it looked as if he might have succeeded in knocking himself off. ("Whither Reuther," 1946, p. 20)

It was not explained why the Luce-du Pont-GM connection alleged to exist by the *Worker* did not make it possible to have a satisfactory and easy settlement with Reuther instead of fighting to the last ditch over a penny. If GM had wanted to promote Reuther's candidacy, all it had to do was to give the penny in dispute early in the strike rather than fight 113 days and still not give in. Thomas was quoted by the *Detroit Free Press,* March 27, 1946, as saying that Reuther was considered a great labor leader only "by the Luce publications . . . which are owned by Morgan and Rockefeller. By the parlor pinks who make a hobby of the labor movement—and by the executive council of the AFL" ("UAW OK's 50-Cent Dues Increase . . . ," 1946, p. 3). The Reuther caucus was not supine in the face of these attacks. In the worst red-baiting story to have emanated from the Reuther camp, the *Detroit News* carried a headline, quoting an anonymous source, "Thomas 'Red Stooge' Reuther Forces Say" (Lauren, 1946, p. 34). Two days later, the same paper had a headline "AFL Link to Reuther Is Scented" (1946, p. 9). It was to get worse

The *Worker* would have considered itself remiss in its political obligation if it had not exposed the machinations behind Reuther's activity in addition to criticizing his strategy. The culprit, of course, was David Dubinsky, president of the ILGWU. The Communists had started early on Dubinsky, noting his generous pledges to the GM strike fund by a headline "Dubinsky Ties Strings to Relief for GM Strikers" (1946, p. 5), continuing, "With nearly a million CIO workers still on strike, a joint AFL-CIO group of Social Democrats under the direction of David Dubinsky has launched a campaign to undermine the leadership of CIO President Philip Murray" (p. 5). On March 12, 17, and 24, 1946, the *Worker* ran stories on Dubinsky's role in the UAW faction fight: "Reuther's strategy was not a mistake. It was a conspiracy, hatched by his Social Democratic CIO-AFL friends headed by David Dubinsky." "The Reuther-Dubinsky Intrigue That Prolonged the GM Strike" (1946, p. 12). "A new threat arises as the Reuther-Dubinsky forces bid for a throttle hold on the organization" ("The Auto Union Convention," 1946, p. 3). Dubinsky's name was used so often that someone not familiar with the union movement might have concluded that he was a high official in the UAW. None of these accusations was accompanied by a shred of evidence. At least the Communists adduced some proofs when they attacked Homer Martin.

In contrast to the *Daily Worker* reporting, the *Wage Earner*'s treatment of the news prior to the convention was factual and accurate, albeit colored by their anticommunism. A legitimate expectation for any newspaper is that, given its biases, it is possible to derive some sense of what is transpiring in the action covered. This was seldom true of the *Worker*, but the *Wage Earner* garnered a national reputation for its coverage. Its treatment of the Ford settlement accurately described the dilemma of the Communist Party fraction. They were for Dick Leonard, as part of their caucus, but they were opposed to the "security clause" that had been negotiated by him to control wildcat strikes. It is no discredit to the Communist Party that it was in such a position; all coalition politics engender such contradictions. However, Rev. Raymond S. Clancy pointed out in a later story that the contract they opposed was superior to the one that they had negotiated when they controlled the local ("Comrades at Fords," 1946, p. 9). The *Wage Earner*'s anticommunism, for the most part, did not preclude decent reporting, except for its irritating habit of using the expression "commie," a term not generally employed in serious political exchange since it smacked of right-wing terminology. It was, however, extremely careful in its labeling. Only those CPers were so designated that even the *Daily Worker* could not take exception to because of their known affiliation with the Communist Party. Nat Ganley was always identified as a Communist, which could not have been a surprise to any of its readers. The *Wage Earner* also reported on the clergymen's statement in support of the 1946 GM strike. They were quoted as saying that the strikes were not only to

gain a more equitable share of our national income and a decent standard of living . . . but to achieve such a balance of purchasing power, production, prices and profits as to benefit the entire nation. . . . The right to strike . . . is as fundamental to human liberty as religious freedom is. The right to a decent standard of living is basic. ("Clergy of Three Faiths . . . ," 1946, p. 5)

The *Wage Earner* ran a straight news story without moralizing on the dinner given for Vincent Lombardo Toledano, Communist Party labor leader from Mexico, by the Wayne County CIO Council. They ran perceptive articles on the wage crisis that accompanied current negotiations in all unions. The foreign coverage was good for a weekly labor press: They reported on the formation of the Fifth International by Pietro Nenni, venerable Italian Socialist Party leader. That was a story not likely to be handled by many members of the labor press. Anti–Franco articles were scattered throughout its issues. They covered the Society of Sentinels, a right-wing organization, who ran an ad in the daily papers advocating repeal of Social Security, the Office of Price Administration, and the Wages and Hour Act. One of the Sentinels, who had opposed the ad prior to its publication, was a top negotiator for GM, causing some embarrassment to the corporation when Reuther asked if he would continue in the capacity of negotiator. The *Wage Earner* covered civil rights material, fights in other international unions, and local fights within the New York City Teamsters (particularly if there was a Communist Party angle).

In contrast to the generally held opinion that ACTU was in Reuther's corner in the battle for the UAW presidency, the *Wage Earner*, as noted, had not endorsed Reuther and the Actists elected to the convention split their votes between the ATL and Reuther caucuses. Their strategy was quite explicit: Isolate the Communist Party from the ATL caucus and create an anti-Communist administration in the UAW composed of both caucuses. On March 1, 1946, just three weeks prior to the convention, the *Wage Earner* had a story that pointed out, "If Addes were to withdraw the non-Communist section of the so-called 'left wing' out from its alliance with the Communists, the latter would be left in an isolated and precarious position" ("Reuther Holds Key . . . ," 1946, p. 2).

The *Wage Earner*, as few of the labor press did, noted the slowness with which Addes committed himself to R. J. Thomas in the 1946 election. Finally, Addes said that "he would plug for the re-election of both Thomas and Reuther to their present posts" ("Addes Favors . . . ,"1946, p. 3). The *Wage Earner* added that "Nat Ganley, National Board member of the Communist Party, said the Communists would not vote for Reuther even for Vice President" (p. 3).

The reporting by the *Wage Earner* in the few weeks prior to the convention was not partisan. There was no labeling of the ATL caucus as "leftwing" or "Communist dominated." They did report the possible lineup on the International Executive Board positions and headed a story on March 15, 1946, "Expect Reuther Candidacy When Convention Starts" (p. 4). The day before the convention, the *Wage Earner* ran two stories: "Reuther Leading in Unofficial Tally" (1946, p. 1) and "Thomas Charges Plot by Dubinsky" (1946, p. 1). The first of these must have been wish fulfillment, for not even the *Wage Earner*, which had an uncanny ability to predict the outcome of elections in the UAW, could have predicted a vote as close as this one. The second story about Thomas was reported straight, without editorializing or comment. The "Gadfly," a humorous political column, did note that the *Automobile Worker* report of the GM settlement mentioned Walter Reuther only once and that was in R. J. Thomas's column (Gadfly, 1946, p. 6).

During the GM strike, both Reuther and ACTU were caught in a development that threatened each of them for different reasons. President Truman appointed a fact-finding committee to make a recommendation on the GM strike and on January 10, 1946, it recommended a nineteen-and-a-half-cent increase in wages without an increase in prices. Reuther immediately accepted the recommendation and GM summarily dismissed it, offering instead thirteen and a half cents. Then the ax fell: UE, a Communist Party–dominated union, also in negotiations with GM, signed for eighteen and a half cents. Even more damaging to Reuther and ACTU, several days later, the Steel Workers signed a contract for the same eighteen and a half cents. Both the UE's and the Steel Workers' contracts were silent on price increases. Thus, Reuther's program of wage increases without price increases had been scuttled by fellow unionists. Reuther was outraged and charged the UE with a "double cross," but he was more circumspect with Philip Murray of the Steel Workers, who was also head of the CIO. The antagonism between the "fancy economics" of Reuther and the business unionism of Murray had led to other conflicts. Even the *Wage Earner*, which ordinarily was disposed to minimize friction between Reuther and Murray, reported on a "secret meeting" between the two in which Murray asked Reuther to drop the demand for wage increases without price increases because he felt the steel industry would not accept it ("Murray Urged Reuther . . . ," 1946, p. 2). The meeting may have been thought to be a secret, but one of the GM negotiators in their sessions raised the fact that Murray told Reuther to get off the thirty percent demand and forget about profits and opening the books. The *Wage Earner* reported that Murray was rumored to be angry with Reuther for stealing a march by striking GM before the steel union could move (p. 2). That seems unlikely, since Murray had no overwhelming urge to strike (Cochran, 1977, p. 252).

After the fact-finding panel had said that GM could afford to pay nineteen and a half cents without an increase in prices, Truman reversed his own panel and made a deal with the steel industry for an eighteen-and-a-half-cent in wage increases for the Steel Workers in exchange for a price increase of $4 a ton. There was a short steel strike anyhow, and the *Wage Earner* entered the fray, charging "Steel 'Doublecross' Reduces Pay Level 18 Cents and $4 per Ton" (1946, p. 3). However, this action put it at odds with Philip Murray, with whom it had an excellent relationship. The following week, in a boxed story entitled "An Explanation of the Steel Story," the editors lamely added, "The editors of the *Wage Earner* thought this story clearly identified the steel industry as the 'doublecrossers' " (1946, p. 1). They added that they were not accusing the Steel Workers Union of double crossing. Just how the steel industry double-crossed anyone was not made clear. The UE was a better target, because it was directly negotiating with GM, as was the UAW, and their Communist Party–oriented leadership made it easy to project a plot against Reuther. The *Wage Earner* had a front-page story: "UAW Heads Demand Hearing on UE-GM 18½ 'Betrayal' " (1946, p. 2). The body of the story quoted R. J. Thomas as being "shocked" by the UE action and George Addes as saying, "I don't know where the Communist Party is going after that one" (p. 2). It also carried a favorable report on Addes's negotiations at Bendix in the same issue.

On February 17, 1946, the *Worker* reported on the steel price raise authorization: "Reuther's caucus wheelhorses are busy spreading stories of alleged 'treason' by Murray. Their Trotskyite allies are even more vocal in this. Their paper . . . calls Murray a 'traitor' and refers to the 18½ cents as a 'sell out' " ("GM Workers Re-Examining . . . ," 1946, p. 4). In the same issue, it said, "Reuther and his social democratic friends are now bringing their attacks upon the CIO leader out into the open. The paper of the Association of Catholic Trade Unionists, Reuther's allies, is also throwing bricks at Murray for accepting 18½ cents" (p. 10). From the Communist point of view, the critical aspect of the discussion was to protect Murray from attack and make Reuther appear as a Murray antagonist.

The strike was soon over, settled for eighteen and a half cents, with a few fringes that Reuther could claim made the total package nineteen and a half cents. Thus, Reuther entered the crucial 1946 UAW Convention with an ambiguous legacy of the GM strike.

Some observers have maintained that Reuther's conduct of the strike was the main factor in his election to the presidency of the UAW. Others scorned the settlement, deeming the strike a failure, a 113-day odyssey that gained the same results as at Ford and Chrysler, led by his opposition, without a strike. The rest of the union movement ignored Reuther's demand of wage increases without price increases and settled for a cent less than Reuther had held out for. No union but the GM Department of the UAW had attempted to create a new kind of public-oriented unionism as opposed to the usual business of unionism of getting higher wages regardless of the impact on the economy. The strike was perceived as a failure by Reuther's opponents, but a sizable number of observers believed that the strike won the presidency of the UAW for Reuther. How could a failed strike have had such a salutary political result?

Reuther's detractors had overlooked the drama of the strike, the ending of war, and the political skills and personality of Reuther. Probably no other strike had as wide a union and public support as this one. R. J. Thomas, the Communist Party, and the press made the criticism that the strike was too long and that its results were the same as other unions gained without a strike. But they forgot that Reuther captured the imagination of the membership and the public by his demands, by the skill with which the strike was conducted, and by the fact that the GM workers were spoiling for a fight after four years of wage restraint.

There was a large public sentiment in favor of the strike. A partial list of those donations over $50 to the strike fund include well-known and unexpected names: Dore Schary; Helen Hayes; Marshall Field, Jr.; Garson Kanin; Henry Luce; Dashiell Hammett; Robert M. La Follette, Jr.; Harold Ickes; and Ruth Gordon. The strike's public supporters included Eleanor Roosevelt; Bishop Bernard Sheil, Walter White of the National Association for the Advancement of Colored People (NAACP); Rabbi Steven S. Wise; Senators Wayne Morris, Claude Pepper, and Glen Taylor; Reinhold Niebuhr; Walter Wanger; Melvin Douglas; Fiorello La Guardia; Karen Horney; Bela Schick; and Gregory Zilborg—in short, famous figures from the religious community, the entertainment world, politics, and the scientific community. Ethel du Pont wired the head of Truman's fact-finding committee during the strike, protesting GM's withdrawal from participation and stating that a large group of GM minority stockholders believed that "no realistic and fair settlement can be reached without determination of the Corporation's ability to pay" (Walter P. Reuther Collection, box 12; folder 16, UA,WSU).

These things cannot be dismissed, as Reuther's critics have done, as only demonstrating his "publicity sense." He certainly had that in abundance. But public relations cleverness could not have produced the support that the autoworkers demonstrated when they elected him president in an upset victory in a union that had known great stability in leadership since 1938. The strike hit a nerve in the public. Reuther's audacity in handling the negotiations was on a level with John L. Lewis's. Reuther wanted the sessions open to the press, but GM refused. Reuther simply turned around and released the verbatim text of all the meetings to the press. This meant that he had supreme confidence that he could handle the sharp negotiators that GM had. It appealed to the workers' sense of outrage at their diminished purchasing power, inflation, and the frustration of the war years, and they could read what their leadership had to say to the bosses. No other union, regardless of its political leadership, had "pioneering" goals at this time or had the sense to seek public support for maintaining price levels. The strike was an effort to break through the isolation of the union movement and to demonstrate that the goals of unions coincided with those of the general public.

Some critics have maintained, in disparagement of both caucuses, that there was no major difference between them and that the outcome had little significance. It depends on your definition. In one sense, there is little difference between a marmoset and a grizzly—both are hairy, mammalian, and quadrupeds. The difference depends on which you would rather meet in the woods. It is true that there were no differences on the order of a conservative, business unionism opposed to a revolutionary union position. Neither was possible given the history of the UAW and the political climate of the times. There was not even the difference between a reformist program contrasted with a revolutionary one. But there were enormous distinctions in the quality of imagination, collective bargaining skills, and leadership resources between the contestants. With Reuther's victory, a distinctive brand of unionism was born.

THE VOTE

Walter Reuther won the presidency of the UAW by 114.187 votes out of 8,821.093, according to the official Roll Call vote of the convention. The Report of the Tellers gave Reuther a majority of 124.388 (UAW Convention Proceedings, 1946, p. 225). Thus, the discrepancies between various writers are accounted for by the source they were quoting.

The purported great ideological differences between the two caucuses on the Communist issue were not evident in the convention debates. There were small differences on the foreign policy resolution between the two groups. The Reuther-sponsored resolution denounced Winston Churchill's "Iron Curtain" speech delivered just three weeks before and attacked the United States, the Soviet Union, and Great Britain for bypassing the United Nations and seemingly to seek out the "old imperialist, war inciting" habits of old.

Philip Murray obliquely supported R. J. Thomas's attack on David Dubinsky without mentioning Dubinsky's name. Murray then referred to Thomas as "that great big guy for whom I have a distinct fondness" (p. 460). This reference was construed by both caucuses as an endorsement of Thomas. It is hard to assess the effect of this mild remark, but Jack Conway and Leonard Woodcock, two of Reuther's closest allies, both of whom claimed a thousand-vote majority for Reuther going into the convention, claimed that the erosion of that majority was attributable to Murray's comment (Conway, 1986; Woodcock, 1987).

With a majority that small, Reuther's victory could be attributed to almost any local or group. An example is Brendan Sexton, pro-Reuther president of Local 50, at the by-then nearly defunct Willow Run Bomber plant. One author states that the Communist Party had made a serious mistake at the convention for not challenging this "paper local" that carried 132 votes for Reuther to the convention where he won by only 114. The Communist Party, whatever else it did, was not likely to miss such an opportunity. It is true that Local 50's membership was down to about 500 because the war had ended, resulting in the consequent cessation of aircraft production.

All aircraft locals had decreased membership at the time of the convention, but they still carried large delegations into the convention because their allocated votes were calculated on the average membership since the last convention. If any advantage obtained from paper locals, it was the ATL caucus, which carried over fifty percent of the aircraft votes in 1946. Halperin (1982) maintains, "At the Convention, Reuther received just over one-third of the reduced aircraft workers' group" (p. 248). Three large aircraft locals, 647, 669, and 927, voting their entire 334 votes for R. J. Thomas in 1946, had been reduced to a combined voting strength of 54 by the 1947 convention. There was no possibility of a successful challenge to Local 50's voting strength. The implication that there was dishonesty involved is nonsense.

It has also been suggested that the support of ACTU was a major consideration in Reuther's victory. However, the *Wage Earner* showed a strict neutrality during the preconvention caucusing. Ten days prior to the convention in 1946, it had an editorial headed "That's Democracy":

The brewing Reuther-Thomas contest in the UAW is nothing more or less than the outcropping of good old-fashioned trade union democracy.

There is no reason for the daily papers to adopt the horrendous view they broadcast during the last week. . . .

The daily papers would do well to join with the WAGE EARNER in keeping their shirts on, refusing to take sides in the Reuther-Thomas affair, and letting the auto workers settle their own problems. (1946, p. 6)

Rev. Raymond S. Clancy, ACTU chaplain, commented in his article:

By the time it [this article] appears in print either R. J. Thomas will have been re-elected to the presidency of the UAW of else Walter Reuther will have been chosen as the new head of the Union. As I am happy to list both of them among my friends, I rejoice in the fact that I am not compelled to make a choice between them as the UAW delegates in Atlantic City must do. ("Convention Comments," 1946, p. 6)

The *Wage Earner* maintained its impartial reporting between the two factions prior to the convention. In January 1946, it headed a page-one story "They Won Their Wage Battles," referring to Thomas at Kaiser-Fraser and Reuther before the GM fact-finding committee. The victories were hardly of equal importance, but they had a flattering story on page two on the Kaiser-Fraser pact and an editorial congratulating Thomas ("They Won Their Wage Battles," 1946, p. 2).

On May 5, 1946, a month following the convention at which Reuther was elected, the UAW ACTU Conference met to formulate its policy on this new development. For two years it had pursued a policy of opposition to the Communist Party, but of neutrality between Reuther and the Addes-Thomas-Leonard caucus. It would much rather have seen a merger of the two major caucuses against the Communist Party than see a fight between Reuther and R. J. Thomas. At the May 1946 conference, a month after Reuther was elected, ACTU passed a resolution supporting Reuther and opposing "all attempts to create a false issue of Reuther vs. Philip Murray" (ACTU Collection, box 3; folder: ACTU-UAW 1946, UA,WSU). There were two dissenting votes, one was John J. McGuire of Local 900, Lincoln Plant. Paul Weber said, in an interview, that McGuire voted for Thomas because Reuther was a Socialist, certainly one of life's little ironies. Other observers noted that McGuire had been an Addes supporter for years and that, ACTU to the contrary, he could not go against his commitment to him. Local 900 was solidly pro-ATL, delivering all sixty-five of its votes to them.

ACTU membership was split on their position toward Reuther. The Communist issue had relatively little importance in 1946, and many ACTU members were committed to caucuses in their locals that claimed a priority on their voting behavior. Of the 190 names gleaned from the ACTU files that indicated ACTU membership between 1939 and 1947, Detroit and Pontiac, who were also identified as members of a UAW local, eighteen of them were elected delegates to the 1946 convention of the UAW. According to the author's own findings, thirteen of them supported Reuther, and five voted for Thomas. Three of those supporting Reuther split their ticket to vote for other ATL candidates. These figures are necessarily incomplete because of the absence of definitive membership lists, but they do indicate a lack of unanimity in ACTU.

Another explanation offered for Reuther's narrow victory was the support of the Trotskyists. From the descriptions in the *Daily Worker,* it would be impossible to derive the actual position of the two very small Trotskyists groups, the Socialist Workers Party (SWP) and the Workers Party (WP), the former estimated to have about 110 members in the UAW and the latter even fewer (Keeran, 1980, p. 243).

The SWP was the "official" party of Leon Trotsky's Fourth International, and the WP (the Shachtmanites) was a splinter group from the SWP. Both were opposed to World War II, and both considered themselves as the true inheritors of the Leninist tradition, viewing the Communist Party (the Stalinists) as corrupters of this tradition. The doctrinal differences between these three groups is not of concern here, but their treatment of each other is. The Communist Party had described the Reuther caucus as a "cabal" of Trotskyists and Actists. ACTU did not support Reuther in 1946, but it did in the 1947 convention. The reverse was true of the SWP. Its paper, the *Militant,* said in 1946 that "to this extent [Reuther's leadership in the GM strike], the UAW militants are correct in supporting Reuther as a more progressive candidate than R. J. Thomas" ("Reuther's Role," 1946, p. 2). Then it enumerated Reuther's shortcomings: support of the

Ford "security plan," the "one at a time" strategy in the GM strike, participation in Truman's fact-finding procedure, and Reuther's support of the "imperialist slaughter" of World War II.

Labor Action, the WP paper, while giving critical support to Reuther, also noted that he was "a milk and water socialist who really fears the logic of his own position" and as a consequence "is weak and ineffective" (Stiler, 1946, p. 2). This was in January 1946. By March, just prior to the convention, one of its reporters described the situation in this way:

> Reuther, as head of the GM local [sic], initiated the strike on the proper basis, but the fact remains that he permitted the real issues in the strike to be pushed into the background. He did not stand up against the Phil Murrays who allowed labor's wage gains to be stolen in Washington-granted increases. (Wilson, 1946, p. 2)

Reuther was sharply criticized "for looking to the White House for direction," for supporting company security plans and for not aggressively fighting Murray (Garrett, 1946, p. 4). It was damned faint praise: "Reuther cannot rise above his own political nature; despite all his talents and imagination, he is not basically a class-conscious, militant working class leader, but rather a pro-capitalist, opportunist labor official" (Hall, 1947, p. 198). (The writer should have observed the old leftist dictum: "Comrades, we do not personalize the conflict with the bourgeoisie.")

By the 1947 convention, the SWP had changed sides and now supported the ATL caucus, along with the Communist Party. After eighteen months in office, Reuther now revealed himself, according to the SWP, as "a dyed-in-the-wool Social Democratic trade union bureaucrat, who aspires to respectability, to rub elbows with the powers that-be, and to come to friendly, round table arrangements with employers" (The Fight Inside the Auto Union, 1947, p. 1). Reuther's caucus had become in eighteen months a red-baiting, "outright reactionary" group whose most influential support was from the "sinister priest-ridden Association of Catholic Trade Unionists" (p. 2). The ATL caucus was described as more democratic, more tolerant of left-wingers, and significantly, less influenced by the Communist Party than in the past. The UAW membership had punished the "Stalinist scoundrels for their innumerable crimes against the working class" (p. 2) without red-baiting or calling on the bosses for help, according to the SWP. While they admitted the many failings of the ATL group, they said that "a confluence of circumstances has forced the Thomas-Addes-Leonard faction into a more progressive role than Reuther's" (p. 2). "More progressive role" or not, the ATL caucus lost, and the *Militant* heralded Reuther's victory with the headline "Red-Baiters Sweep UAW Convention, Strong Minority Resists Retreat on Taft-Hartley Slave Labor Measure" ("Red Baiters Sweep UAW Convention," 1947, p. 1). This position will have to provide its own defense, but it should be noted that it is a pleasure to see an opponent characterized as a scoundrel rather than as a Fascist.

In any event, neither of the two Trotskyist groups were critical to Reuther's success. It is impossible to even venture a guess as to the numbers that were at the convention. Some informants insist that they were excellent activists and effective unionists, but their numbers were so small that it is not creditable that they greatly influenced the outcome. In 1947, the larger of the two groups, the SWP, left Reuther and supported ATL, and Reuther still won overwhelmingly.

It is difficult to account for Reuther's victory on the basis of race, sex, plant size, or geography. For example, the vote according to size of local shows very little difference. In those locals having from 1 to 10 votes, Reuther and Thomas split them almost down the middle: the former had forty-seven percent; the latter had fifty-one percent—they split two and a half percent (that is, neither commanded over seventy-five percent of the vote). This held true for the other groupings. Of those having 11 to 50 votes, Thomas, forty-one percent, Reuther, thirty-seven percent; twenty-two percent split. With 51 to 100 votes, Thomas and Reuther both took thirty-two percent and split the remaining thirty-six percent. In those locals with 101 plus, Thomas took 2 of them (seventeen percent), Reuther took 3 (twenty-five percent) and 7 of them split (fifty-eight percent).

When the delegates are counted by race and sex, the results are astonishing—not for the distribution but for the smallness of the numbers. There is an enormous problem with counting minorities at the 1946 convention. Since no records were kept by race and sex, it was necessary to have actual delegates or members of the locals at the time of the 1946 convention identify the delegates. Some 78 people were interviewed, most of them face-to-face; the rest were contacted by letters. They were able to provide answers for ninety-five percent of the locals represented at the convention. African-Americans ($n = 56$) represented three percent of the delegation and had three and four tenths percent of the votes. They cast seventy-seven percent of their votes for R. J. Thomas. Reuther garnered just twenty-three percent. The 3 African-American female delegates all voted for Thomas.

During the research, several respondents said that they did not expect the African-American delegates to exceed ten percent. Shelton Tappes who, prior to his defection to Reuther, had been a longtime supporter of the Communist Party in Local 600, one of its strongholds, expressed dismay when interviewed in 1987 at the small number of African-Americans in the local's delegation—16 Black males out of a total of 76 delegates. He said, wistfully, "And we were such a progressive local" (Tappes, 1986). In fact, two locals, 453 and 600, accounted for 39 of the African-American males at the 1946 convention. As B. J. Widick pointed out at a Labor History Conference in Detroit, Locals 51 and 155, both Communist Party strongholds, had no African American delegates out of a total of 39 delegates (Widick, 1987). This is no criticism of the Communist Party. This is the result of the hiring practices of the auto industry, which, incidentally, was not fought vigorously enough by any faction.

It must be noted, however, that many of the Reuther supporters recognized the deficiencies of the Reuther caucus on racial matters, noting a "lack of sensitivity." One African-American longtime Reuther supporter, Horace Sheffield, said of the Communist Party:

They articulated issues such as discrimination. . . . Walter, he spoke to these issues, but it was an ongoing thing for the left wing. . . . They were in the vanguard of the movement to create a color blind trade union movement. . . . [The left wing] makes it almost a passion. (Sheffield, 1986)

The female vote was even smaller. There were 55 female delegates, 3 of them African-American, two and nine tenths percent of the total delegation. They voted sixty-six percent for Reuther; thirty-four percent for Thomas. The combined female and African-American delegates represented under six percent of the delegation. Those locals that had substantial numbers of minority representatives, for the most part, had leftist leadership, either Socialist or Communist, or were from foundries, a traditional workplace for African-Americans.

Because of the concentration of the automobile industry in Michigan, the Detroit area was critical in the 1946 election. Michigan had thirty-five percent of the locals at the convention. Detroit and its contiguous suburbs (Dearborn, Hamtramck, and Highland Park) had eighty-one locals represented, twelve and a quarter percent of all locals at the convention. However, due to the large size of the plants, these Detroit area locals had thirty and eight tenths percent of all the delegates at the entire convention.

Since all of the locals were easily accessible to both caucuses because the distances were not great, there was enormous political activity. The result of the delegate election mirrored the final vote for president. Reuther got fifty and four tenths percent of the delegates, and R. J. Thomas got forty-nine and a half percent.

The one variable that seemed to explain the outcome of the election was the political leaning of the regional directors (see Table 4.1).

In almost every case where the regional director had a firm commitment to a candidate, that candidate carried the region. In the two large Detroit area regions, 1 and 1A, the vote was evenly divided because all the locals were easily accessible to both candidates. In region 9A, Charles Kerrigan permitted the region's staff complete freedom to campaign for whomever they pleased. Two of the most effective staffers, Irv Bluestone and Mike Svirdoff, were Reuther supporters and did an excellent job of counterbalancing the ATL forces on the staff.

The commitment of the regional director was crucial in the campaign. In the three Ohio-based regions, 2, 2A, and 2B, neither geography nor types of industry were markedly different. But the three regional directors were among the most committed to their caucuses. They overwhelmingly carried their respective regions for their candidates. In a highly political union like the UAW that had experienced an extraordinary level of rank and file participation in its organization period, it was to be expected.

Table 4.1

Distribution of Vote by Region and Regional Director

Region		Percentage of Vote to Reuther	Regional Director Prior to Election	Alliance
1	(Detroit)	51	Norman Matthews, Melvin Bishop	ATL[a]
1A	(Detroit)	49.5	Richard Leonard, Percy Llewellyn	R[b]
1B	(Pontiac)	78.8	William McAuley	ATL
1C	(E. Michigan)	56.6	Carl Swanson	ATL
1D	(W. Michigan)	61.1	Kenneth Forbes	R
2	(Cleveland)	23.5	Paul Miley	ATL
2A	(Cleveland)	6.3	Richard Reisinger	ATL
2B	(Toledo)	84.1	Richard Gosser	R
3	(Indiana)	39.4	Arnold Atwood	ATL
4	(Illinois, Wisconsin)	40.3	Joe Mattson	ATL
5	(Southwest)	53.5	John Livingston	R
6	(California)	23.4	Cy O'Halloran	ATL
7	(Canada)	35.8	George Burt	ATL
8	(Southeast)	64.4	Tom Starling	R
9	(Northeast)	78.0	Martin Gerber	R
9A	(Northeast)	50.2	Charles Kerrigan	ATL

[a]Matthews was formally committed to the ATL caucus but had strong leanings toward Reuther.
[b]Melvin Bishop was a member of the Reuther caucus but had a long relationship with George Addes.
Source: Compiled from UAW Convention Proceedings, 1946, by author.

When the voting records of the Big Three—Ford, GM, and Chrysler delegates—are counted, the same pattern emerges. The number of delegates from the Big Three represented twenty-nine percent of the total delegates voting for president at the 1946 convention. Reuther, who was GM director and leader of the GM strike, received sixty percent of the delegates from GM locals. Ford and Chrysler, to the contrary, gave only forty-two percent of their delegates to Reuther. Dick Leonard was Ford director, and Dick Frankensteen had been director at Chrysler. They managed to carry their constituency for the ATL caucus. The vehicle for this ability was, of course, their respective staffs. As a consequence, Reuther received only forty-nine percent of the Big Three delegates.

If neither race, sex, geography, radical groups, nor religious sectarianism could account for Reuther's victory, certainly Reuther's leadership in the GM strike and old-fashioned politics could. The formal bureaucracy became one of the keystones for political success and the International representatives one of the most vital factors. In Reuther's case, this could be overstressed because he went into the convention against the top officers who had been in office for years. But Reuther was able to neutralize some of his opposition and take votes from an area where he might have not been expected to prevail.

Staff members are all appointed. The regional director and top officers are elected, and they appoint their staffs with the concurrence of the president, although it is unlikely that a president would veto the selection by a regional director. When there was a clear division between the president and the International Executive Board (officers and regional directors) on appointments, as there was after the 1946 convention, they sat down and horse-traded.

Staff positions are highly coveted jobs in unions. The original formula for an International rep's pay in the UAW was based on the wages of a skilled worker working six days a week. Hence, the pay was greater than the average worker's. But there were skilled workers who refused to go on the staff because of a cut in pay, and there were cases of staff members who returned to their factory jobs because of the loss of wages.

A good job, away from the intense politics of the local scene or away from the grueling work in the factory, caused considerable competition for these staff positions. Being an intensely political union with high levels of rank and file participation, political turnovers meant job turnovers. Predictably, the charge is made that after Reuther was elected with a majority of the IEB in 1947, he "purged" the staff of his opponents. Horace Sheffield, an African-American retired UAW rep, and longtime Reuther supporter, said that this was the ordinary practice in the UAW. "If your director lost the election at the convention, you'd buy your snuff, your Copenhagen, your work clothes and go back to work" (Sheffield, 1986). Even when there was no particular factional dispute in effect, a change of leadership in a department meant wholesale turnovers in staff. For example, with Thomas as president, in the absence of a major political division, only one Education Department staff member, an Addes supporter, out of about a dozen survived the change of directors from Deverall to Levitt. Staff changes were common and expected under all leadership changes. Leonard Woodcock ran for regional director in 1947, and one of his main platforms was a promise to replace every staff member if he were elected. He was and he did.

On the other hand, Paul Miley, Richard Reisinger, and Joe Mattson, anti-Reuther regional directors, were given jobs after Reuther's 1947 victory. Dave Sherwood, Ken Robinson, Alan Strachan, and Walter Sowles went to the IEB between the 1946 and 1947 conventions to protest their discharges from the staff because of their Reuther sympathies. The charges and countercharges before the IEB of political partisanship got so heavy that George Addes said, "No international representatives or officers have guaranteed lifetime jobs. It should be specifically understood that the union is not making a lifetime commitment" (UAW IEB Minutes, March 17–26, 1947, p. 219). Matthews, by now supporting Reuther, when challenged for firing three anti-Reuther representatives, William Buckley, Carl Bibber, and Kenneth Groves, said, "He was willing to reinstate these boys if Dick Leonard reinstates Alan Strachan and Kenny Forbes reinstates every person he fired for political reasons" (p. 137). It got so threatening to the staff of the UAW that they made sporadic efforts to form a union to protect their rights, not succeeding until the 1960s(For a comparison of the Education staff, see, Linton, 1965, pp. 96, 99, 100; Keeran, 1980, p. 229).

NOTE

1.   This argument was not used when Local 248, UAW, a CP-dominated local, went on strike against Allis-Chalmers.

5

UNION ISSUES BETWEEN THE CONVENTIONS

ALLIS-CHALMERS STRIKE

Reuther's victory over R. J. Thomas was so small (114 votes out of over 8,000, carrying only eight members of the twenty-two-member International Executive Board) that his brother Victor later reflected, "I was fearful that we might face years of gradual build up of strength" (Reuther, 1988.)[1] Instead, Reuther, at the next convention, just eighteen months later, had only token opposition and defeated George Addes, R. J. Thomas, and Richard Leonard, effectively destroying the ATL caucus as a factor in UAW politics.

The intervening months between the 1946 and 1947 conventions was a period of intense shop floor political activity and acrimonious exchanges at the officers' level. Some of it was ludicrous, some libelous.

Three union issues dominated the exchanges: the Allis-Chalmers (AC) strike by Local 248, the proposed merger with the Farm Equipment Workers of the CIO, and the Taft-Hartley Bill. The AC strike was the most important battle on the union front even though it was not as significant a political factor in the internal life of the union as the FE merger. The Taft-Hartley (T-H) Act requirement that officers must sign an anti-Communist oath or be denied access to the National Labor Relations Board had a depressing effect on the entire union movement and occasioned intense debate in the UAW.

The essential facts of the AC strike are well documented. UAW Local 248, with a strong Communist Party leadership dating back to the 1930s, had organized 8,500 of the 11,500 employees of the AC shop in West Allis, Wisconsin. On April 29, 1946, the membership voted 8,091 to 251 to strike against the company, one of the most reactionary in the United States. The owners and managers of AC had long been identified with isolationists and pro-Nazi tendencies in the country. The union demands included the usual pattern settlement of eighteen and a half cents, but the company offered thirteen and a half cents and wanted unusual changes in the grievance procedure and maintenance of membership provisions of the contract.

The tough local leadership, oriented toward shop floor militancy and preservation of their hold on the membership against raiding AFL unions, could not give in on these crippling management demands. Seven plants struck against AC, including those shops organized by the Communist Party–dominated FE and UE. Because of the purported national emergency of delaying peacetime reconversion, the government talked of seizing AC and forcing the resumption of production. Some officials of the Labor Department maintained that there was no threat to reconversion. Truman refused to take over the plants even though other members of his administration were for it. The unions would not have been opposed because it would permit the local to retain the favorable wartime contracts.

By October 1946, the other AC plants, UE and FE included, accepted inferior contracts and went back to work. Regional Director Mattson, who was anti-Reuther, complained that "the demoralizing effect of the United Electrical Workers and the Farm Equipment Workers has hit the Union [Local 248, UAW] rather hard" (Mattson, 1946, p. 11). Reuther had commented in the same vein on the UE and FE settlements at the same Special Session of the IEB on October 18–20, 1946 (p. 7). The J. I. Case local of the UAW had, at this time, been on strike for ten months and AC for four months. The agricultural implement industry was notoriously antilabor, never having been humbled by major union victories as had the Big Three in auto. At this same Special Session of the IEB, Mattson noted that AC and J. I. Case "have refused to bargain or even renew the contracts that have been in existence, let alone any improvements" (p. 10).

With most of the other AC plants settled on the company's terms, the West Allis management launched a major offensive: They started a back-to-work movement. Congress cooperated: both the House Un-American Activities Committee (HUAC) and the House Committee of Labor and Education held hearings in February and March of 1947. Setting the stage for these witch hunts, the two Milwaukee papers, the *Sentinel* and the *Journal,* ran an astounding series of red-baiting stories. One cartoon, two columns wide, front page, showed a dagger entitled "Local 248" thrust into the back of Walter Reuther, impaling dozens of workers also ("Target and the Victims," 1947, p. 1). The dagger also was emblazoned with a hammer and sickle. The "Red Issue" had become ubiquitous. AC management went before HUAC with copies of the Communist Party nominating petition for governor of Wisconsin, demonstrating that most of the officers, committee persons, many members, and lawyers of Local 248 had signed it. The Wisconsin Employees Relations Board (WERB) added to the difficulties by ordering that mass picketing be stopped, limiting each gate to two pickets.

In November, as the local situation reached the critical stage, R. J. Thomas took over the direction of the strike, after George Addes had refused, owing to the press of other assignments. By January 1947, the strike was in almost total disarray; 4,000 employees were crossing the picket line. Despite differences of opinion on the conduct of the strike, both factions had been very careful to treat the issue as a trade union question. The political implications of the Communist Party leadership of the local had been largely ignored. Both sides agreed on the reactionary character of the AC management and publicly deplored the red-baiting by the company.

The tenor of the strike was established by the company in September 1946. The *Wall Street Journal* of September 21, 1946, quoted an Allis-Chalmers official as saying that "the strike would end when the 'union capitulates or the union is broken'" (McWethy, 1946, p. 2). The UAW leadership was unanimous on the handling of the strike. In August 1946, Reuther recommended that all locals contribute ten percent of their strike funds to Local 248 (Reuther, IEB Minutes, 1946, p. 163). This was part of a seven-point program Reuther offered, including asking Murray to try to persuade the government to intervene to give the local some relief. The War Labor Board had made several recommendations favoring the union, but the company had adamantly refused, as it did with the local's offer to arbitrate all disputed issues.

By December 1946, everyone recognized that the situation was grave. At the IEB meeting of that month, Reuther ruled that locals could use their strike funds to transport their members who support Local 248 (UAW, IEB Minutes, December, 1946, p. 10). The report of the agricultural implement strikes was equally dismal. The J. I.Case plants in Racine and Rockford had back-to-work movements. At Rockford, out of 800 employees, all but 200 had returned to work (p. 7). R. J. Thomas reported that the AC local in Boston, represented by the UE, had voted to return to work (p. 16). George Addes made the unprecedented suggestion that the local 248 leadership "on their own initiative" step down and be replaced by a UAW administrator (p. 11).

Then the split in the UAW leadership at the International level erupted into the open over the strike. The dispute was precipitated by the intervention of the Rev. Ensworth Reisner, a Methodist minister in Milwaukee. Reisner was a liberal who had served on the Executive Committee of the American Labor Party in New York and had been present at R. J. Thomas's wedding. Through the offices of Dr. Henry Hitt Crane, a liberal Detroit minister and close friend of Victor Reuther, Reisner got word to Walter Reuther that he had met with AC management and that they would welcome the intervention of Reuther and Philip Murray. The UAW Executive Board authorized Reuther and Murray to meet with AC. They met on January 11 and 14, 1947, with AC company representatives, John Brophy representing Murray.

On January 26, 1947, R. J. Thomas wrote Reuther a letter with a bill of particulars about Reuther's conduct during meetings with the AC management and released it publicly. He charged that Reuther and Brophy were authorized "to discuss with them solely the question of permitting Brother Mattson [the UAW regional director] or me to enter the negotiations. Failure to arrive at agreement on that question, there was to be no negotiating." In addition, Thomas said that Reuther had asked Thomas for wage and contract data, despite the prohibition against negotiating. Professing surprise, Thomas said, "Nevertheless, I complied with your instructions" (Walter Reuther Collection, box 36; folder 13, UA,WSU).

After the January 11 meeting, Reuther and Brophy briefed Thomas about the discussion with AC management on wages, grievance procedure, and union security. When asked by Thomas about Thomas's presence at subsequent meetings, Reuther indicated that the company objected. Thomas maintained strongly that at that point Reuther was obliged to end the meeting.

Thomas further charged in his polemic against Reuther that Reuther had notified him by phone that Brophy and Reuther would meet again on January 14. On January 15, at the IEB Policy Committee on the AC strike, Reuther reported that there was no progress, and the Policy Committee "made the unanimous decision that there were to be no more negotiations unless all four International officers were present." (This position, incidentally, was also a violation of the UAW constitution.) On Tuesday, January 21, Reuther called Thomas to inform him about a meeting at Reisner's house with all four officers of the UAW. Thomas insisted that Robert Buse, president of Local 248, also be present. Reuther told Thomas to call Reisner, who agreed reluctantly, according to Thomas's document. That afternoon, Buse, Richard Leonard, George Addes, Thomas, Reuther, and Brophy met with four AC representatives. Reisner asked Buse to leave, and Thomas responded that if Buse left, he would also go. Reisner then, according to Thomas, allegedly invited everyone to lunch but Buse. No one complained but Buse and Thomas stayed (Walter Reuther Collection, box 36; folder 13, UA,WSU).

The negotiations were going nowhere, and after a recess, all agreed to leave. Then Thomas, in his narrative, dropped the bomb, "Mr. Story heatedly stated to you not only that the company's proposal which had been offered at this meeting were the same as had been discussed with you and *agreed to* [emphasis added] by you in your previous private meetings, but also that you led him to believe that the strike could be ended at this meeting on these terms" (Walter Reuther Collection, box 36; folder 14, UA,WSU).

The thrust of Thomas's charges against Reuther revolved around Reuther's allegedly breaking the UAW constitution and the express wish of the IEB that negotiations were not to take place unless local union representation was present. These were serious charges in a union that had genuine cases of secret meetings with companies during the Homer Martin time as president. While the principle and the fears of "sellout" were real, as Emil Mazey pointed out in a board meeting, R. J. Thomas had met with Briggs while Mazey was president of the local without Mazey's approval or even knowledge. The practice was not unheard of, even in the UAW (Walter Reuther Collection, box 36; folder 14, UA,WSU).

Judging from the number of drafts that Reuther made of his answer to Thomas, he must have been furious. One draft was twenty-six pages long, but the final answer was just ten pages. Reuther said in one version that he would have preferred to have responded after the AC strike was over, which is what he did on February 11, 1947, relating that the WERB election (assumed by everyone to herald the end of the strike, mistakenly) was won by Local 248 by just 2 votes out of 8,259. "There are, however, still seventeen challenged ballots," Reuther continued, "to be acted upon by the Wisconsin Employment Relations Board. Since most of these challenges were made by our union, it is easily possible that the present majority may be dissipated" (Walter Reuther Collection, box 36; folder 14, UA,WSU).

What was omitted from the final letter that appeared in the various drafts is interesting. One draft pointed out that the "political complexion" of the competing UE and FE unions was close to that of Local 248. In the same draft, Reuther pointed out that "a split movement developed within local 248" to get rid of the Communist Party leadership, adding that Philip Murray had warned that if the leadership was not cleaned up, there was danger of losing the strike. In another draft, Reuther recounts the twists and turns of the leadership of Local 248 on foreign policy, reflecting their obedience to the Communist Party line. "No amount of hysterical invective . . . can deny the fact," Reuther continued,

that officers, committeemen and stewards of Local 248 circulated 37 percent of all petitions gathered by the Communist Party in Milwaukee County and that these petitions were circulated on the picket lines during the time when our union was fighting for its life. . . . Will the charge of redbaiting hide and excuse this colossal blunder and stupidity? (Walter Reuther Collection, box 36; folder 13, UA,WSU)

Reuther added, "There are those in our union who hide behind the charge of redbaiting to escape from sober judgment and cool analysis of fact. . . . There are Communists in our union and our industry. I do not propose that they be driven from our union or from our industry." But these fulminations against the political leadership of Local 248 came to nothing because they were expunged from the published letter (Walter Reuther Collection, box 36; folder 13, UA,WSU).

Reuther maintained that he delayed in responding to Thomas's January 26, 1947, polemic

because I felt that any harm I might suffer personally by your unwarranted newspaper attacks was of little consequence compared to the tremendous injury our union would suffer in the midst of this critical struggle at West Allis. . . . This sensational attack by the Vice President of the CIO's largest union on the President of that union brought streamer headlines in the press of the nation and joy to the hearts of the reactionary politicians in Congress and the company executives of our industry and, especially, to the management of the Allis-Chalmers Company. (Walter Reuther Collection, box 36; folder 13, UA,WSU)

Reuther insisted that he had never gone to "the anti-labor, reactionary press." "I defy you or anyone else to cite one single instance where I have resorted to the capitalist newspapers with an attack on any fellow officer of mine." Thomas, according to Reuther, first attacked him on Sunday, January 26, 1947, carried in the *New York Times* and the Milwaukee papers. After that, Thomas then wrote the letter that was released to the "Hearst *Detroit Times*" and printed before Reuther received a copy. Reuther said that Charles Bioletti, a member of Thomas's staff, used it in an attack on Reuther at Local 7 before Reuther had received his copy (Walter Reuther Collection, box 36; folder 13, UA,WSU).

Unction was as thick as class-conscious vocabulary in most of these exchanges.

Reuther then set down a point-by-point refutation of Thomas's charges, noting that the UAW Policy Committee, which had oversight responsibility for the strike, met on January 10, 1947, with all members present, except Thomas, who was at the strike scene.

I then asked . . . specifically for instruction as to procedure in the event the company would not agree to your inclusion [in negotiations]. Brother Stevenson [a Thomas supporter] said I should then explore the position of the company as to a possible settlement. All persons present, including Regional Director Mattson, agreed to this.
"I then drew the committee's attention to Article 19, Sections 2 and 3 of the International Constitution. You quote these on page 3 of your letter. The Policy Committee gave it as its opinion that we should proceed with the conference because of the extreme emergency existing in the strike." All present were polled and agreed to meet without formal approval by Local 248. (Walter Reuther Collection, box 36; folder 13, UA,WSU)

John Brophy, Philip Murray's representative at the meetings with AC management and a highly respected unionist, wrote a letter substantiating Reuther's version of events. Reuther quoted Brophy's letter that Thomas had agreed that if the company would not meet with Thomas present, then Brophy and Reuther were to proceed to explore the company's proposals. "One proof of this understanding is the fact that Thomas supplied us with the information about previous negotiations which we would need in the discussions" Reuther added, "Neither you nor he [Buse] expressed any disapproval and you definitely consented to the procedure outlined." Further, Reuther insisted that at the Policy Committee meeting on January 15, where he and Brophy reported on the meetings with the company, Maurice Sugar, a longtime Reuther antagonist, and others proposed that he and Brophy continue to meet in order to create the impression that a settlement was at hand to enhance the UAW's chances in the upcoming WERB election. According to his undisputed account, Reuther refused, wanting all four top officers there, and provided that the meeting "should not be held unless the company should show some evidence of making a concrete proposal" (Walter Reuther Collection, box 36; folder 14, UA,WSU).

The good pastor Reisner also wrote a letter to Reuther, substantiating his account of the events. Reisner made a particular point about these meetings not being negotiating sessions but merely exploratory. He quoted Reuther as saying that Thomas must be at any meetings "where there were negotiations." Reisner pointed out that "Geist [AC representative] had made it clear that his negotiating committee would do the bargaining for his company" and that if Thomas were present, it would be a negotiating session and the entire AC committee would then have to be present. This was a convoluted argument by Reisner to get Reuther and Brophy off the hook of actually "negotiating" rather than "exploring."

Reisner also explained some of the social niceties of the meeting at his house. It was true, he said, that Buse was asked to leave but that George Addes protested that Buse's presence "might be necessary . . . purely and simply to acquaint them with some of the facts." He also reported that George Addes "ate two pieces of pumpkin pie with honey and whipped cream," proving a "delightful" luncheon. Apparently, a good time was had by all (Walter Reuther Collection, box 36; folder 9, UA,WSU).

Charges and countercharges can be expected in a situation as tense and important as this was. But there is no evidence that Reuther acted with anything more than complete union propriety during the struggle with an obdurate and reactionary management. As the situation deteriorated, some Reuther supporters became more and more disenchanted with the Local 248 leadership and their tortuous reactions to the critical exchanges and picket line brutality. Reuther promptly pulled his troops back in line and sent a telegram to all the locals in the area, insisting that the victory of Local 248 was paramount and that "any differences . . . must be subordinated to the job of winning the Allis-Chalmers strike" (Walter Reuther Collection, box 36; folder 9, UA,WSU).

It is equally true that the pro-Communist leadership of Local 248 cannot be faulted for conducting a political strike to inhibit the country's reconversion from wartime production. The pro–Communist Party leadership of the FE and the UE scurried to cut their losses when they recognized that AC, J. I. Case, and other agricultural implement companies were out for blood. The pro-Reuther leadership of striking agricultural implement workers faced the same horrendous resistance of companies that refused to settle on a decent union basis and conducted punitive tactics against all the locals involved. Local 248 leadership undoubtedly made some major mistakes, but they were not the result of hewing to some, in this instance, mythical "Communist line."

The upshot of it all was that, facing yet another WERB election that they knew they could not win, and having been denied access to the NLRB because the local officers had not complied with the Taft-Hartley anti-Communist oath, the Local 248 bargaining committee recommended "that the strike be called off . . . and that all Allis-Chalmers workers return to work as soon as reasonably possible" ("Report of the Bargaining Committee," 1947). The company promptly fired ninety-one workers, including all the strike leadership.

Whatever its union significance, the AC strike had a serious effect on the political aspirations of R. J. Thomas. George Addes was the original choice of the IEB to direct the strike, but he begged off under the pressure of work. It seems more likely that he wanted to avoid a situation in which no one could possibly survive politically. Thomas threw himself into the conflict with a passion that suggests that he felt it might provide him with a road back to the presidency, as Reuther had done in the GM strike. Thomas was a tough, decent unionist, who most writers describe as "bumbling." Even Christoffel compared him unfavorably with Reuther. Thomas was a real working-class guy, with little of the sophisticated polish that many unionists had. Brendan Sexton told the story of Victor Reuther's meal with Thomas at one of the early conventions. Victor said that Thomas casually shifted his cud of chewing tobacco to one side of his mouth and continued to eat and talk with the cud undisturbed.

Thomas loved to drink with the boys and play poker, but he was somewhat diffident about his union duties. Reuther's notes on the IEB meeting of December 9–18, 1946, claim that Thomas had agreed that the AC strike would be first on the agenda at the December 10 meeting, so that Thomas could give a report on the strike. He did not show up until 4:10 P.M. with Joe Mattson, who had been sent to find him, and "had obviously gotten him up and out" (Walter Reuther Collection, box 36; folder 10, UA,WSU). Reuther complained in his notes that Thomas even missed a breakfast with Secretary of Labor Lewis B. Schwellenbach in November 1946, even though Reuther had stopped at his room the night before to remind him of the morning meeting (Walter Reuther Collection, box 36; folder 13, UA,WSU).

The public accusation against Reuther for having broken the UAW constitution by meeting with a company without authorization of the IEB was a serious mistake on Thomas's part. He was clearly wrong about the events in his news release, and it antagonized John Brophy, Murray's representative. Murray had given a near endorsement of Thomas over Reuther at the 1946 UAW convention, and it was impolitic to alienate the highly regarded Brophy at this point. The silence of Addes, Leonard, and other anti-Reuther board members was significant.

Thomas's most egregious fault was his inability to analyze the strike itself. He became so partisan that his judgment was distorted. Prior to the WERB recognition vote in January, AC offered a weak contract to the union. Reuther was for it, believing that a settlement would strengthen the hand of the local in the election. The leadership of the local refused. A majority of the IEB supported the local, reasoning that a better contract could be secured after the local had shown strength in the election. It all hinged on the prediction of who would win and the size of the majority. It was a simple union difference on strategy, and Reuther went along. Thomas had been predicting a large majority for the local (on the order of eight to one) that did not materialize. The results were so ambiguous that another vote was scheduled for March. By that time the strike was a shambles, and the local capitulated, leaving Reuther with a considerable edge on an important union issue.[2]

FARM EQUIPMENT MERGER

If there was one turning point in the battles between the ATL and the Reuther caucuses, it was the proposed merger between the UAW and the Farm Equipment Workers offered by the ATL group to the UAW Executive Board. There was ample union reason for the merger of the two organizations. For one, it would stop the jurisdictional battles between the two unions for those workers in farm equipment. The discussion between the two unions had been going on since 1940 when the FE was still an organizing committee (Farm Equipment Workers Organizing Committee [FEWOC]). The CIO National Office had repeatedly urged the merger, but the two unions could never reach agreement. By April 23, 1941, the FEWOC Executive Board rejected merger with some very harsh language:

Any further dalliance with this problem of jurisdiction can only mean that the unity within our own workers would be sacrificed to certain selfish interests who seek first to foist their political policies upon the farm equipment workers rather than organizing the farm equipment workers on the basis of rank and file controlled industrial unionism, embracing all workers regardless of craft, creed, color, religion or political affiliation. (Walter Reuther Collection, box 93; folder 8, UA,WSU)

The FEWOC Executive Board minutes of the same date reveal even stronger language. FE Director Frank Silva charged the UAW with rule or ruin tactics, and FE Vice-Chairman John Shaffer "charged political racketeering" in the approach to the merger. Addes expressed extreme disappointment in a letter of May, 12, 1941 (Walter Reuther Collection, box 93; folder 8, UA,WSU).

The FEWOC in November 1941 was in full throat for support of the war, demanding "repeal of the Neutrality Act, arming of merchant ships, convoying of American war supplies . . . defeat of Hitler and Hitlerism." They also condemned the UAW for claiming jurisdiction of Farm Equipment Workers and called on President Franklin Roosevelt to confer citizenship on Harry Bridges and pardon Earl Browder. A series of stickers was issued by the FEWOC in October 1942: "Support FDR Second Front Now" and "Stalingrad Week. Let's Do Our Part, 2nd Front Now" (Walter Reuther Collection, box 93; folder 9, UA,WSU).

In June 1945, the issue of merger had surfaced again with much of the same acrimony of the past. Addes complained to Grant Oakes, president of FE, that Addes's request for details of a proposed merger was answered by Oakes "flagrantly" misrepresenting the history of the negotiations, told of FE's "lofty objectives," "purity of purpose," and "by more than implication, what a terrible organization the UAW-CIO is." Addes continued in this five-page letter, "Apparently it is unpardonable for your membership to obtain even the slightest information about our negotiations. All such information must be kept from them, we presume for their own good!" In exasperation, Addes concluded, "Why are you so damned secretive about this business [merger], anyway?" (Walter Reuther Collection, box 93; folder 10, UA,WSU).

May and June 1945 produced more of this bitter exchange. Charles E. Lawson of FE telegraphed Addes that "5 Goons representing the United Auto Workers of America" broke into FE headquarters, broke down the door, attacked the office, and wrecked the files. One FE local asked for affiliation with the UAW, claiming that the FE was not representing its members, had UAW sympathizers fired, suspended fifty stewards and officers illegally, and had libeled the UAW. "The Report to the Membership" of June 22, 1945, of the IEB, FE-CIO, employed such refined expressions as "Pearl Harbor," "plotter," "disrupter," and "quisling" (Walter Reuther Collection, box 93; folder 10, UA,WSU). Perhaps these caustic exchanges could be accounted for by a remark of Allan Haywood, the CIO representative, before the IEB Special Session of the UAW to discuss the FE merger on June 20, 1947. The minutes read: "Brother Haywood announced to the board that he had dealt with the FE for a long time. It was quite some time since Addes, Thomas and he had tried to get them in the UAW. The proposal was rejected then because Thomas was then considered a war monger" (UAW IEB Minutes, Special Session, June 20, 1947, p. 56).

Two years later, the situation had changed. Reuther was now the president of the UAW and a beleaguered "left-center" coalition was being badly pressed by his aggressiveness. Now was the time to make the best deal, and the FE did. It got such a favorable agreement from the ATL caucus that it probably was its undoing. In the final analysis, it meant that the FE would enter the next UAW convention with from 400 to 500 votes, all securely in the pocket of the ATL slate. The transparency of the motives was so blatant that it was easy to expose.

Caucus activity on major issues was generally conducted by having the major caucus prepare a position paper that could then be adapted for local situations. Ten days after the IEB passed the motion that the merger "be sent to all local unions to be voted on and have it returned by July 15th, if at all possible," Reuther was in print with a letter to all the local unions with a denunciation of the proposal, followed by a longer, more thorough letter June 30. From an organizational point of view, the motion was, at best, hasty. Reuther claimed that the IEB was allowed only fifteen minutes to study the proposal before the vote. Since they had the votes, the "mechanical majority," as Reuther called his opponents, simply voted it into effect and sent it to the locals for their vote (UAW IEB Minutes, June 14, 1947, p. 164).

It was a calculated risk on the part of the ATL group. The provisions of the merger were suspect, but it meant a possible victory for the anti-Reuther caucus by the addition of the FE votes at the convention. The unanticipated result of the referendum was that it galvanized the Reuther forces into a level of activity they might not have employed on a lesser issue. The referendum had to be defeated, and it was fought on every local union floor. Either side had to take a majority of those voting at the special meeting, and they received all the votes that the local carried into the past convention.

Reuther's main propaganda letter denounced the merger on every possible ground. Constitutionally, it should have been brought to the convention for approval; it set up a special division in the UAW that no other major department enjoyed; the meetings with the FE were held without the knowledge of the president; and it provided "representation without taxation," that is, the FE locals would be allowed to vote without ever having paid any per capita dues. The document also compared the past mergers of the UAW and the Airline Mechanics Association, plus that of the Aluminum Workers and the Steel Workers, showing that these efforts had not been done in an unconstitutional manner. Some of the merger provisions were so sloppy and pro FE that they presented wonderful targets. It appeared from the wording that the UAW guaranteed that all FE staffers would be retained despite any possible turn in the economy. The director of the new FE division would have a seat on the Executive Board of the UAW and would be elected only by FE representatives, thus creating a "union within a union" (UAW Washington Office, D. Montgomery Collection, series 9, box 25-c-3 (1); folder 80-16: FE Merger with UAW, 1945–1947), (Walter Reuther Collection, box 108; folder: FE-UAW merger, UA,WSU).

This administrative letter was the basic Reuther piece that was used in his drive to defeat the merger. It was reproduced very effectively with embellishments by a "Committee of UAW-CIO Agricultural Implement Workers." Local 180, UAW, representing the J. I. Case workers, who had been on strike for fourteen and a half months against that reactionary, agricultural implement manufacturer, blasted the merger proposal and got in a few digs against the anti-Reuther regional director, Joe Mattson. This basic piece, with one exception, argued against the merger on a straight union basis. Whether it was right or wrong, the arguments were on its constitutionality, democratic procedure, and sound unionism. The one slight exception: the piece issued by Local 180, in which there was a sly quote from Grant Oakes, FE president, stating that the merger would create a "powerful, unified and autonomous FE Division of the UAW-CIO," thus contradicting George Addes. The source given for Oakes's statement: "Daily Worker, June 12, 1947" (Walter Reuther Collection, box 108; folder: FE-UAW Merger, UA,WSU; UAW Washington Office, D. Montgomery Collection, series 9, box 25-c-3 (1); folder: 80-16: FE Merger with UAW—1945–1947).

If ever a political situation was ripe for some good, old-fashioned red-baiting, this was it. One writer, sympathetic to the FE, stated that it was the "most left-wing of the CIO unions" (Keeran, 1980, p. 278). This same author recognized the "organizational and ideological role" that "the Communist Party played for the Addes-left-wing faction" (p. 254). Given these two facts—a Communist Party–dominated FE and the ATL caucus in the UAW that was dependent on the Communist Party—a murderous, red-baiting attack could have been leveled at the Addes group. Instead, the fight was fought on trade union issues, with one quote from the *Daily Worker* of an innocuous nature. That does not mean that shop level discussion was quite as decorous. If the written record on other issues at this time is any indication, the oral arguments must have been more brutal where it is not possible to hold one to account. It does mean, however, that the Reuther forces did not use their press, a most powerful tool in such battles, to advance the charge of communism.

It may be that failure to use the press was of no consequence. That seems to argue against the importance that both unions and radical sects have placed on the press. Some writers have suggested that the radical press did not exist because of the organization, but the sect existed because of the press. It is hard to assess statements like the following: "The impact of the issue of communism in the factional battle should not be exaggerated [*sic*]. As we have seen, the Communist issue was rarely debated openly, but formed the underlying context for the loss of legitimacy by the left caucus" (Silverman, 1982, p. 295). Perhaps other, more parsimonious explanations have greater validity.

TAFT-HARTLEY AND ECONOMIC ISSUES

Section 9 (h) of the Taft-Hartley on "Representatives and Elections" states:

No investigation shall be made by the Board of any question affecting commerce concerning the representation of employees . . . unless there is on file with the Board an affidavit executed . . . by each officer of such labor organization and the officers of any national or international labor organization of which it is an affiliate . . . that he is not a member of the Communist Party or affiliated with such party, and that he does not believe in, and is not a member of or supports any organization that believes in or teaches the overthrow of the United States Government by force or by any illegal or unconstitutional methods. (Taft-Hartley Act, Labor Laws, Vertical File, UA,WSU)

President Truman vetoed the act, but it was overridden. Both the AFL and the CIO immediately denounced it as a "Slave Labor" bill. Philip Murray was outraged about the total bill but was particularly provoked by the anti–Communist Party affidavits because it was obviously a class-biased piece of legislation. No such requirement was made of management. The UAW officers and Executive Board excoriated the bill and mounted a major offensive against its passage.

The choices facing unions were limited. Not to sign the oath meant to lose the NLRB offices in certification and recognition elections, a nearly fatal blow as dissident unions discovered. Several unionists simply resigned their offices, including Max Perlow, secretary treasurer of the United Furniture Workers, and Bill McKie of UAW Local 600. But that reduced effectiveness as surely as the provisions of the bill did. Some unions tried to reduce the number of officers and play around with titles, but the NLRB soon stopped that. Another option was to sign, even if the organization to which you belonged was on the subversive list, and let the NLRB prove your membership. This was highly dangerous, particularly if your name had long been associated with a group. There were personal and organizational decisions to make. Despite early protestations on the part of the CIO and refusal of several high officials to sign the affidavits, it was clear that unions were going to comply or lose substantially.

A Committee for Defense of UAW-CIO from the Taft-Hartley Slave Labor Law was established and pointed out an alternative: "The same alternative used before the Wagner Act—use of our economic strength. Unions are today winning elections, and winning contracts without the 'services' of the Board" (Walter Reuther Collection, box 108; folder: Taft-Hartley Issue, UA,WSU). It is true that even today not all unions use the Board, but they are generally confined to large powerful building trades locals that do not face competing unions.

The reality of not signing the Taft-Hartley affidavits is demonstrated by the plight of the FE local representing Caterpillar Tractor in Peoria. It was the largest FE local, and the officers refused to sign the non-Communist oaths. Caterpillar promptly withdrew its recognition of the local, the local struck unsuccessfully, and a new election was ordered, without FE on the ballot because of its non-compliance. In the first election, the UAW-AFL got 4,707 votes; the UAW-CIO got 2,656; the International Association of Machinists (IAM), 1,170; and "no Union" (the FE position), 2,112. The runoff election was between the UAW-CIO and the UAW-AFL, the top two vote-getters. The UAW-CIO won 7,702 to 5,655 (Blackwood, 1951, p. 117).

The ATL caucus fought the signing until several of their faction switched sides, permitting Reuther to wire the National Labor Relations Board that the UAW would comply. Still, Addes and Thomas refused to sign. Thomas, in a telegram to Robert Denham, general counsel of the National Labor Relations Board, stated that the provisions of the act required all officers of the union to sign and that he would not sign until the UAW convention, just weeks away, would make a decision. Thomas's position was reported in a front-page story in *Ford Facts*, newspaper of Local 600, written by Carl Haessler, November 8, 1947 (Walter Reuther Collection, box 108; folder: News Clips, November 1947, UA,WSU).

Part of the propaganda surrounding the T-H Act was the story that not only did Reuther favor compliance with the act, but he was also in favor of it. R. J. Thomas referred to the hated bill as the Taft-Hartley-Reuther bill. It was only a short step to the story, propagated by Drew Pearson, that Robert A. Taft, planning to run for president on the Republican ticket, wanted Walter Reuther to be his running mate for vice-president. The ATL committee's *Issues and Answers* piously stated, "We don't know whether this story is true or not. . . . But UAW members know that Reuther has been FOR compliance with Taft's Labor Board, which is in itself a contribution to the G.O.P campaign [emphasis in original]" (Walter Reuther Collection, box 108; folder: Factional Statements on Convention Issues). *Suggestions for Editorials*, issued by the ATL, concluded: "We can't dismiss the Taft-Reuther story as too fantastic. It's all so logical" (Local 9, Collection, box 97; folder: Pre-Convention Propaganda, 1947, UA, WSU).

An open letter from an influential New Jersey local president was an attack on Reuther, calling him "ambition-crazed," "would-be dictator," faulting Reuther's "sly, underhanded and unprincipled factional campaign" and announcing his opposition to Reuther "because of his avowed support of Taft-Hartley principles." In another attack on Reuther, two UAW members are having a fictional discussion of the Taft-Reuther story. One of the workers, Mike, concludes: " I don't know. It's not important whether the red-head [Reuther] is running with Taft. He denies it, but to me its [*sic*] enough to know that he's eligible" (Walter Reuther Collection, box 108; folder: Factional Statements on Convention Issues, UA,WSU).

The UAW Public Relations Department put out a release on October 12, 1947, that said, in part,

President Roosevelt called Drew Pearson a chronic liar. Pearson's broadcast that I was a possible running mate for Senator Taft in 1948 proves him not only to be a chronic liar but also a fool. . . . This fantastic story was planted by the newly hired publicity agent of George F. Addes and R. J. Thomas in an effort to influence UAW delegate elections now in progress. (Walter Reuther Collection, box 143; folder 8, UA,WSU)

The 1947 UAW convention brought all of the discussion to a stand still when the delegates voted to comply with the Act, to seek to overturn it in the courts and to work for its repeal.

Several economic issues arose during the time between conventions, which, if they had been taken seriously, would have set back the study of labor economics for decades. Reuther had prepared under the direction of Don Montgomery, of the UAW Washington office, a brief for the upcoming UAW wage negotiations entitled "Wages, Prices, Profits." Because of the seriousness of the occasion, it was reviewed by Robert Nathan Associates, a prounion economic consulting service in Washington. The demand was for a twenty-three-and-a-half-cent pay increase, buttressed by such arguments that increased productivity "is a sound prescription for labor's wage demand in years ahead" and noted "the wide profit margins which already exist"—thus setting the stage for a major increase out of current high profits and increased productivity in the future (Ganley Collection, box 1, series 1; folder 1–38, UA,WSU).

Reuther issued a press release that the wage statement (over fifty pages long) would be the subject of a press conference on April 8, 1947. On April 4, 1947, R. J. Thomas wrote to Reuther requesting that the report be postponed on the basis that "no such study has been reviewed or approved by the International Executive Board or the International Officers." Thomas added that confusion would result if the report were released because "current rumors that the UAW's wage demand is limited to 6 cents per hour arising from materials already released by you confirm this impression" (Walter Reuther Collection, box 108; folder: Factional Statements on Convention Issues, UA,WSU).

Reuther's chagrin was obvious: He noted that when they had met just two days before Thomas's letter, Reuther had invited Thomas to the press conference, and Thomas had not expressed any reservations about the report at that time. On the procedural issue, Reuther said that the report was shown to George Addes, who made some suggestions for revision. The changes were made, and on March 14, 1947, Addes, Montgomery, and Reuther met again, where Addes announced himself "well pleased." The final proof was passed out at the IEB meeting in Louisville. Thomas's letter had the effect of stopping the release of the report "in order to protect the membership of our union against repetition of the same kind of damaging and irresponsible press statement which you made during the Allis-Chalmers strike" (UAW IEB Minutes, Special Meeting, April 15, 1947, p. 21, UA,WSU).

Thomas wrote again on April 11, 1947, claiming that the first thirteen pages of Reuther's wage statement "mean nothing at all" and that he had taken the wrong base year "for estimating the workers' real hourly wages" (p. 20). He continued with an analysis of the brief that betrayed a sophistication that Thomas had not demonstrated prior to this time. Regarding his failure to protest earlier, Thomas said that he was not given a copy until April 8. The entire board had only the briefest look at the proposal at the earlier board meeting, and it was impossible, according to Thomas, to form an opinion in such a short time. At the April 15 meeting of the IEB, Don Montgomery answered questions regarding the wage brief, and a motion was made to accept the report. The motion carried, with Thomas dissenting. Thomas was again unable to mount and sustain a frontal attack on one of Reuther's positions. Most of the board, even those in his caucus, failed to support Thomas.

Local 155, a Communist Party stronghold, added to the merriment and confusion on the wage question in the June issue of its local press, *Common Sense*. It attempted to create a factional difference on the IEB and "repudiated the personal statement on policy filed by President Reuther" and supported the IEB position. In fact, the IEB position was now the one proposed by Reuther. The editorial noted the following differences between the IEB and Reuther: The IEB was against higher wages obtained through speedup, while Reuther was for higher wages coming from profits and productivity. It also pointed out that Reuther recognized the need for higher prices in those industries *"which can not otherwise raise their wages to a decent level* [emphasis in original]." The Local 155 editorial further asserted that the board was opposed to "supporting higher prices in return for higher wages in all cases." It is not clear whether Local 155 was talking about the International Executive Board or the Local 155 Executive Board (Ganley Collection, box 10; folder 21, UA,WSU).

In addition, there was the usual attack on David Dubinsky and the charge that Reuther was red-baiting. However, this spurious leftism was not being accepted by their ideological counterpoints in the UE. They settled for eleven and a half cents, with fringe benefits that they estimated brought the total to fifteen cents. For the second year in a row, the UE signed with GM, again undercutting the UAW demands. Reuther charged that there was an agreement that no one would sign until a decision was made by the CIO. William Stevenson, an ATL supporter, made a motion that James Matles, head of UE, be invited to a UAW IEB meeting and asked not to accept the fifteen cents. The motion passed, but there is no indication that Matles accepted the invitation (UAW IEB Minutes, Special Meeting, April 15, 1947, pp. 3–6, UA,WSU).

Coupled with the wage policy dispute was a statement by the National Planning Association (NPA). NPA was one of those postwar efforts like the chamber of commerce plan to get labor and management together to study economic problems and, if possible, to reach some agreement on policy statements. They were feckless efforts, but most union leaders went dutifully through the motions to avoid public criticism. Labor leaders from Philip Murray on down were involved in the NPA.

On August 7, 1947, the NPA released a statement that thirty-three labor leaders had endorsed the following positions:

Labor has as great a stake as anybody in Labor Management efficiency leading to increased production per man hour.

You don't pull increased wages out of thin air or out of your hat. They come out of the rising production.

Workers are increasingly realizing that high wages are made possible by the high and increasing efficiency of our economy. (Walter Reuther Collection, box 108; folder: News Clips, September 1947, UA,WSU)

Walter Reuther's name, along with other CIO and AFL presidents and officers, was appended to the statement.

Local 45 was the point for this attack. Their September 12, 1947, edition of the *Fisher Eye Opener* slammed Reuther with a reproduction of the NPA statement and further assaulted him for remarks allegedly made to the membership of

Studebaker Local 5, urging it to accept the management proposal to lay off 1,000 workers and have the remaining work force maintain the same production. This became the "speed up" issue.

There was an extraordinary spate of materials put out on this issue. George Hupp, president of Local 5, branded the report by Local 45 about the situation at Studebaker "a disgrace to true unionism" (UAW Local 51 Collection, box 22; folder 12, UA,WSU). Reuther slashed back at his attackers with a denial of having seen the NPA statement prior to publication, and he repudiated it. In the same correspondence, he berated Local 45 on the Studebaker story. Since Local 51 and Local 45, both with strong Communist Party leadership, had joined the attack, Reuther added a section on "How the Communist Party Uses UAW Local Unions." In this section, he recounted the history of these locals and their adherence to the Communist Party line, including supporting piecework proposals during the war. In addition, the Reuther caucus put out a one-pager "How They REALLY Stand on Piece Work and Speed-Up." Here R. J. Thomas's "straddling" position at the 1943 convention was compared with the Communist Party's *New Masses* article on Addes's support of piecework in 1943 and Reuther's 1946 position against speedup and piecework. The flyer added that this last position of Reuther's was defeated by the "mechanical majority" on the IEB, which was true but not for the reasons implied by Reuther (Walter Reuther Collection, box 108; folders: Speed-Up and Unmarked, UA,WSU).

The *Wage Earner*, the newspaper of ACTU, reported on a debate between Thomas and Reuther in Flint, Michigan. Thomas charged Reuther for support of the NPA statement.

"Show me Phil Murray's . . . name on the NPA. The NPA is a stooge for the National Association of Manufacturers! It has Reuther's name, but show me the NPA letterhead with Phil Murray's name on it!" . . . Suddenly, the UAW President [Reuther] darted over to Thomas, unfolding a sheet of paper on the way.

He placed it on the desk and, with gestures showed Thomas not only Murray's name, but Emil Rieve's [Textile Workers president] . . . and James B. Carey, CIO Secretary Treasurer. All three were on the NPA list! ("Was His Letterhead Red," 1947, p. 6)

They also noted that the NPA Advisory Committee on the Aircraft Industry listed Addes, Frankensteen, Reuther, and Thomas (p. 8).

That there was considerable demagogy in a situation as tense as this is to be expected. But to be demagogic and so transparently wrong is fatal. The ATL caucus—actually Thomas seemed to be on his own at this point—fudged stories; they confused production and productivity, claiming that any discussion of productivity meant speedup when it obviously did not. They imputed ideas to Reuther that he was easily able to refute; they failed to note or did not care that their supporters were also on the NPA advisory boards. The attacks on Reuther got more and more fierce to the point that they were unproductive.

NOTES

1. *Newsweek,* April 8, 1946: "The man who really emerged from the [1946 UAW] convention with increased power was Addes" ("UNIONS: Three Header UAW," 1946, p. 67).

2. After Reuther's victory in 1947, he appointed Pat Greathouse, newly elected regional director, as administrator over Local 248, who designated Tony Audia as the responsible International representative to revive the local. It was in a shambles, there was no contract, the rank and file were convinced of "Communist invulnerability" in the local, and it was described as a "desert." Rebuilding began in December 1947. By late January, 2,000 members had rejoined. Reuther spoke at the local to reinforce the UAW's dedication to reconstitute Local 248.

An education program was started, a voluntary organization committee was established, and handbills were distributed to revive the membership. By May 13, 1948, the local had 5,000 members. One handbill "on pink paper showed a one-armed bandit with the revolving fruit varieties and explained: 'Here's a machine that never pays off. Turns up three lemons every time. They call it "The little Commie Vending Machine." To operate, insert copy of the Daily Worker in the slot, then watch the jaw begin to wag and the mouth begin to flop' " (Harrison, 1948, pp. 68–69).

In the election of union officers, 2,500 voted, giving an eight-to-one margin for the administration candidate against the Christoffel slate. At the installation of officers, 1,500 members attended the ceremony. August and September local meetings drew 900 to 1,200, almost unheard of figures except in extreme crisis.

Harrison concludes: "Thus, at Allis-Chalmers, Audia's foremost job was selling the Reuther program in positive terms. . . . He makes much of the fact that the Red label was saved for election propaganda . . . and used only on top of six months of constructive appeal. 'Just windowdressing,' he laughs" (pp. 69–70).

Audia's cheerful cynicism is symbolic of Reuther's attitude toward defeating an entrenched Communist opposition. Basic, hard caucus work determined victory. Simple use of anti-Communist slogans, however valid, did not win elections. Local issues, program, and organization were the keys to success.

6

POLITICAL ISSUES
BETWEEN THE CONVENTIONS

STATE OF THE UNION

The tradition in the UAW is that the local union press is not to be used for factional political purposes. Like most traditions, it is often honored in the breach. Some of the most political locals in the union were careful to keep partisanship out of their newspapers. Local 212, Emil Mazey's home local, issued a weekly *Voice of 212* that dealt overwhelmingly with local news from January 3, 1947, to November 21, 1947, when it carried a report of the convention at which Walter Reuther and Mazey were elected top officers of the UAW. On February 28, 1947, it carried an attack on Governor Kim Sigler's red-baiting speech about unions. At the time of the proposed FE merger, it carried both Reuther's and Addes's statements (De Gaetano Collection, UA,WSU).

In the same tradition, Local 3, which had given a majority of its votes to Reuther in 1946, had no mention of the November 1947 convention or of the politics leading to it. There was not even a notice of the election of delegates in the local's press. The pro-ATL Canadian Region, in the *Canadian Automobile Worker*, ran straight news stories with no mention of the convention, even in November 1947, the month it was held. Local 200, Ford Canada, had no factionalism in its stories in Canadian *Ford Facts*. On October 9, 1947, it ran an article from the Canadian *Financial Post* entitled "Communist Bogey Won't Solve Labor's Problems." Page two carried an editorial "Let Employers Fight Communism," arguing that the exploiters cause communism, so let them change the conditions leading to communism (De Gaetano Collection, UA,WSU).

Local 22, an ATL stronghold, had no mention of factionalism until the month of the convention, November 1947. In that issue of the *Cadillac Steward*, front page, it had a picture of R. J. Thomas with a story "R. J. Thomas Outlines a Program for UAW Convention." Much of the article was an attack on red-baiting. The president's column, page three, by Dave Miller, was a blistering attack on Reuther on local union issues, avoiding most of the ATL positions (De

Gaetano Collection, UA,WSU). No mention of the ever-so-popular Dave
Dubinsky.

Reuther's home Local 174 started early, March 1947, with a story on page
one: "Rump Meeting, Lies and Communist Party Interference Blot Vote
Campaign." The story in the *West Side Conveyor,* described an "illegal" meeting
that was, apparently, only a caucus meeting. Pages four, six, and eight had either
attacks on Thomas or the Communist Party. April 1947, page four: "Communists
Menace Progress of Union." July, August, and October of 1947 also had pro-
Reuther articles or attacks on the Communist Party. Although the Ternstedt unit
of Local 174, in its separate press, *Ternstedt Flash,* endorsed Reuther in October
1947, in the entire year it made no mention of the Communist Party or factionalism (De Gaetano Collection, UA,WSU).

Local 155, Communist Party stronghold of the UAW, started in April 1946,
just after Reuther was elected president, to attack him—and Dave Dubinsky, of
course. From January to November 1947, only three of the monthly issues of
Common Sense, did not carry a partisan article. In April 1947, when Reuther
berated Michigan governor Kim Sigler for a red-baiting attack on unions, an article appeared assuring its readers that Reuther, "a foremost red baiter," must feel
better "for having repudiated the line begun by Hitler, Togo and Mussolini—the
boys who were 'saving the world from Communism' and killed 35 million people in the process." By September 1947, ACTU was also attacked, quoting Dan
Tobin of the Teamsters and Albert Fitzgerald, president of UE, "a practicing
Catholic himself" (De Gaetano Collection; Walter Reuther Collection, box 65;
folder 7, UA,WSU).

Local 600 kept up a steady barrage against Reuther. Local 51, in September
24, 1947, had a banner headline "Reuther Aids Labor Enemies/Our Union Must
Keep United" that was three inches high. There was also a picture of Thomas and
Henry Wallace marching together in the Labor Day Parade (De Gaetano
Collection, UA,WSU).

Other locals, however, had no mention of factionalism or faction fighting—
for example, Locals 651 *AC Sparkler,* 659 *Searchlight,* and 142 *Spotlight.* Local
45 was violently anti-Reuther, attacking him on the Studebaker issue and
speedup. Local 455 reprinted Local 45's "Open Letter to Walter Reuther" on
October 8, 1947. Local 5, Studebaker, defended Reuther on his position in the
local. Both sides of the FE merger were reported by Local 262, *Forgemen.*
Locals 280 and 190, as expected, were dramatically anti-Reuther (De Gaetano
Collection, UA,WSU).

The larger anti-Reuther locals were more vociferous in their use of the
local's press for partisan politics than were the pro-Reuther locals—that is, until
Reuther, in a political coup, used the *Automobile Worker* in September 1947 for
one of the most inflammatory partisan uses yet experienced.

The president of the UAW is mandated by the constitution to submit a report
to the membership quarterly on "The State of the Union." Reuther did so in the

September 1947 issue of the *Automobile Worker*. An introduction to the report cited the problems facing the country and the union and stated that factionalism was impeding the progress toward solving those problems. There was a ringing cry that "Factionalism Must End" ("Report to the Membership," 1947, p. 5). Every faction said that. Reuther's program for achieving this end included the following points: verbatim minutes of the IEB meetings, election of a three-person board of trustees to oversee the finances of the union, creation of a strike fund, improved organizing, and an end to patronage. The blame for failure to achieve these objectives was, of course, laid to the "mechanical majority" of Reuther's opposition.

Then Reuther called for the implementation of section 8, article 10 of the UAW constitution that prohibited Communists, Nazis, or Fascists from holding office in the UAW. "For Democracy—Against Totalitarianism" was the heading of the next section. The Fascists must be fought for their "technique of smearing every decent liberal and progressive with the brush of Communism" (p. 7). But the Communists must also be fought when they smear as fascist or red-baiter "everyone who has the courage to oppose or criticize the Communist Party line" (p. 7). "The Communist Party is not a political party in the legitimate sense," Reuther insisted, but is governed by the foreign policy of the Soviet Union (p. 7). There followed a twenty-four-item program covering everything from "Atomic Power for Peace" to "Women Workers."

Clayton Fountain, an ex-CPer autoworker who was on Reuther's staff, wrote in his book *Union Guy* that Reuther was required to submit a report by the UAW constitution,

and Addes had no legal ground for trying to prevent the publication of the report. But we knew that, if Addes found out that we intended to print the report, he would try to hold it up. So we went ahead without telling Addes—although he could have found out about it if he had been smart enough to post a lookout at the printing press in Indianapolis. (Fountain, 1949, pp. 210–211)

The outrage of the majority of the IEB was palpable. In the morning session of the IEB on September 24, 1947, it passed a motion condemning Reuther for the partisan nature of his report. The resolution denounced Reuther "as a whole hearted advocate of the restrictive features" of the Taft-Hartley bill. "Reuther has exposed himself as the working ally of Labor's enemies" and "by his irresponsible campaign antics, Walter P. Reuther has divorced himself from the main body of the American Labor movement" (UAW Local 9, Collection, box 97; folder: Pre-Convention Propaganda, 1947, UA,WSU).

In the afternoon, Thomas made a further motion that since the minority group of the board had their position represented in the report, the majority of the board also be given access to the *Automobile Worker* for a rejoinder. Reuther insisted that his statement was his report and not a caucus document. Martin Gerber maintained that the president has a constitutional obligation to make a report and that the IEB has no such right. Gerber further argued that the majority "chastised" the president for an action they now wanted to perform themselves (UAW IEB Minutes, September 22–24, 1947, pp. 241–242, UA,WSU).

Bill Stevenson quoted the *Wage Earner*, the ACTU paper, on the Reuther report, which had treated it as a gleeful trick on Reuther's part and a sly but perfectly honorable tactic. Dick Leonard noted that the IEB was the governing body of the UAW and that it was its "prerogative" to state the majority position of the board. Norm Matthews insisted that this proposed action by the majority of the board entitled the minority to also have the *Auto Worker* pages open to it. The juridical turn of the argument did not last for long. It soon ranged over the entire campaign since the last convention and became increasingly political, even though it maintained a veneer of a discussion of the constitution (pp. 243–245).

Reuther soon entered actively into the dispute. Reacting to Stevenson's mention of the *Wage Earner* story, Reuther asked, If Stevenson based his request for rebuttal to the report on a *Wage Earner* story, could Reuther therefore request rebuttal space on the anticipated article in the *Daily Worker* and the *Michigan Herald*, as the Michigan *Worker* was now called? Then he took on *FDR*, an ATL newspaper, and other ATL propaganda:

You have already taken care of that by telling the whole world, including the membership, that Reuther is a working ally of the enemies of labor, that Reuther has divorced himself from the main body of labor and that Reuther has sold out to the enemy and is now collaborating and working with the Tafts and the Hartleys. (pp. 245–246)

Reuther insisted, accurately, that he had never stooped to personal vilification in his programmatic positions. He said that his proposals for more precise financial handling of the union's funds specifically stated that the proposals were a matter of good organizational method and that no attempt was made to suggest any financial culpability on the part of any officers (pp. 246, 247, 250).

After the recess, the dispute turned from a rousing factional exchange to a personal cry of anguish from several sources. Paul Miley reported that someone had taken a picture of his house in Cleveland and surmised that some local was going to run a picture of the house "indicating that is where some of the money of the Thompson Products drive went." He continued:

I have got to live in this community . . . and my child is being raised in that community. . . . You can laugh about it, if you want to. You think it isn't serious for me to be condemned as a crook in my neighborhood or community or any place else, but I think it is serious, and believe me, I'm not going to sit around and watch it happen. (p. 285)

None of this did or had happened, of course. It was only Miley's apprehension. Reuther responded after others had spoken.

You can accuse the father of my children of selling out to the bosses. That is all right. That is lovely for my kids. I am going to fight for my kids just as you fight for yours, and whenever you can get so you can act decently toward other people, maybe you will have the right to have other treatment. (p. 287)

The tension continued for the rest of the meeting. The effect of the sixteen-month-long campaign was wearing on everyone's nerves. It had been such a brutal campaign that all the board members were frayed. Thomas said to Reuther in one exchange, "I am afraid to say anything. I am getting to where I am afraid to say anything, because you might get started on an hour's speech" (p. 297). That statement not only reflected the exhaustion of the participants, but it suggests who was dominating the discussion.

Addes, Thomas, and Leonard put out a special issue of the *Automobile Worker*, dated October 1947, entitled "Report on the State of Your Union." They said that since Reuther had not issued a quarterly report, as required by the constitution of the UAW, "therefore we determined weeks ago to prepare this report" ("Report on the State of Your Union," 1947, p. 1). Reuther's belated report "is now being used by labor's enemies to discredit the whole labor movement of this country" (p. 1). Then they tried to enlist Philip Murray as an ally. "He [Murray] rightly said that this so-called report was the most devastating attack on labor he had known in a life time of service for labor. He was astonished and indignant" (p. 1).[1]

It was a brutal polemic, but it was also curiously reactive. The by-now-familiar charges that Reuther was pro–Taft-Hartley and for speedup were coupled with statements that "Factionalism Is Over Stressed," as if the monkey of continued factional dispute was on their backs. If factionalism was overstressed, the question arises about why they called for the dissolution of all caucuses in their document. They successfully rebutted Reuther's charges that the failed Thompson Products organizing drive cost $500,000. It had only cost $287,836.41, without appreciable results. For the first time, the ATL caucus did more than just reject Reuther's program for three trustees to oversee the finances of the UAW. They proposed that a committee be selected to go over the reports of the president and the secretary treasurer before they are issued "to satisfy itself as to the accuracy of the reports" (p. 2). Not quite the same as Reuther's platform, but close enough to warrant the suspicion that the ATL caucus felt it should be responded to.

The ATL report was at its intellectual best on the question of civil liberties. After affirming their patriotism (expected of everyone addressing the Communist issue), they entered into a defense of a trial for all of those charged with a violation of article 10, section 8 of the UAW constitution that forbade Communists, Nazis, or Fascists from holding office in the UAW. Incidentally, neither side rejected the constitutional provision itself. The question became a procedural one: What is the mechanism for removing anyone from office? "The Issue Is a Fair Trial," the ATL document intoned. They quoted Victor Reuther to great effect from the 1941 convention when he insisted that a trial would be granted. The real issue was whether a democratic union should have such a proviso. But in the context of the campaign, the ATL forces were surely right and Reuther was just as surely wrong when he insisted that a known Communist can simply be dismissed from office without a trial.[2]

The weakness of the ATL argument was not a logical one; it was political. They spent twenty-one and a half inches of double-column print on this issue, fifty percent more than Reuther had spent. That was eight inches more than they wrote on the Thompson Products drive and nearly twice as much as they had spent on the Taft-Hartley bill. Reuther had obviously provoked them on the Communist Party issue, and they had reacted in excess to the demands of the stimulus. The ATL caucus spent more time defending Communists than Reuther did attacking them. That was a tactical blunder.

DIRTY TRICKS

Blackwood (1951) reports the following incident during an election at UAW Packard Local 190:

In the race for president the left wing had entered a man named Al Crebole against Pat Zombo. At an opportune moment Crebole had his name changed to Patsy Zombo. This particular maneuver was sanctioned by the local financial secretary, a left winger, who had the ballots printed. However, the International Executive Board refused to allow the change of name. Meanwhile, inasmuch as the chief left wing candidate was named John K. McDaniel, the right wing had persuaded a member named J. McDaniel to enter the race. In this strange contest Pat Zombo was elected. (p. 236)

Not all of the political campaigning used by the factions in the UAW were as outrageous and ludicrous as this. Some of it was mean spirited, libelous, and nasty. Some was borderline illegitimate from a trade union perspective; some were dilatory and disruptive. Reuther sneaked his "State of the Union" report past the censorship of George Addes. On July 1, 1947, Reuther wrote to Addes protesting that his statement explaining his position on the FE merger had been mailed to the membership by third-class mail, an unprecedented move. A year after his election in 1946, Reuther still could not get a master key to the UAW headquarters or get the UAW mailing list from the printer unless Addes gave his permission. The IEB Minutes of April 4–29, 1947, had twelve pages of discussion summary on Reuther's right to sign checks, which he clearly had. Granted.

The ATL caucus had two propaganda blockbusters, *FDR* and *The Bosses' Boy*, that were used extensively during the campaign. *FDR*, obviously playing on the initials of the revered President Roosevelt but said by some to mean "Fuck

Dirty Reuther," started out innocently enough as a tabloid concerned with union and political issues, much like the New York paper *PM*. It ran about eight pages and published irregularly, from two to four weeks apart, from June 1947 to October 1947.

The Bosses' Boy, however, was a one-shot, twenty-four-page pamphlet, signed by twenty-nine presidents of UAW local unions or large units within amalgamated locals. It was an earnest, well-written document, demonstrating considerable, if badly cited, research. Its most effective parts were quotes from the leading periodicals praising Reuther. The first page of the text "The Real Reuther" (*The Bosses' Boy*, 1947, p. 3) quoted Reuther from the *Ternstedt Flash* in 1937, condemning red-baiting, contrasting this statement with the present scene.

These reactionary forces red-bait our Union because they want once again to go back to the open-shop, because they seek to change our Union from a militant, fighting union— of, by, and for the workers—into a "Labor front" in the service of the employers. (p. 3)

Reuther was obviously the agent for this right-wing attempt to convert unions into a docile, Nazi-like "Labor front."

The pamphlet had favorable quotes for *Look* and The *Saturday Evening Post*, noting that the author of the latter article, Joseph W. Alsop, Jr., was from a wealthy Republican family from Connecticut. It also claimed that *Colliers, Time, Life, Fortune,* and the Chamber of Commerce had praised Reuther. Harold W. Story (Allis-Chalmers Company) was quoted as saying that there is "no question about the Americanism of Mr. Reuther" (p. 5). Reuther certainly received good press[3] as had R. J. Thomas at an earlier period, not to mention an avuncular Joseph Stalin peering from the magazine section of the *New York Times*, April 12, 1942 (Davies, 1942, p. 3).[4] But this was good, effective propaganda of a Populist variety.

The familiar "speedup" charges against Reuther were trotted out again, as well as Reuther's position to comply with the provisions of the T-H bill requiring non-Communist oaths from union officers. Reuther's "betrayal" of the AC Local 248 was introduced again, as was the support given Reuther by the conservative New York *Daily News*. But then *The Bosses' Boy* slipped into its demagogic best: "GM Loves Reuther!" (p. 9). Reuther "quietly" supported Kim Sigler, Republican candidate for governor (p. 10), it alleged. And "the anti-labor U.S. Chamber of Commerce look to Reuther to provide leadership in their campaign to destroy labor" (p. 10). It could, and did, get worse.

World politics raised its head in the internal union battle. In November 1945, Victor Reuther had written to UAW locals inviting them to attend a lecture by a "certain Paul Hagen," (as described by *The Bosses' Boy*). Victor Reuther identified Hagen as a "militant labor and political leader in pre-Hitler Germany and [who] is thoroughly familiar with the trade union situation today" (p. 14). Nearly two years later, the authors of *The Bosses' Boy* ominously asked, "Who is this Paul Hagen?" They, of course, had an answer.

Paul Hagen is, in the words of the Anti-Nazi Society for the Prevention of World War III [Who is this Anti-Nazi Society for the Prevention of World War III?], the "most dangerous protagonist of Pan-Germanism in the United States," an undercover agent for the forces who seek to rebuild Germany. Hagen is one of the leaders of the rebuild, re-arm Germany group. (p. 14)

Paul Hagen? A left-wing Socialist leader in the German Social Democratic Party who had spent time in Nazi concentration camps, as had his friend Kurt Schumacher, head of the Social Democratic Party. Schumacher was considered so dangerous by the State Department that he was refused a visa to enter the United States.

Here the looming international battle with the Soviet Union entered the UAW contest for president. It is hard to imagine what UAW workers thought of this allusion to German and international politics, assuming any UAW rank and filer read a twenty-four-page piece. But the authors understood that the role of Germany was central to the settlement of the peace in Europe. The Soviet Union wanted what was left of Germany's industry shipped to the East. The German Socialists, and others, did not want a Germany reduced to a state of helplessness, as it was after World War I, with all of its attendant consequences. (The Left was once again warning the faithful: "Comrades, we must confront this revanchist renegade.")

But it was not enough "that Reuther—who has apparently forgotten the concentration camps, the slaughter houses, and the cremation furnaces of the Nazis, has shown a soft spot in his heart for the Nazis but not for the victims of the Nazis" (p. 12); it was also necessary to prove the affiliation of Reuther and the indigenous American Fascists. They produced a photostatic copy of a purported confidential letter (*"Destroy this letter immediately upon reading its contents!"*) from Gerald L. K. Smith to his key supporters. It said, in part:

This is to warn all key workers in the Nationalist movement to avoid enthusiastic praise of Walter Reuther. He is doing such an excellent job from our point of view that any public statements complimentary to him . . . might limit sensational usefulness in curbing the leadership of such men as Thomas, Addes, Sugar and Hillman. (p. 13)

It ends: "Inside informers tell me that Mr. Reuther is thoroughly alert to the Jewish issue" (p. 13). That sentence must have amused Reuther's Jewish wife.

The Bosses' Boy then undertook to investigate Reuther's alleged racism, asserting that he had stuck "a knife in the back of Negro workers." Proof? The publication quoted Reuther's remarks before a Senate committee supporting a national Fair Employment Practices Committee: "The real discrimination, that which occurs at the point of hire, we cannot touch" (p. 16). And another Fascist plot had been detected and exposed. This attack fell on deaf ears. The *Michigan Chronicle*, a liberal Detroit African-American newspaper, wrote in September 27, 1947:

> While we do not believe that the top leaders of the so-called left wing of the UAW-CIO are Communists, we do believe that the right wing leadership as represented by Walter Reuther offers the soundest course in the long run for the best interests of the UAW and the Negro memberships.
>
> Despite the long tenure of the anti-Reuther leadership in the UAW, there are no Negroes at the policy making level in the organization and, with the possible exception of Walter Hardin, there never was.
>
> The so-called left wing seeks to develop its own brand of Negro leadership and in some respects, they have done a good job. These same leaders will confess privately, however, that their progress is carefully controlled and they are always expendable when the line shifts. ("UAW Factionalism," 1947, p. 6)

In addition, Phil Murray on September 18, 1947, gave Reuther the CIO Award for outstanding work on behalf of Fair Employment Practices. Eleanor Roosevelt, Walter White, A. Philip Randolph, and Lester Granger were quoted in support (Walter Reuther Collection, box 107; folder: Convention 1947, UA,WSU).

The pamphlet continued with more earthbound union matters—GM wages and working conditions, the weakness of the GM steward system, discrimination against women at GM. All of these alleged failures were laid at the door of Reuther because he was the GM department director. Corporate strength, the conservatism of GM management, and antiunion resistance and similar failures in other contracts were never mentioned as possible reasons for some of these purported weaknesses. But they were union arguments and legitimate ones to use in a campaign, accurate or not. World affairs are a proper platform for union debate and always had been in the UAW. It was the "King Charles's Head" syndrome of the ATL's concerns that was disconcerting and dishonest.

Again, the ATL caucus, undoubtedly influenced by the Communist Party, made an issue of Irving Richter, who was a UAW representative in the Washington, D.C., office. Richter had long been associated with the Communists. Reuther sought his dismissal on the grounds that he had supported the wartime May-Bailey Bill, which was a "work or fight" piece of legislation that proposed to draft strikers. Congressmen of both sides offered statements that Richter had supported or not supported the bill, with the pro-Richter advocates outnumbering the anti-Richter. The Communist Party had supported the bill, and the unions, naturally, opposed it. Reuther maintained that Phil Murray supported him in the decision to fire Richter. The issue had been confined to the IEB until *The Bosses' Boy* raised it again. Apparently seeking a reason for introducing the subject, the pamphlet resorted to a story in the *Wage Earner* that was over a year old. It was of no immediate public concern and put the ATL faction in the vulnerable

position of again defending a spurious issue involving the Communist Party
(Walter Reuther Collection, box 108; folder: Factional Statements on
Convention Issues, UA,WSU).

FDR started out innocuously enough with reports of Henry Wallace's
speeches and pro-Wallace articles. The first issue also had a headline on page
two, "Callahan Measure Hit by Reuther," and reported his blast at the proposed
legislation. The editors characterized the Callahan Bill as a bill "which pretends
to curb subversive activity in Michigan" ("Callahan Measure . . . ," 1947, p. 2).
It was actually a bill addressed to the activities of the Communist Party. Reuther,
ACTU, and other organizations of the Left-liberalism position opposed it.

The second issue was confined to union issues, all pro-ATL. There were
articles in favor of the merger proposal with the FE and a laudatory article on
Richard Leonard and the Ford pension plan, which was not actually agreed to
until 1949. On page four, there was a headline "Scholle Wins But Reuther Loses
as UAW Majority Goes to Fraser." Gus Scholle was the candidate supported by
Reuther, and Doug Fraser ran against him for president of the state CIO. A
majority of the UAW delegates, according to *FDR*'s count, had gone against
Reuther's endorsement and voted for Fraser. They concluded, "It was argued that
this was important as an omen for the UAW International Convention in
November" ("Scholle Wins . . . ," 1947, p. 4). Not much of an omen, since
Reuther faced no serious opposition at the convention. Obviously, the UAW del-
egates supported Fraser because he was a UAW member and very popular in
UAW circles.

Issues three, four, and five continued the pro-ATL positions, supported
Henry Wallace, took pro–civil rights stands, and were consistently anti-Reuther.
As the year wore on, *FDR* became increasingly pro–Communist Party, offering
a story on a Nat Ganley article in the *Michigan Herald* on "amending seniority
provisions so that an undue proportion of Negroes are not discarded in the next
round of lay-offs" ("Communists Offer . . . ," 1947, p. 7). Ganley was identified
as a "veteran Detroit Communist leader" (p. 7).

The last two issues, September 25, 1947, and October 9, 1947, just prior to
the November UAW convention, went all out.[5] The September issue reran the
Gerald L. K. Smith story about supporting Reuther from *The Bosses' Boy*. It also
covered some of the material on other right-wing alleged support for Reuther.
The center pages had a headline: "Reuther's Speedup Policy Stirs Revolt in
Ranks" (1947, p. 4). The NPA charges and the Studebaker local dispute became
central again. R. J. Thomas had a lengthy editorial responding to Reuther's
"State of the Union" report. In the same issue of the *Automobile Worker* that
Reuther's *State of the Union* report appeared, there was a boxed article entitled
"*FDR*." It said, in part:

FDR is not a UAW publication. Its editorial policies and treatment of the news for the
most part follow the Communist Party line. . . . The paper is actually published in the
interests of a factional clique in the UAW-CIO. The editor of the paper is one Roy

Lancaster, who for many years has associated with Communist groups. (*"FDR,"* Report to the Membership, 1947, p. 4)

This boxed statement was undoubtedly surreptitiously introduced in the same fashion that Reuther's report was printed. Thomas attacked Reuther's report and the boxed denunciation of *FDR* by saying that everyone "knows full well that both R. J. Thomas and his associates have no connection or sympathy with the Communist party or any of its affiliates or its program or methods. We are against them" ("Thomas Replies," 1947, p. 6).

Reuther responded to the Gerald L. K. Smith story by threatening to sue *FDR* for libel, but he was angry enough about the story to seek allies. In answer to an enquiry by Reuther, Oscar Cohen, executive director of the Jewish Community Council of Detroit, on October 15, 1947, replied by quoting an America First Party circular, a Smith group, hitting Reuther for "playing into the hands of those who are engineering the Red Revolution in the U.S.A." Cohen concluded by saying, "We here as well as the best fact finding people in the country with whom I have been in contact are convinced that the FDR letter is a fake" (Walter Reuther Collection, box 64; folder 3, UA,WSU).

L. M. Burkhead, national director, Friends of Democracy, telegraphed Reuther: "The Smith letter is obviously an awkward forgery. . . . I heard him myself denounce you as a 'Jewish stooge, a revolutionary left winger and an enemy of Christian Nationalism.' . . . We consider the attack in FDR Bulletin outrageous and tricky deceitful propaganda."

In the September 25, 1947, issue of *FDR*, another traditional enemy was attacked, the Association of Catholic Trade Unionists. Dan Tobin, Teamster president ("71 years a Catholic"), "roared" his opposition to ACTU, along with Albert Fitzgerald ("a practicing Catholic himself"). Tobin proclaimed, "It was the Catholic unions in Germany which split that mighty German workers' movement and made things easy for Hitler with the bosses' money in his jeans" ("Catholic Labor Leaders . . . ," 1947, p. 7). Fitzgerald, a leader of the UE-CIO, was quoted from a letter that he had written to a "high dignitary of the Catholic Church" about an unnamed priest whose activities left the "impression that unionists of the Roman Catholic faith cannot be assured of freedom from ecclesiastical interference and coercion" (p. 7). ACTU again had become an issue in the contest.

ACTU

The Protestant *Christian Century* found itself in sympathy with the position of some of Tobin's earlier charges against ACTU, adding that "it is not the business of the Church to attempt to control labor organizations." But they differed with Tobin when he had the effrontery to include Protestants, "particularly

Methodists," in his attack. The editors noted that "Tobin is really complaining about the activities of ACTU. . . . who *are* organized for the purpose of infiltrating into unions" ("Catholic Infiltration . . . ," 1945, p. 573). They were probably right: Tobin's target was undoubtedly ACTU, but in the interest of openhandedness, he felt compelled to include Protestants.

Paul Blanchard, stalwart Protestant observer of the Catholic church, was less critical of ACTU than might have been expected. He wrote in *American Freedom and Catholic Power* (1958) that ACTU was a "small and relatively unimportant organization that has never attained the menacing proportions of the dual Catholic organizations in Quebec" (p. 200). Blanchard's main concern was not with the influence of the Catholic church in unions but coincided with many American unionists' fear of dual unions. In Quebec and in Europe, there were often separate union movements, Socialist, Communist, and Catholic, representing their ideologies. Dual unionism had plagued the American unions for decades, but not on a religious basis. Attempts to organize outside of the existing unions made the charge of "dual unionism" almost as potent a political weapon as the charge of "communism" to a later generation of unionists.

In addition to the charges of Dan Tobin, ACTU was also attacked by other labor representatives of the Left, Right, and Center. Frank X. Martel, head of the Detroit AFL Central Labor body, charged in the early 1940s that the ACTU newspaper, then called the *Michigan Labor Leader*, "looks like a second edition of the *CIO News*." He contended that the paper "seems to be under the control of the CIO" (ACTU Collection, box 1; folder: Clippings, 1939–43, UA,WSU). The ACTU leadership in Detroit were very sensitive to charges of a pro-CIO bias, maintaining that they had a position of strict neutrality between the two federations.

The *Wage Earner*, as the Detroit ACTU weekly *Michigan Labor Leader* became known, in 1947 reported on Mike Quill's attack on ACTU and on the Catholic church's social policy. Quill, president of the Transportation Workers Union (CIO) and one of the leaders of the Communist Party–dominated faction in the CIO, was quoted as expressing

criticism of the labor policy of the Catholic Church in New York, where he is a member, and described the labor movement of the Church as a 'hindrance, a nuisance, and a strike breaking outfit' which he said could not get a dozen followers. ("Quill Assails . . . ," 1947, p. 3)

Bettan (1976) quotes Quill as using even stronger language, calling ACTU "a strike breaking agency," their newspaper was the "official organ of scabs," and "their cliques are shot through with stool pigeons" (p. 120).

Quill was under severe attack from the ACTU membership in his own union, predominantly Irish Catholic, for his pro–Communist Party positions, and as a colorful and polemical unionist, he had no compunction about attacking the Catholic church any more than he had in attacking the Communist Party a few months later. The *Wage Earner* did not comment on their own story of Quill's assault in either a news story or an editorial.

The *Wage Earner* was a conscientious, well-written, and -edited newspaper, but like all publications, it occasionally got trapped by its own cleverness. It ran a book review on October 10, 1947, on a book written by an anti-Communist on the Communists' union tactics. The reviewer described the CP's tactics at union meetings.

Another tactic is the "It is no accident" gag. This is used when somebody criticizes the action of the Commie leadership.

The Commies then say, "It is no Accident" that the attack comes just at the time when all labor is under attack, when reaction is in the saddle, when Taft-Hartley are on the loose, etc., etc. The inference [*sic*] is that critics of Communist leadership are part of a general conspiracy to wreck the union. ("It Is No Accident," 1947, p.3)

On the same page, The *Wage Earner* had an editorial stating, "The revival of the Comintern should occasion no surprise among those who understand the Communist mentality." The headline over the editorial: "It is no Accident."

Daniel Bell, then the *Fortune* writer on labor news, amplified on Kermit Eby's position in his notes on the articles that were not published. Bell wrote: "Eby thinks Jesuits do not like ACTU because of direct interference of ACTU as an organized group and thus they became targets. Jesuits want to train individuals. National Catholic Welfare Conference [Fr. Higgins] does not like ACTU" (Bell Collection, box 4; Wagner Library, NYU). Eby was correct that some Jesuits preferred to train individual unionists in their labor schools. It is doubtful, however, that there was a Jesuit position on ACTU. Paul Weber, head of Detroit ACTU during the late 1930s and the turbulent 1940s, said in an interview that ACTU had good relationships with some Jesuits and bad relationships with others, just as they did with other orders.

The Catholic press itself, divided by ideological positions, was not uniformly favorable to ACTU. The more liberal magazines such as *Commonweal* printed stories about and by ACTU members, particularly John C. Cort, cofounder of the New York chapter. The *Guildsman*, a Catholic publication, was anti-ACTU and wrote against all sit-downs and accused all unions of creating class conflict and being opposed to what the editor, Edward Koch, considered to be repeated papal injunctions to eliminate class conflict.

ACTU was separated from liberal and radical thought by its position on various issues, for example, released time for religious observance in the public schools. While it cautioned against raising the matter as inappropriate and "not in the field of competence" of unions, it did advise members to be prepared for such debate if it were raised by the "enemies of Catholicism" (ACTU Collection, box 2; folder: ACTU Convention, 1947, UA,WSU).

The traditional conservative Catholic position on women and the family also separated Catholics from liberal thought. In a patronizing editorial, "A Fair

Policy on Women in Industry" (1947, p. 4). The *Wage Earner* faced this problem that became more intense as the war drew to a close and the veterans returned to their jobs. ACTU was cautious about proposals for nursery schools for women who stayed in industry. On the UAW's role toward working women, the ACTU paper said, "It [UAW] has no energy which can safely be wasted on projects designed to make it possible to earn a new fur coat while the city takes care of your kids" (p. 4). Conceding that many women are economically forced to work, ACTU was opposed to a policy of encouraging women to enter industry in preference to clerical and sales "for which they are biologically and spiritually better fitted" (p. 4). It did not desert its basic union position of equal pay for equal work but mentioned that "it must be recognized that there are biological and mental differences between men and women. . . . Nature designed man to earn a living for the family, and women to keep the home" (p. 4). In a denouement, it raised an issue that had plagued the women's movement for years. It said that it was more important that African-American men get a decent job than providing jobs for women. In an insufferable flourish, it concluded: "This may be denounced . . . as 'Women's-place-is-in-the-homeism,' a horrible variety of fascism. But no amount of denouncing will alter the facts of nature. One look at the attractive Miss Hawes [a pro–Communist Party UAW staffer] demolishes many of her arguments that there is no distinction between the sexes" (p. 4).

Central to its political ends was the corporatist concept of the organization of industry. This, more than any other Catholic position, was the basis for repeated leftist charges against the Church of Fascist leanings. Paul Weber, editor of ACTU's paper, The *Wage Earner*, was compelled to answer these accusations as the battle with the Communist Party heated up after World War II. In 1940, Philip Murray, president of the CIO, advanced his Industrial Council Plan, which had a strong resemblance to the papal corporatist position. It did not create much of a stir at the time. Earl Browder almost perfunctorily endorsed it, as did many UAW Communist Party–dominated locals (UAW Convention Proceedings, 1941, p. 552; UAW Local 51 Collection, box 14; folder 12, UA,WSU).

As the conflict grew in the CIO, the charges of Fascist doctrine reemerged. Weber, in a May 1946 editorial, pointed out that the similarities between Mussolini's "Corporate State" and the papal "Corporatism" are the same superficial similarities that exist between the American Congress and the Supreme Soviet: They both take votes, and both are allegedly representative bodies. "There the resemblance ceases." The distinction between the Fascist and papal approaches is marked by the fact that Mussolini ("a screwball radical") "took away the freedom of both owners and workers. . . . Strikes were forbidden and industry and all labor became subject to Mussolini's fiat." Weber maintained that the corporatist position and the Industry Councils "are democracy in economics," based on voluntary cooperation, with no dominant factor, either capital, labor, or government ("The Corporate State," 1946, p. 6).

Whatever the political or intellectual failings of the corporatist concept, it is politically indecent to call ACTU a Fascist organization. One author, highly critical of ACTU, gave a list of the strike activities of the New York chapter and it was a very impressive list. It fought against Mayor Frank Hague of Jersey City, New Jersey, and was in numerous battles all over the United States in the name of trade unionism (Seaton, 1981, p. 149).

By 1946, Detroit ACTU had created a Basic Training Course for its members that refined its ideology. One section dealt with the "Errors of Individualism." The lecture notes pointed out that individualism was "a revolt against authority and external restraints. Makes 'self' the center of one's life and the final judge of right and wrong" (ACTU Collection, box 1; folder: ACTU Basic Training Course, 1946, UA,WSU). Capitalism ("the economic expression of the individualistic philosophy") leads to monopoly, war, revolution, and dictatorship because "economically, it is a bad system. . . . Its lack of social or democratic planning ignores the complexity of economic life and allows the evils to go unchecked," and "morally, it is un-Christian" (Lecture III, p. 2).

That collectivism also had its errors and was inadmissible as a guide for Catholics stated a moral position, but it did not constitute a policy of action toward these groups. It was necessary to have a section in the lectures on "What to do about Communism" to make it clear that collaboration was impossible. "We can work with socialists, Mohammedans [*sic*], Presbyterians and others with whom we do not agree: but Communism, because of the essential dishonesty of its tactics and the essential evil of its ends, cannot be so treated" (Lecture IV, p. 2). Nonetheless, Christian charity asserts itself on the individual level: "DISTINCTIONS: Communists are people, and we must often work beside and with them. We must never hate them or treat them uncharitably. But the Papal warning bars any united front, alliance, or joint effort on a program of common objectives" (p. 2).

Financially, the influence of the Church was also felt. The chancery gave Detroit ACTU $4,000 out of total receipts of $4,850, which made up a large portion of The *Wage Earner*'s budget from June 1948 to September 1949 (ACTU Collection, box 2; folder: ACTU Convention, 1947, UA,WSU). John C. Cort also reported on Cardinal Francis J. Spellman's contribution to ACTU. In 1949, the cardinal's support for New York ACTU amounted to $3,000, which paid for Cort's salary with about $1,000 left over. Hardly a princely salary (Cort, n.d.).

The real test is when the lay membership confronts the hierarchy. In 1949, the cemetery workers went on strike against the Calvary Cemetery in Queens, New York, run by St. Patrick's Cathedral.[6] Cardinal Francis J. Spellman, never one to mince words, denounced the strike, according to Cort, as "an anti-American, anti-Christian evil and a strike against the Church" (p. 246). Among the demands of the union was a forty-hour week with no reduction in take-home pay. The trustees of the cemetery refused to bargain with the union initially, possibly because it was a local of the Communist–dominated Food, Tobacco,

Agricultural and Allied Workers (CIO). ACTU immediately supported the strikers, and just as promptly, Cardinal Spellman suspended the $3,000 a year subsidy to ACTU. This behavior is not the performance to be expected of a clerically dominated religious organization, particularly when it was taken against one of the most powerful prelates in the country (p. 25).

There is an unpleasant myth about Catholicism that is completely unrelated to the legitimate criticism of the conservative, sometimes wretchedly reactionary, role that the Catholic church has played in political life. One element of this mythomania is that the secret councils of the Vatican reach into the life of every Catholic and dictate the minutiae of his or her existence. This belief is harbored in many minds despite the manifest diversity of Catholic life. As one of the many social action groups within the Church, ACTU was not a creation of the hierarchy. It was created to meet a need conceived of by active Catholic unionists for a Catholic voice in the unions.

The finances and the number of members of the branches are difficult to determine. Certain vital facts are available that it might have been more circumspect to conceal (chancery subsidy), making it likely that the paucity of information is the result of bad record keeping rather than a conscious effort to hide data. Membership is difficult to ascertain. Probably no one knows what the numbers were. The best estimates are that ACTU had 1,000 members nationally in 1940, 250 of which were in Detroit, and about 2,000 nationally in 1947. Most writers frankly admit that their figures are estimates or guesswork.

In all of the tedium of organizational life, perhaps nothing is as debilitating as the constant internal fighting. As a new social action group within the Church, ACTU was continually being attacked from within the Church and in ACTU itself. Catholic workers, even ACTU members, complained to their priest or the bishop that the organization was Communist or Socialist or that Richard L-G Deverall, executive secretary of ACTU, was a Communist (ACTU Collection, box 3; folder: ACTU Executive Board Minutes, 1939–1940, UA,WSU). Usually these complaints were filed and ignored. Some Catholic members of the UAW, caught in heated political battles, were occasionally bitter in their denunciation of ACTU. Those with a long-term affiliation with the leadership in a local, with or without Communist influence, had a difficult time when ACTU took a position that jeopardized their political alliances in the local. This often happened in locals with strong Communist Party leadership. More than 1,500 Catholic members of Local 51, according to the local's newspaper, where the Communist Party was well entrenched, signed a petition in 1941 protesting ACTU's action supporting a list of candidates in the local's election. A letter in the newspaper further complained of its action, saying that "it was a written rule that no slates be permitted" (a strange rule, indeed).[7] The 1,500 petitioners blasted ACTU as a dual union, compared it with Homer Martin's tactic of red-baiting, and asserted that the *Michigan Labor Leader* "works to create dissention [*sic*]" (Brown Collection, box 1; folder: Association of Catholic Trade Unions, UA,WSU).

Catholic workers in Local 600, representing the huge Ford Rouge plant, reacted the same way at the 1941 convention of the UAW. They sent a telegram to Buffalo, asserting, like the Declaration of Independence, "We the honest Catholic industrial unionists of Ford Local 600 . . . resent the intrusion of the ACTU paper in its unfair and unprincipled attack upon the leaders of our union" (UAW Convention Proceedings, p. 270). They said that it was reminiscent of Gerald L. K. Smith, Henry Ford, chamber of commerce, and other reactionaries. Not content with assaulting ACTU, they turned to the Church: "The Catholic Church and its papers have no more right in trying to control the policy program of our organization than have the Ku Klux Klan Black Legion . . . Manufacturers Association Socialist Communist Party Opposition Trotskyites New American Communists Republican or Democrats" (p. 270). There was one signature on the telegram. The punctuation is the responsibility of the Western Union.

The differences within the ACTU chapters were great. Those started by the priests (Maryland and Pittsburgh) tended to diminish the role of the workers in favor of the clergy. The chapters that were started by the lay members (New York, Detroit, and Chicago) tended to be more radical and had an orientation against collaboration with companies and less disposed to want government agencies like the House Un-American Activities Committee to interfere in their battles. It is no secret that Fr. Charles Owen Rice of the Pittsburgh ACTU worked with HUAC and the FBI. Fr. John F. Cronin, unlike Fr. Rice, was less interventionist and more given to questionnaires and censuses of parish members and their willingness to fight Communists.

The endeavors of Fr. Charles Owen Rice in Pittsburgh and Fr. John F. Cronin in Maryland were broader and had an almost sinister quality. Broader because a clerically dominated apparatus, with the rank and file as their hand-maidens, essayed the organization of anti-Communist groups where unionism became secondary to anticommunism; sinister because there was a definite attempt to involve employers in the fray and to utilize HUAC as an ally.

Always a believer in the up-to-date census and a well-formed questionnaire, Fr. Cronin, early in 1945, sent out a Confidential Questionnaire on Communism from the National Welfare Conference to ACTU chapters (ACTU Collection, box 29; folder: National Catholic Welfare Conference, 1945, UA,WSU). It asked five general questions on public attitudes such as the "current state of public opinion in regard to communism, . . . fear of communism as a factor in the labor movement," and other national and international political aspects that might involve the Communists. In assessing Communist strength, the respondents were asked to identify those individuals they had named as "A. *Communist,* . . . B. *Communist Sympathizers or Fellow Traveler,* . . . C. *Communist-minded Opportunist,* . . . and D. *Communist Tool or Dupe*" (p. 1). Apparently on a descending scale. An explanatory definition of each classification was provided for the uninitiated. Information also requested was the estimated number of Communist Party members and sympathizers in the receiver's area. "If possible, also list origin, racial or cultural background of the communist-minded persons. If any are apostate Catholics, please note the fact" (p. 2). While national origin might be a legitimate matter of concern, if the validity of such a poll is accepted, and—while religion was not requested except for backslid Catholics—it is notable how often the Jewish Communists were so identified. Respondents were also asked to provide information on "communist activity among Negro groups," foreign born, unions, and government and to ascertain whether the American Youth for Democracy (a Communist Party front group) was active in the area. Detroit ACTU replied, point by point, with a sophisticated analysis of the local situation, providing a list of Communist activities in the unions that was accurate and discerning.

If Fr. Cronin was the archetypal bureaucrat, Fr. Rice was the charismatic leader. He started the Pittsburgh ACTU; he *was* the Pittsburgh ACTU. Fr. Rice's involvement in actual labor disputes was greater than that of Fr. Cronin. Rice first started, with four other priests, the Catholic Radical Alliance and in 1938 launched the Pittsburgh ACTU. No bureaucrat he, Fr. Rice catapulted himself onto the labor scene. In the postwar years, his main activity was to fight the Communists in the UE-CIO. The intervention of the Pittsburgh ACTU into the politics of the UE was direct and involved the apparatus of the parish priests. Harrington (1960) reports that in Local 601 a Communist sympathizer was laid off or fired, and the Communist Party wanted him back. When it was taken to the local's meeting, Rice got the parish priests to have their parishioners attend the meeting and defeat the move (p. 17). The FBI files[8] on Pittsburgh ACTU indicate that, probably borrowing from Fr. Cronin, they, too, were going to employ a union census in each of their parishes. The questionnaires asked for the usual demographic data; then the questioner was asked to check such questions as "Willing to fight Communism?" and "seems to be pro-Communist." An affirmative answer to the last question would be marked if the respondent said, "What's wrong with the Communists?" or "to me it's nothing more than red-baiting" (Goode Collection, FBI, ACTU file, pp. 2, 3, and 5, UA,WSU).

Fr. Cronin's crusade had a strong pro–business group bias and a disposition to have the network dominated by priests. Cronin, several years later, had made a contact with some GM officials and wanted to approach Walter Reuther with his information. This was part of the strategy used by Cronin: Approach businessmen and even speak to the Baltimore Association of Commerce about Communists in the union movement. This was probably the most selfdefeating ploy imaginable. It would have been a field day for the Communist Party to have a record of an ACTU-associated priest speaking to a business group on the danger of communism in unions. Ten priests were indicated by name as having a part-time involvement in his project, and the information gathered was to be coordinated by priests.

ACTU itself was ambivalent about HUAC. The *Labor Leader* on March 31, 1946, noted, "While we can by no means endorse all the activities of the

Committee in the past, particularly when such activities have been stupid and inept, nevertheless, there is little doubt the Committee has served a useful pur-pose—at times in spite of itself" (ACTU Collection, box 16; folder: Fr. John F. Cronin, 1943–46, UA,WSU). As ambiguous as this statement is, it is still a long way from actively soliciting cooperation.

These differences in approach by the clergy and the laity did not preclude cooperation and friendship; John C. Cort was obviously very fond of Fr. Rice. But there were certainly tensions between the New York and Detroit chapters, initiated by the laity, and Pittsburgh and Maryland, the clerically run chapters. In 1947, Fr. Cronin asked Paul Weber to review a directive that he had written to guide anti-Communist workers. Weber had several criticisms, one of the sharpest of which was, "The advice to consult the so-called Dies Committee records for material on Communists or pro-Communists in the labor movement is very dan-gerous, and in my opinion would lead anyone who follows it to make grave errors in identifying Commies" (ACTU Collection, box 14, folder: Communism in Labor Movement—1947, UA,WSU). The evidence suggests that where ACTU was started by lay unionists, the chapters tended to be more liberal and were more prounion and anticompany. Where the clergy originated the chapters, the contrary was true: Communism became almost the sole enemy, and there was a tendency to cooperate with government and business groups. Fr. Cronin's approach, using a cadre of priests to conduct a search for Catholic allies using the parish census, was the grandiose creation of a bureaucrat and probably ineffec-tive. Harrington (1960) notes that ACTU's "tactics were often contradictory and their cohesion was almost non-existent. In almost every case, one is struck by disorganization and lack of liaison, but not by the activity of a monolithic force" (p. 233). Rather than a rightist Catholic plot, the Detroit ACTU was quite inde-pendent of the rest of ACTU and easily adapted "itself to the social democratic ambience" of Detroit and the UAW (Cochran, 1977, p. 287).

RED-BAITING AND CIVIL LIBERTIES

The UAW has a well-deserved reputation of being a highly political union with considerable membership involvement. But that does not mean that all political battles in the UAW were fought on principled, well-defined programs. Most locals confined their caucus activity to local issues. This was reflected in the names of their slates. In Briggs Local 742, Detroit, a dozen different slates were offered at some point. Their names generally were innocuous: Progressive, Independent Progressive, Four Freedoms, Progressive Unity, CIO Policy Slate, Liberty, All American, Clean Sweep Slate, Blue, Rank and File (Sam Sweet Collection, box 5; folder 19, UA,WSU).

While Local 742 showed a greater level of caucus activity than other locals, it was still true that loyalties on the shop floor were formed by networks of friendship, favors, and patronage with little concern for earthshaking issues. The intrusion of sophisticated (left-wing or right-wing) exchanges was mostly associated with real issues, for example, the Lovestone-Martin relationship and the Communists' support of piecework during World War II. If it was proper to assail Homer Martin for his alliance with Jay Lovestone, then it was equally just to criticize the ATL group and the Communist Party for their positions.

The Homer Martin split in the UAW highlighted a problem that runs throughout the early history of the union—the question of red-baiting. After the actual split, Martin's AFL version of the *United Automobile Worker* had a front-page head "Reds Rule Dual Union." The "dual union," of course, was the UAW-CIO. On page three, in a boxed one-quarter-page statement, was a story headlined "Red Chieftains Who Plotted to Seize Your Union, UAWA." The story listed the names of well-known, avowed CPers, Israel Amter, and so on, and also provided the real names of some who were only known by their party names, for example, "Fred Brown (correct name Alpi)" (Sugar Collection, box 1; folder 24, UA,WSU). Only ex-members of the Communist Party could have known the real and the party names of those persons listed in the story. It would be easy to dismiss this as a mildly amusing story of the minute, exotic Left in the United States. However, it raises a critical problem: Was it red-baiting when these two minority parties hurled charges against each other? They identified their opposite number by name and political affiliation, charged a plot on the other's part, and generally behaved like old-time reactionaries.

It is easy to recognize red-baiting when Mayor Richard Reading of Detroit ran for reelection in 1939 with a handbill emblazoned "Vote American—Defeat Communism—Defeat the CIO." Or when Michigan Congressman Claire Hoffman said of the 1937 Chrysler strike, "This is nothing but a Communist plot to Sovietize Detroit" (UAW Local 51 Collection, box 8; folder 8, UA,WSU). Clergymen inevitably had to join the chorus. Fr. Coughlin warned that "communism is sweeping the automobile industry and threatening to challenge all America" (*The Searchlight,* 1986, p. 1). Protestant observers, not to be outdone, in the person of Rev. Paul Coleman, a Flint, Michigan, minister, said of the sit-down strike, "This strike is a part of a carefully laid program, originating in Moscow to Communize America" (p. 1).

The "Original Pioneer" slate in Local 212 asked in one piece of literature, "Isn't it true that" so-and-so supported the Communist Nat Ganley for such and such a position? "Isn't it true that" these four local members "voted for and actively supported the same ticket that was supported by Fred Williams and John Anderson, the Communist Party wheel-horses in the UAW-CIO?" There was no discussion of issues, just name-calling. Labeling is one form of political definition, but it is the lowest form (John Croft Collection, box 1; folder 15, UA,WSU).

This is old-fashioned nativism, associating communism with the union movement, no discussion of issues, a simple appeal to the worst prejudices of

Americans. Some of the company statements were rhapsodic. After the recognition election at Ford's was won by the UAW, one Ford attorney said:

As a result, the Ford Motor Co. must now deal with a Communist-influenced-and-led organization whose first objective is to raise additional millions with which to finance its drive to control all American industry, and whose ultimate objective is, through strikes and general turmoil, to produce that public confusion and bewilderment which is essential to Communist seizure of governmental power in the United States.[9] ("Statement from Ford . . . ," 1941, p. 3)

During the Flint sit-downs in 1936, one newspaper explained that "Lewis and Martin were dupes of the Communists and were being used by them to spread Communist influence in the United States" (Fine, 1969, p. 113).

These company accusations are arrant nonsense. The Communists did not dominate the UAW; they were, in fact, a very small but important element in the formation of the UAW. But, putting aside the reactionary claims of management, the role of the Communist Party bedeviled the UAW for years, particularly after the faction fighting began in earnest during World War II.

Criticism of the Communist Party has caused some bizarre reactions, particularly in radical circles. While most of the critics felt no compunction about their vociferous views, some of the critics, mainly ex-party members, have steadfastly refused to publicly condemn the activities of their erstwhile comrades. The denunciations of their more acquisitive peers who had left the party and shown themselves overly pliant regarding the truth caused many to abjure any commentary. Apostasy was vilified by most radical groups, very often in the grossest terms. One non-Communist, radical leader is alleged to have informed his following: "Comrades, the class struggle continues despite this renegade relaxing his bowels across the pages of history." Even some of Reuther's old Socialist comrades were critical of his public discussion of communism. They felt that, given the use by conservatives, all disapproval of the party's activities should be confined to internal discussion within the UAW.

Was Reuther justified in making the Communist Party part of his target during the campaign? Or was this action merely seeking a target of opportunity, vulnerable to the conservativism of American political life? The Communist Party was certainly central to the operation of the ATL caucus. The Communists were the ideological mentors of the group. While they held no commanding office in the UAW, they did supply the tactics, strategy, and much of the writing for the ATL position. Just as Lovestone provided political skills for Homer Martin and ACTU did the same for locals in the East, the Communist Party gave counsel to ATL. This is one of the functions that small ideological groups provide for larger, more naive organizations.

The Communists had a history in the UAW, as did Reuther and the other leading political figures. To refer to that history is perfectly legitimate. When John Anderson claimed that Reuther had been in his house, met with

Communists, and helped formulate policy with them, he was within his rights. When Reuther reviewed the Communist Party's positions in the UAW, he, too, was within recognized political boundaries.

Major political decisions were to face the union within several years: the 1948 presidential election, the Marshall Plan, and positions on Europe and the Soviet Union. The UAW had taken foreign and domestic policy positions in the past and certainly could be expected to in the future. The Communist Party was never a threat to the security of the United States, but a significant section of the American labor movement dominated by the Communist Party did represent a threat. Despite the nonsense spoken and written about communism, there was a legitimate basis for criticism.

The Communist Party wanted to subsume all criticism of it as red-baiting. In this way, all critics of the Communist Party were joined with the reactionaries, the "know-nothing" elements in American society.[10] The *Daily Worker*, in a particularly defensive mood, had this description of red baiting:

A good example of what red-baiting means is the case of Richard T. Frankensteen, vice president of the UAW, who announced that he will not run for reelection because he is considering some "lucrative offers" from many sources. . . . Social Democrat Reuther may seek to utilize his desertion to scatter progressives at the Convention. (Morris, 1946, p. 9)

Len DeCaux (1970) takes the argument another step: "Jew-baiting, Negro-baiting, the baiting of any scapegoat group, were always blood-brothers (and bloody brothers) to red baiting. Hitler's anticommunism and his anti-Semitism were one in style and purpose" (pp. 352–353). Thus, according to DeCaux, anti-Semitism, Negro-baiting, and scapegoating are "always" linked to criticism of the Communist Party. DeCaux takes notice of the liberal argument that calling a person a Communist if he is one is not red-baiting, but he dismisses it because of the particular vulnerability of the Communists in the United States, unlike their situation in European politics. But this is a flawed argument; neither gender, race, religion, age, nor political vulnerability can legitimately exempt any individual or political movement from democratic scrutiny and judgment.

To extend DeCaux's argument, if labeling a person by his or her political affiliation, however accurately, may subject that person to unwarranted harshness, what do we make of R. J. Thomas's response to a *Detroit Free Press* reporter's question about whether he would accept Communist support? " 'I would even accept support from a Reuther style Socialist,' he said laughing" (O'Shea, 1946, p. 1). Walter Reuther and David Dubinsky, President of the International Ladies Garment Workers Union, were always referred to by the *Daily Worker* as "socialist" or "social democrat": "Walter Reuther came into the UAW from the Socialist Party ranks and brought with him that organization's unprincipledness and opportunism" ("Reuther-Dubinsky Intrigue . . . ," 1946, p. 2). Brendan Sexton, president of the critical Local 50 in the 1946 UAW convention, was labeled "Socialist Branden [*sic*] Sexton" (1946, p. 2).

The *Worker* not only labeled the Trotskyists at every opportunity; it also saved some of its most furious fulminations for them. Just in case political analysis was inadequate for its reading public, the writers for the *Worker* used such descriptive gems as "fifth column," "enemies of the people" and "tools of the most reactionary and darkest forces" (Howard, 1941, p. 5). The main "enemies of the people" were Reuther, the "Norman Thomas socialists" (or the social democrats), the Trotskyists, and ACTU, with the Coughlinites sometimes attributed, without evidence, to ACTU, with the America Firsters thrown into the pot on occasion. The net effect of this lumping of the opposition was that the Communist Party publications were totally unreliable on these issues. On the lineup on such questions as the no-strike pledge during the war and the composition of Reuther's support in 1946 and 1947, they were simply wrong.

It was even worse when in their desire to identify their enemies, they mislabeled them. In one issue, the *Worker* said that "the debate for the Reuther forces was led off by Trotskyite Ben Garrison" ("Murray UAW Talk . . . ," 1946, p. 2). Trotskyists and other knowledgeable political persons in Detroit never knew Garrison as a member of any of the political sects, let alone the Trotskyists. If it is true that he was a member, he was certainly one of the most undisciplined adherents to the movement because as the Trotskyist sects were supporting Reuther, he nominated R. J. Thomas at the 1946 UAW convention (UAW Convention Proceedings, 1946, p. 213). Paul Silver and Emil Mazey were also erroneously tagged as Trotskyists ("Murray UAW Talk . . . ," 1946, p. 2).

Delegates to the 1946 convention also hit heavily at Brendan Sexton. A Communist Party partisan from Local 600 attacked him in his speech from the floor:

I understand—I don't know whether it is true or not, but I have heard that the present President [Sexton] . . . saw to it a motion was carried at a packed meeting turning that treasury over to him unaccountable, to spend as he sees fit, supposedly to find more work for the Willow Run workers. I think it is a sin and shame, and it is a blot on the record of the UAW, when one individual can have anywhere between fifty and one hundred thousand dollars in order to spend as he sees fit unaccountable. (UAW Convention Proceedings, 1946, p. 195)

Sexton finally got the floor on a point of personal privilege, since he had been attacked, pointing out that no such motion had been adopted, and the only place the money had been spent was on the Frankensteen race for mayor, the Ford Windsor strike, and the General Motors strike. Sexton had voluntarily removed himself from the payroll five months prior to the convention because of the diminishing treasury. He did not sustain any serious political misfortune, except for having to hear his character maligned in a vicious manner (p. 197).

The myopia evidenced by the Communist Party on the political divisions in the union on any specific issue was so inaccurate as to appear deliberate—all of its opponents had to be collectively guilty of every crime. In 1943, when John L.

Lewis was threatening a strike in the coalfields, Earl Browder, in a speech in St. Louis, Missouri, attacked Lewis for the threatened strike and then associated Lewis with Reuther, maintaining that "this banner of Lewis has been taken up by Walter Reuther in an open revolt against the chief leaders of the Union" (Browder, 1943, p. 19). Browder added such elegant epithets that observers had come to expect of the Communists: "treason," "betrayal," "unprincipled demagogy," and "lying." Reuther had waffled on the no-strike pledge, responding to pressure from his own caucus. He recognized that some of the strikes were eminently justified by the intransigence of employers and had not become the enforcer of the pledge as had the Communist Party. One labor leader long known for his cooperation with the Communists, Joe Curran, wrote on the no-strike pledge in his column in *The Pilot*, the NMU paper, headlined by "Pass the Word—Keep'em Sailing," "The Reuthers, Trotskyites, ACTUers are also bent on destroying the war effort" (Curran, 1943, p. 5). It is not true that ACTU opposed the no-strike pledge. In their Policy Convention in 1944, they passed a resolution "that all ACTU members and conferences be urged to continue their support of labor's no-strike pledge as a general rule of conduct during time of war" (ACTU Collection, box 2; folder: ACTU Convention, 1944, UA,WSU). Even Nat Ganley had praised Paul Weber, ACTU leader, saying, "Rising above power politics the ACTU leader, Paul Weber (Newspaper Guild) fought against the revocation of our no strike pledge" (ACTU Collection, box 24; folder: Local 155, UA,WSU).

For the Communist Party, there were no civil liberties as a separate issue apart from its own well-being. Since it was usually the target of the government's inquisitorial activities, it felt it was only necessary to defend itself, not some abstract notion that had universal application. Less than two months after Germany invaded the Soviet Union, the U.S. government indicted nine members of the Trotskyist Socialist Workers Party under the provisions of the Smith Act, the same act that subsequently was used against the Communist Party. The Communist Party attacked the Smith Act as a "sedition" law but at the same time, regarding its use against the nine Trotskyists, said, "The American people . . . can find no objection to the destruction of the fifth column in this country. On the contrary, they must insist on it" (Howard, 1941, p. 5). The rights of unions against government interference were asserted "WHILE AT THE SAME TIME GIVING NO SUPPORT TO THE TROTSKYITE FIFTH COLUMNISTS" (emphasis in original) (p. 5). In effect, according to the Communists, it was proper for the government to persecute the SWP, but it must make it clear "that it is fighting the Trotskyists not as a workers' revolutionary organization, but because it is a fascist fifth column masquerading falsely as a worker's organization" (p. 5).

This failure to take a decent position toward the civil liberties of the SWP led many people mistakenly to ignore the plight of the Communist Party when it was attacked by the same undemocratic law. In a like manner, the *Daily Worker* chortled "UAW Local Upholds Ban on Trotskyite Rag" when Local 735 of the UAW banned the *Militant* "from the union hall, picket lines and the strike kitchen" (1941, p. 5). Local 51, a Communist Party stronghold, showed a similar lack of sensitivity to minority political rights in its position on slates of candidates in its local. "Pop" Edelen, president of the local, appeared before the International Executive Board in 1941 and explained that Local 51 was opposed to the creation of slates and forbade the passing out of such "propaganda" at the plant. It was not made clear what the rights of an opposition group were or how they were to form or make their positions known (UAW IEB Minutes, July 14, 1941).

Probably the worst reporting during this period was the *Daily Worker*'s assessment of the composition of the Reuther caucus. In the month prior to the April 1946 convention, *Worker* readers were assailed with such stories as this: "Meanwhile, all the shady elements in the UAW are concentrating behind Reuther's candidacy. The Trotskyites are tooting their horns for him. So are Norman Thomas' Socialists and the Association of Catholic Trade Unionists, whose Detroit organization is filled with Coughlinites" ("The Auto Union Convention," 1946, p. 3). And: "Reuther in this period is maintaining a coy silence as to 'whether he will run' while the cabal of Socialists, Trotskyites, ACTUers and Lewisites are out beating the bushes" (Allan, 1946, p. 5). The role of ACTU as Reuther supporters had become part of the mythology about the 1946 UAW convention, when, in fact, it did not support him.

ACTU was of several minds on civil liberties. It urged all unions to write provisions in their constitutions barring all CPers or fellow travelers from office. While the intention was not to bar Communists from membership, only from union office, John C. Cort, on later reflection, said:

I find it difficult to deny the reasoning that such bars are a form of coercion in a matter of belief that should have no place in a semi-public organization like a union which ought to be open to any law abiding person, and that therefore anyone who qualifies for membership should be free to run for office or be appointed to an office. Exclusion from office should be the result of full discussion and free election, not a trial procedure. (Cort, n.d., p. 25)

From a civil libertarian point of view, ACTU would have been seen in a better light if it had held Cort's position from the outset. The Pittsburgh ACTU, started by Fr. Rice, had a more "expedient" point of view. The chapter had disbanded during the war, and at its reorganization meeting in 1947, it resolved that "this body call for the exposure of Communists and Communist fronts by democratic measures and . . . that though we recognize the right of Congress to suppress the Communist Party or any other subversive group, we deem it expedient at this time to use other means such as education and counter organization" (ACTU Collection, box 2; folder: ACTU, Pittsburgh, 1947–1950, UA,WSU).

Several incidents involving civil liberties came up in 1947, one involving a Catholic group. Max H. Sorenson, national commander of the Catholic War Veterans, had advocated that all Communists, citizens or not, be deported (it was not clear where those having citizenship were going to be sent) and that the Communist Party be outlawed. The *Wage Earner* greeted this as a "horrendous" proposal and offered a two-point program to combat communism, exposure and "basic correction of the evils of monopoly capitalism, and extension of our democracy to all areas of life" ("Curbing Commies," 1947, p. 6). The repressive Callahan Bill in Michigan was dismissed as "union wrecking" by ACTU. The newly chartered Utility Workers Union (CIO) started out barring Communists from membership in the union. This was as far as any union had gone in antide-mocratic procedures. In fact, there is not much left to do after that. The *Wage Earner* countered with a story in opposition to this action, headed: "Barring CPs from Union Draws Catholic Criticism" (1946, p. 9). They also protested when the dissident Bridgeport local of the UE, in 1947, expelled twenty-seven members for "communism." The national ACTU paper, *The Labor Leader*, wrote in the February 28, 1947, issue:

It was not only a clear violation of the UE constitution, but it was, we believe, wrong in itself. Under the maintenance of membership contract these workers had to be discharged from their jobs. Even if they were all Communists, we still believe that no union should take the terrible responsibility of throwing men out of work. (Cort, 1947, p. 5)

Contrast this with the Communist Party leadership in the UE toward some wild-catters in one of their locals who were expelled from the union and then the local insisted that the company fire them (Preis, 1964, p. 137).

Several of ACTU's defenses of civil liberties came about as the result of ini-tiatives by government figures. Secretary of Labor Lewis B. Schwellenbach, in 1947, publicly advocated barring the Communist Party from the ballot. The *Wage Earner* pointed out that "barring communists from the ballot could easily lead to barring most, or all other minority parties too—a situation which would give the two major parties . . . a political monopoly" ("Keep Them Out in the Open," 1947, p. 9). To bar the Communists, it continued, would mean legislation and then interminable court battles, a procedure of "dubious value." The *Daily Worker* noted that Local 174, "home local of President Walter Reuther" also voted against this proposal ("Big Auto Local Opposes . . . ," 1947, p. 4).).

Michigan's governor, Kim Sigler, provided the most excitement in 1947 regarding the Communist Party. He had testified before the House Un-American Activities Committee on Communist infiltration into unions, claiming that Addes, Thomas, and Leonard were captives of the Communist Party. ACTU reacted, "Sure, Governor, turn the light on 'em," but cautioned about where that little light shone, for if innocent people were hurt, "we will be the first to tie a can on you" ("Let the People Know . . . ," 1947, p. 11). Reuther did not take Sigler's testimony in such a cavalier manner; he took it as an attack on the union movement and retorted, "Unwilling and unable to meet and solve the serious social and economic problems which presently confront the American people, reactionary forces are resorting to the traditional red scare." He added: "The reactionaries of the country have launched a red hunt whose ultimate victims are intended to be, not Communists, but all effective labor leaders and labor unions" (Walter Reuther Collection, box 143; folder 4, UA,WSU). In the next issue of the *Wage Earner,* there was a call to avoid hysteria about Sigler's comments, and it presented a special hysteria award to Reuther's advisers who had confused everyone "by rushing to the defense of his political opponents and denying facts about them known to everyone in the UAW" ("Too Much Hysteria . . . ," 1947, p. 9). It then went on to hit "hysterical lawmakers" for wanting to deny funds to Wayne University because of the presence of a well-known Communist Party front group, American Youth for Democracy, on the campus. Reuther's perception of the governor's attack was more astute than ACTU's, and it astounded the ATL caucus. The latter could not distinguish or wanted to confuse the difference between a principled criticism of the Communist Party and a conservative piece of red-baiting.

NOTES

1. That ploy failed. Ken Bannon, Reuther's caucus chair and later vice-president of the UAW, wrote to Murray regarding the quote. Murray vigorously denied it. In truth, Murray had attacked the level of the factional exchange in the UAW, not Reuther's report (Walter Reuther Collection, box 88; folder 3, UA,WSU).

2. The question of a trial for Communists, Fascists, or Nazis was settled expeditiously after the 1947 election. At the March 1948 IEB meeting, Leonard Woodcock moved that anyone charged under article 10, section 8, be asked if he or she is a member of the Communist or a Fascist party. "If the answer is Yes, the candidate shall be disqualified. . . . If the answer is No, the candidate shall be allowed to run unless he or she is found to be a member of such Communist, Fascist or Nazi party through the regular trial procedure of the International Constitution." It carried unanimously (UAW IEB Minutes, March 1948, p. 788, UA,WSU).

3. The very conservative *Chicago Daily Tribune,* on November 11, 1947, just prior to the UAW convention, attacked Reuther for supporting rent control. During the GM strike, on January 8, 1946, the *New York Sun* assailed Victor Reuther for attempting to "overthrow the American system of free enterprise and establishing a Socialist government" (R. J. Thomas Collection, box 14; folder 4, UA,WSU).

4. Earlier in 1941 and 1943, prior to and during the war, R. J. Thomas had received excellent press in the *Saturday Evening Post,* December 18, 1943 (Lahey, 1943, p. 17); *Time,* January 27, 1941 ("Labor," 1941, p. 16); *Business Week,* December 6, 1941 ("How They Bargain at Ford," 1941, p. 92); and *Survey Graphic,* November 1941 (Weybright, 1941, p. 652).

5. Carl Haessler, longtime associate of the Communist Party, had agreed to edit *FDR* on the proviso that it "would include nothing that was false or fraudulent in argument and

nothing libelous" (Haessler, 1957, p. 199). The pressure of the campaign "led to demands that I pep up the paper beyond the limit. I respectfully declined and left it. It was taken over by another editor and the paper became quite a rag" (p. 200).

6. Fr. Clancy, in 1941, had signed with a CIO union representing the employees of Holy Cross Cemetery in Detroit ("Fr. Clancy Signs with CIO," 1941, p. 1, UA,WSU).

7. The Minutes of the International Executive Board, July 14, 1941, record that the president of Local 51, "Pop" Edelen, appeared before the board to explain this position. "He pointed out that Local 51 was opposed to the establishing of so-called slates for the election of Delegates and would not permit the passing out of any such propaganda at its gates or around the plant" (UAW IEB Minutes, 1941, p. 27).

The election committee of Local 51 put out a leaflet during World War II explaining:

The election Committee has accepted a rule of long standing in our Local Union against the use of printed slates. We do this in the interest of unity and democracy. Where there is printed slates, there are also caucuses. Where there are caucuses and slates, trade union democracy is not. Where there is not full trade union democracy, factionalism thrives. Where factionalism is, disunity prevails and the immediate grievances and the interest of the workers, as well as the whole war effort suffer. (UAW Local 51 Collection, box 26; folder 8, UA,WSU).

8. Obtained through the Freedom of Information Act, these files were very limited, confined largely to minutes of two ACTU meetings in Pittsburgh in 1947. The informant did note that one ACTU sympathizer observed that ACTU was not much of a threat to the CP: "I believe that one communist puts up a better fight then ten ACTU members" (Goode Collection, FBI, ACTU file, p. 1, UA,WSU).

9. The *Michigan Labor Leader,* newspaper of the ACTU, cautioned its readers: "The charges, of course, are ridiculous, irrelevant and unworthy of credence. With whatever small credence we may possess, we warn Catholics, particularly, not to be deceived" ("Cheap Tricks," 1941, p. 6).

10. Roger Keeran, a pro-ATL writer, is an exception to this practice. He recognized "Reuther's liberal anti-Communism" that used such weapons as "exposure, free debate and social reform" (Keeran, 1980, p. 263).

7

CONCLUSION

The 1947 UAW convention provided few surprises.[1] Reuther was elected with only token opposition. Thomas, Addes, and Leonard were all defeated, and Reuther carried the Executive Board with a solid majority. Most of this was predictable from the defeat of the "left wing" in the Michigan, Wisconsin, Ohio, and Indiana CIO councils since the last UAW convention. All of the Reuther program prevailed. The delegates elected to comply with the Taft-Hartley bill while opposing it and seeking its repeal. Reuther, in his opening address, assailed American industry, maintaining that every worker could have been given twenty percent wage increases without any price increase and "still have made $8 Billion in profits after taxes." In a homely example, he examined the price of beer in New Jersey. The wholesale price was up sixty-two cents a barrel; the bar owners promptly went from a ten-ounce glass to an eight-ounce glass to create a profit of $17 a barrel to meet the sixty-two-cent increase, since there are 700 eight oz. glasses of beer in a barrel. "That is, if they do not put a head on the glass and I am told they do" (UAW Convention Proceedings, 1947, p. 10, UA,WSU).

Philip Murray, president of the CIO and the Steel Workers, was the main speaker. He noted his affection for the UAW and endorsed Reuther: "I have no words that can flow from me that would provide adequate appreciation for the splendid support that the little [!] red head has given Phil Murray since his incumbency." Of Thomas: "There is old R. J.—he makes mistakes, yes. He has a big heart. Sometimes a little mischievous, but nonetheless not a bad guy." Both statements were so patronizing that it is not hard to infer that the politics of the UAW were more of a pain than a joy to him (p. 66).

The question persists, How could Reuther have destroyed the ATL caucus in a mere eighteen months of politicking? Two anti-Reuther authors suggest possible answers. Keeran (1980) maintains that all of the Communist parties in western Europe and the United States "have been revolutionary parties in non-revolutionary situations. Consequently, they had two choices: they could continue to act as revolutionaries and face almost certain isolation, or they could plunge into reformist activities and risk the necessary compromises" (p. 23). Accepting none of this "Communism as revolutionary" talk, Cochran (1977) said: "If the Communist organization could have continued along its chosen path for another half-dozen years, it would have congealed into a party of the social-democratic type" (p. 15). The final disparagement!

Keeran's assessment of the alternative open to the Communist Party is undoubtedly accurate. But having adopted reformist politics and the attendant risks, was it necessary for the Communists to have made so many egregious mistakes?

The problem of being caught in an ideologically impossible situation is a real one, particularly for belief systems of perfectibility. ACTU also had true believers. Paul Weber's lectures on religion in the *Wage Earner* were stilted and catechistic. But in his political behavior, he recognized the tough reality that sacerdotal Catholicism had to give way to the prevailing politics, largely Social Democratic. The trade-off was a small contribution to the defeat of the CP-led Addes faction. Neither the Communists nor the Catholics had the troops or a favorable prevailing political setting to accomplish a political victory. Weber wisely settled for a compromise and supported Reuther. That option was not open to the CP, but it could have dropped its polemicizing for better analysis, unhampered by vicious personal attacks.

Nat Ganley points out that some of the Communists' failures had nothing to do with being in a nonrevolutionary situation. For example: the failure to carry on a "mobilization of the rank and file of the auto workers with the big economic battles that were bound to develop"; "wartime opportunism"; and allowing Reuther to appear as a "super militant" ("Hence, Reuther could ride in as a great hero on the white horse leading the crusade of the downtrodden masses, which he did and did very successfully"). Cochran's denigration of the members of the Communist Party that they were becoming "social democrats" does not answer the question of why they were so ineffective and dangerously wrong (Ganley, OH, pp. 33–34, UA,WSU).

Halperin's (1988) position is a faint echo of Keeran's. He asserts that "the decisive reason for Reuther's victory . . . was that the rank and file viewed him as a more pragmatic leader for the difficult times that union was facing" (p. 234). If radicalism is opposed to pragmatism, what could have been more pragmatic than the Communist Party's drifting with the rest of the union movement while Reuther raised explosive issues during the 1946 GM strike? All during the war, the Communist Party and the ATL caucus were the most "pragmatic" of all the tendencies. There was nothing, except the important race issue, that distinguished the Communists after 1941 as a radical alternative to Reuther's pragmatism. Ganley was right: There were basic weaknesses in the CP's positions and activities.

The choices were not between a pragmatic Reuther and the more ideological ATL caucus, whose brain trust was the Communist Party, or between the dynamic, antitotalitarian Reuther and the subversive Left. The choices for the UAW members were of another order.

There were certainly ideological differences between Reuther and the ATL caucus. Reuther was a longtime Social Democrat, and the CP was the brain trust of the ATL group. But that was not how the conflict was played out before the rank and file. Most of the definitions of ideological distinctions were carried out in the pages of the *Daily Worker*, which did not have wide circulation in the ranks of autoworkers, or at the IEB, whose deliberations were not generally shared with the public. There was no major public effort to differentiate the ideological positions of the participants by either side. The occasional sniping by both parties was a form of guerrilla warfare.

The contest was won on strategy and tactics about trade union issues. Reuther's strength was in his program, his tactical and strategic skills, and the blunders of his opponents. It was precisely on the "plane of policy," as Cochran (1977) phrased it, that victory was achieved.

On July 7, 1947, Wyndham Mortimer, who had been fired from the UAW staff as a result of his activities in the North American Aviation strike in 1941, wrote to R. J. Thomas:

I feel very strongly that you should fight to make it [UAW-FE merger] at the convention, and commence NOW to cut this bastard down to size. . . . I think we have got to start comparing him to Homer Martin. . . . If this is done, he will soon go on the defensive, and then we can trim his ass for him. One thing is certain Tom. That red head is not going to be licked by our staying on the defensive. . . . If this bastard isn't a stool pigeon, I never saw one. Don't forget Tom, I said Martin was a stool pigeon before you did, and this present bird is another one, or else I have lost my sense of smell. (R. J. Thomas Collection, box 10; folder 7, UA,WSU)

Thomas assured Mortimer that his olfactory capacities were undiminished and promised an aggressive campaign on the FE merger.

Mortimer's letter was not the basis of the ATL's strategy, but it was a reflection of the thinking of the Communist Party in the earlier formation of the strategy. The letter demonstrated two postulates of the ATL position: mounting aggressive attacks and labeling Reuther as a company stooge. The rank and file autoworker responded favorably to warlike leaders, the presumption being that they would be more militant toward the company. But an attacking mode no more wins elections than the "pedal to the metal" psychology wins auto races. More than mere assertiveness is necessary. Skills in tactics are required, knowing when to slow down, credibility. Otherwise, shrillness is substituted for sense. Stridency alone could not carry the 1947 UAW election.

Halperin (1982), a pro-ATL writer, notes:

The Reuther caucus, in fact, dropped the anti-Communist theme and instead concentrated on such issues as wages, prices, civil liberties, consumer cooperatives, and political

action. The Thomas and Addes forces were slower to recognize the limited impact of neg-
ative-sounding campaign literature and continued to sound the anti-Reuther theme. The
principal reason for this approach was that Reuther had gained the political initiative, and
his opponents felt themselves compelled to respond to his moves. The terms of the debate
were set by Reuther's proposals, ideas, and actions. (p. 221)

The ATL caucus, with the Communist Party directing the attack, erred
grossly in various areas. Thomas's charges against Reuther's "selling out" of the
AC strikers is a case in point. The accusations were easily refuted both by IEB
minutes and by the testimony of John Brophy, Murray's representative at the
attempted settlement. The list is extensive. The Taft-Hartley Act provided for a
new use of injunctions and the postponement of strikes by the government and
permitted courts to accept breach of contract damage suits against unions. To
impugn Reuther for purportedly supporting this odious legislation could only
cause the charges to be dismissed as "Stalinist vilification." Reuther was indicted for being a racist, when his subsequent support for the NAACP, Martin Luther
King, Jr., and Caesar Chavez of the Farm Workers Union reduces this indictment
to silliness. Subsequently, Reuther distinguished himself as an opponent of
Senator Joseph McCarthy and the Vietnam War. Hardly the acts of an arch conservative.

But it was not only the extravagance of the recriminations against its enemies that damaged the ATL caucus. It made major blunders during the course of
the campaign. The proposed merger with the FE was outstanding for its duplici-
ty. If any one issue turned the tide toward Reuther, this was it. The ATL caucus
was on bad UAW constitutional ground, it ran counter to other mergers in the
UAW and the Steel Workers, and the motive was so transparent that it self-
destructed. Perhaps it would have been possible to accomplish the merger (and
the 400 or so votes at the November convention), but not in the hurried, skitter-
ing manner that was used.

Even on issues where it had a decent position, such as the demand for trials
before anyone could be removed from office for being Communist, it discarded
a straightforward approach for a dissembling one. Reuther's position was that
when there was no doubt about membership in the Communist Party, "*and where
such facts are proven to the satisfaction of the Local Union membership at a regular membership meeting, after giving member in question a fair hearing before
membership meeting* [emphasis in original]," the accused can be automatically
disqualified (UAW IEB Minutes, April 28, 1947, p. 223). This was a significant
retreat on Reuther's part. Addes, however, submitted a legal brief of over fifteen
pages stressing that article 10, section 8 of the UAW constitution dealt only with
holding office, not *running* for office. This brief must have been written by
Maurice Sugar, but what it hoped to accomplish is unclear. It is clear that it muddied an issue that should have been straightforward.

It was not that Reuther failed to make mistakes; he did make them. Percy
Llewellyn charged that some Reuther supporters, following his 1946 election,

were raising money for a Victory Ball. In the process, they had approached some companies for money and gotten it. Reuther claimed to be innocent of these doings, agreed that it was wrong and made a public statement repudiating such activity (UAW IEB Minutes, August 16–18, 1946, p. 191, UA,WSU). In another case, Victor Reuther had accused Joe Mattson of sabotaging the educational program in Region 4, where Mattson was the director. After the debate at the Executive Board, Reuther said, "Joe, I think that you have been wronged, certainly you are entitled to that consideration [a retraction and correction of misstatement]" (UAW IEB Minutes, September 22–24, 1947, p. 305, UA,WSU). But the ATL board members would not even agree to as simple a request as verbatim minutes of board meetings and three trustees to oversee the finances of the UAW, which every local union had. Intransigence became confused with militancy, and as a consequence, they looked like they were trying to hide something.

The Left-Right designation for the combatants was dismissed by the *Wage Earner*: "One of our readers takes pen in hand to suggest that we stop referring to 'right wing' and 'left wing' elements. He says the current 'left wing' in American labor is topped by the Communist Party which . . . is far to the right of Francisco Franco" ("Gadfly," 1946, p. 6). The *Detroit Free Press* also had trouble with Left/Right specification. Prior to the 1947 convention, it ran a cartoon on its editorial page entitled "A Strange Bird Is the Pelican." Pictured was a pelican with two left wings, labeled "Reuther Faction" and "Thomas-Addes-Leonard Faction." A top-hatted figure, "Automobile Manufacturers," says, "Now let me see . . . which is the left wing?" ("A Strange Bird Is the Pelican," 1947, p. 4).

Another proffered explanation for the defeat of the ATL caucus, Reuther's red-baiting, is weak. When Reuther had major opportunities to criticize the Community Party, he refused to do so. The Communist Party was extremely vulnerable on the issue of the Farm Equipment-UAW merger and the Allis-Chalmers strike, but Reuther did not use the Communist issue during those protracted battles. He was tempted, but he altered his early drafts in his reply to R. J. Thomas on the AC strike to omit mention of the CP. Reuther did not win on a negative campaign of attacking Communists. He knew that this tactic could not win elections in the UAW.

The battle in the UAW was not decided by red-baiting or the activities of ACTU. ACTU's numbers were too small and its discipline nonexistent. In the few locals where it had strength (Locals 7 and 600), it was indistinguishable from the Reuther caucus. At the important conference meeting called by ACTU to formally support Reuther after the 1946 UAW convention, it could barely muster forty delegates. Joe McCusker, president of Local 600 and later regional director in the UAW, did not even bother to join ACTU, according to Tom Doherty, a leading Actist. The touted Kremlin-Vatican battle in the UAW was a product of the febrile imagination of some observers.

The victory of Walter Reuther presaged, according to some critics, the creation of a new era, where unions became instruments of social services and retreated from their old radical social reconstruction days. There is some truth to this, but Reuther did not create this new era. It was a product of the enormous expansion of American capitalism that had doubled its productive capacity during World War II while the rest of the world lay devastated. The resulting prosperity meant a more satisfied working class in America, and the conservatives managed a resurgence. The unions prior to World War II were not as radical as some assumed; the AFL was hardly radical, and the CIO was started by quite conservative figures, but there were dramatic strikes at Auto-Lite, Flint, Minneapolis, and San Francisco. In a few unions there were intense factional rivalries that reflected ideological differences.

But these were few in number. It is a mistake to assume that pre–World War II days were times of revolutionary upsurge. The actions of the Flint sit-downers were radical, but their ideology was not. The events that could lead Paul Weber of ACTU, in the late 1930s, to call for "[a] minority passionately devoted to something *positive*, something which has the qualities connoted by the words 'revolutionary' and 'utopian,'" (ACTU Collection, box 2; folder: ACTU NY, 1939–1943, UA,WSU) were gone. Millenarianism had been killed by the Cold War. What remained was an expanding economy and a massive array of national and international problems.

The factionalism in the UAW was brutal, which may have accounted for its demise. Every faction found it imperative to inveigh against the very system that is now applauded. The ATL caucus, Reuther, the Communist Party, and ACTU roundly condemned factionalism (while continuing to act as factions), because they knew that autoworkers would not tolerate this fighting for long. It was just too destructive. A rank and file that had supposedly been careful to keep power divided among the different groups now apparently wanted a resolution of the conflict.

What is exceptional in the labor movement is the sameness of the activities of the major unions, Communist (Harry Bridges), Republican (John L. Lewis), and Social Democratic (Reuther), particularly in the collective bargaining field. Levenstein (1981) points out that while Reuther drew criticism from various leftists for signing a five-year contract, Bridges had signed a seven-year contract several years before that (p. 334). The question of productivity was handled in slightly different ways, but the results were the same. Lewis agreed to the mechanization of the mines in exchange for a comprehensive hospital system for his members. It was a great success until the tonnage declined, and the system was severely constricted. Bridges signed a contract allowing containerization of cargo that provided job security for the privileged "A" card holders, less so for those in the "B" category. Productivity increases in the auto industry were used to respond to the UAW problems raised in the 1945–1946 GM strike. The UAW raised the twin problems of an improved standard of living for its members and the need for protection against inflation. GM, in subsequent negotiations, offered an annual improvement factor (AIF) based on productivity growth and a cost-of-living adjustment (COLA) to adjust wages to inflation. Thus, three important industrial unions responded to the need for productivity increases. They responded according to the structure of their industry, but they all accepted the need for such increases.

What choices, then, existed for autoworkers who were tired of the acrimony of the factional battles? At the time, the alternatives were an ATL caucus, whose propaganda was excoriating and shameless, versus Reuther, who had shown great militancy in the GM strike and great skills as a factional strategist. Reuther had a program; ATL had anti-Reutherism. Reuther had a sense of the potential of collective bargaining as a tool for general social betterment. While he was fighting for pay increases without price increases to siphon off profits and control inflation, the Communist Party was engaged in the most pedestrian of simple trade union arguments, with a dash of Populist rhetoric (mass picketing).

Reuther's later use of collective bargaining was imaginative. The first UAW-Ford Pension negotiated in 1949 called for a maximum $100 pension, composed of Social Security benefits plus the negotiated pension. If Social Security benefits went up, the company's obligation was reduced. As a consequence, there was a motivation for the company to favor increases in Social Security benefits. Thus, everyone benefited. The Supplemental Unemployment Benefits (SUB) was another negotiated benefit that served a dual purpose. Short workweeks bedeviled autoworkers. The supplement was negotiated to lessen the financial shock of layoffs. The result also tended to level out production schedules and avoid the overtime/layoff pattern in auto. Eventually, SUB provided up to ninety-five percent of take-home pay for layoffs and short workweeks. The Communists never showed the slightest imagination about collective bargaining as an instrument for social change. While it is a limited instrument, it has value and should be exploited.

The UAW staff became a collection of some of the best minds in the union movement, most of them tough, experienced unionists. Many of them later distinguished themselves by their writing and became leading academics. Others made reputations in the diplomatic service, philanthropic organizations, or political action groups. Their service in the UAW produced imaginative union programs and provided an intellectual leavening for the UAW that was unique in the union movement. At the same time, the Communist Party was howling, "Mad dog, jackal, Fascist, hyena."

ACTU ceased to become a major figure in the UAW or national politics after 1947. It continued as an organization with a press but became increasingly conservative. By the 1950s, the *Wage Earner* was attacking the Michigan CIO for a series of articles by Bill Kemsley, the education director, in support of the German Social Democrats and in opposition to the Christian Democratic Party. Both sections of the Trotskyist movement continued their splitting ways and never recovered the respect they once held in intellectual life in America. The smaller of the two sects eventually joined the Socialist Party. The CP, victimized shamefully at the hands of the government and raided by the other unions, was reduced to a harassed grouplet, spending much of its time unsuccessfully warding off government attacks and successfully beating back internal attempts to liberalize the party. The world was frozen by the Cold War, its potential for a transforming vision of human society stalled.

Now, even with the demise of the repressive eastern European political systems and the nearly forgotten judicial and military suppression of unions in the United States, there is little reason for optimism. The second great scourge of working people, economic depression, threatens the effort to create a just, honorable, and rewarding human life. The 1946–1947 battle for leadership in the UAW, however, was fought in an entirely different economic climate. The United States emerged as the single world power with its economy not only intact but double its prewar capacity. There were problems with a restless work force in the auto industry that Walter Reuther recognized and exploited in his rise to the presidency of the union. The Communists were partially disabled by their conservative positions taken during the war and their alliance with the ATL caucus. The unions that had strong Communist leadership—the FE, the UE, and the International Longshoremen's and Warehousemen's Union (ILWU)—were trying to maintain, in their vernacular, the "left-center" coalition with Phil Murray. This coalition was largely a figment of the Communist Party's imagination. Murray felt no political need for such an arrangement and soon broke it off when it became an embarrassment to him. The result was a distinctly conservative stand by the Communist Party unions on collective bargaining issues. Contrary to some popular opinion, these unions did not distinguish themselves by either their militancy or imagination regarding union issues. Their overriding concern was with the relationship between the Soviet Union and the Western bloc.

In short, Reuther won the UAW presidency in 1946–1947 in almost the same way that you get to Carnegie Hall: Praxis, praxis.

NOTE

1. The *Michigan Herald*, Michigan edition of the *Daily Worker*, October 26, 1947, in a demonstration of cloudy clairvoyance, predicted in a banner headline: "Reuther Plans A-Bomb Scare." The article, by Nat Ganley, began: "Walter Reuther will try to stampede the UAW-CIO convention this coming November 9 with a flag waving hysterical call for labor to support Wall Street's plan of aggression and war" (p. 1).

APPENDIX: FBI FILES

These files are punctuated with missing pages (the omissions are noted), inked-over names, and entire paragraphs deleted; occasionally, entire pages are sent with nothing on them but censored, inked lines. There is an elaborate rationale for these deletions, all described in the Freedom of Information Act, but the reader is still left with the sense that while the criteria are known for these judgments, they are so broad that it is obvious that decisions had to have been made for the deletions in accord with those criteria.

Fortunately, they occasionally slip. A letter was released from the FBI, for a researcher in 1975, involving a possible strike against General Motors in 1941. It said, in part:

There has been confidentially obtained from Communist Party sources a brief report of a mass meeting of the United Auto Workers of America, which meeting was held in Flint, Michigan on April 20, 1941. The report makes evident the position of several leaders of the United Auto Workers of America who are urging that General Motors Corporation be compelled to grant wage increases. (Goode Collection, FBI files, UA,WSU)

The body of the report has a series of deletions that seem to make no sense.

Apart from the dubious intelligence value of concealing which UAW leaders felt that GM should "be compelled to grant wage increases" (they all must have felt the same way), there is the question of the other deletions. Why were they made? What was the justification for them? Luckily, for some unknown reason, the same archival source has an unexpurgated copy of the same letter. The nature of the omissions is interesting, if puzzling. For example: "John Edgar Hoover, Director" is inked over; various stamps and penned notations of transmittal are obliterated, as is the notation "*Personal and Confidential*"; the recipient of the cover letter is deleted, a Captain Alan Goodrich Kirk, Director, Office of Naval Intelligence; and the names of the four UAW officials who spoke at the meeting and parts of their speeches and, finally, the ending of the letter are deleted. The deleted ending reads in full:

These persons are referred to in the report by their last names only. The report is attached hereto for your confidential information. Respectfully, John Edgar Hoover, Director, *By*

Special Messenger, cc: Brigadier General Gene Sherman Miles, Assistant Chief of Staff, G-2, War Department.

Only one word at the end of the letter was not deleted—"Enclosure." Intelligence is an arcane pursuit, by necessity, but one wonders what vital secrets would have been revealed to a researcher if the end of that letter had been left intact.

Other censored parts are equally strange. For example, one UAW speaker was quoted as saying: "Either ———— sends the goons back to the penitentiaries for their stripes, or puts them in uniform, so everyone can see who they are standing around." The excised name was "Bennett," Harry Bennett of the notorious Ford Service Department. Certainly Bennett's sensibilities would not have been offended by leaving his name in—he had heard worse—and no discernible intelligence reason seems to exist for the omission. Another example: "————, making money hand over fist in defense orders. Made 37½ million on GM stock alone." Deletion: "The Dupont family." Similarly, the names of some GM officials were expunged, but their salaries, bonuses, and dividends were left intact as reported by the speaker, George Addes, the secretary-treasurer of the UAW. The other speakers whose names were expurgated were Walter Reuther; R. J. Thomas, president of the union; and Mike Widman and Carl Swanson, both of whom were on the UAW staff. Precisely the people expected to speak on such an occasion.

The meeting was a typical agitational prestrike meeting, including statements that defense industries would not be struck. Hardly very subversive. Hardly any need to censor the report (Goode Collection, FBI files, UA,WSU).

BIBLIOGRAPHY

ARCHIVAL MATERIAL ✓

ACTU. Collection. Box 1; folder: ACTU Basic Training Course. 1946, UA, WSU.
ACTU. Collection. Box 1; folder: ACTU—Chicago, 1943, UA, WSU.
ACTU. Collection. Box 1; folder: ACTU 1938, UA, WSU.
ACTU. Collection. Box 1; folder: ACTU 1941, UA, WSU.
ACTU. Collection. Box 1; folder: ACTU undated, UA, WSU.
ACTU. Collection. Box 1; folder: Clippings 1939–1943, UA, WSU.
ACTU. Collection. Box 1; folder: General Meetings Minutes, UA, WSU.
ACTU. Collection. Box 2; folder: ACTU Convention, 1944, UA, WSU.
ACTU. Collection. Box 2; folder: ACTU Convention, 1947, UA, WSU.
ACTU. Collection. Box 2; folder: ACTU Pittsburgh, 1947–1950, UA, WSU.
ACTU. Collection. Box 2; folder: ACTU Pontiac, 1939–1949, UA, WSU.
ACTU. Collection. Box 2; folder: ACTU 1939–1943, UA, WSU.
ACTU. Collection. Box 2; folder: ACTU 1940, UA, WSU.
ACTU. Collection. Box 2; folder: ACTU New York, 1939–1943, UA, WSU.
ACTU. Collection. Box 2; folder: Communist Party, 1939–1945, UA, WSU.
ACTU. Collection. Box 2; folder: National Catholic Welfare Conference, UA, WSU.
ACTU. Collection. Box 3; folder: ACTU Handbills—1939, UA, WSU.
ACTU. Collection. Box 3; folder: ACTU-UAW 1946, UA, WSU.
ACTU. Collection. Box 3; folder: ACTU Executive Board Minutes, 1939–1940, UA,WSU.
ACTU. Collection. Box 3; folder: General Meetings Minutes, 1937–1940, UA, WSU.
ACTU. Collection. Box 3; folder: Parish Captains Minutes, 1939–1941, UA, WSU.
ACTU. Collection. Box 3; folder 21, UA, WSU.
ACTU. Collection. Box 8; folder: AC—1941, UA, WSU.
ACTU. Collection. Box 14; folder: Communism, UA, WSU.
ACTU. Collection. Box 14; folder: Communism in Labor Movement—1947, UA, WSU.
ACTU. Collection. Box 15; folder: Communist Party, 1939–1945, UA, WSU.
ACTU. Collection. Box 16; folder: Fr. John F. Cronin, 1943–1946, UA, WSU.
ACTU. Collection. Box 18; folder: ACTU NY 1939–1943, UA, WSU.

ACTU. Collection. Box 19; folder: Food, Tobacco, Agricultural and Allied Workers (CIO), UA, WSU.

ACTU. Collection. Box 20; folder: Carl Haessler, 1942–1945, UA, WSU.

ACTU. Collection. Box 22; folder: Jews, UA, WSU.

ACTU. Collection. Box 24; folder: Local 155, UA, WSU.

ACTU. Collection. Box 25; folder: Briggs Forge 742, UA, WSU.

ACTU. Collection. Box 25; folder: UAW Convention, 1946, UA, WSU.

ACTU. Collection. Box 29; folder: National Catholic Welfare Conference, 1945, UA, WSU.

"Addes Backs Reuther Against Communist Party Demands to Strike All Plants." 1946. *Wage Earner* (January 18): 1, UA, WSU.

"Addes Favors No Change in UAW Administration." 1946. *Wage Earner* (March 8): 3, UA, WSU.

Addes, George. 1941. *Michigan Labor Leader* (September 26): 4, UA, WSU.

" 'Back to Work' Move Is Smashed." 1939. *Michigan Labor Leader* (November 17): 1, UA, WSU.

"Barring CPs from Union Draws Catholic Criticism." 1946. *Wage Earner* (April 26): 9, UA, WSU.

Bell, Daniel. Collection. Box 4, Wagner Library, NYU.

Bell, Daniel. Collection. Box MB3, Wagner Library, NYU.

Bell, Daniel. Collection. Box MB4, Wagner Library, NYU.

The Bosses' Boy. 1947. Walter Reuther. Collection. Box 108; folder: Factional Statements on Convention Issues, UA, WSU.

Boxed Statement. 1941. *Michigan Labor Leader* (August 15): 1, UA, WSU.

Brown, Joe. Collection. Box 1; folder: Association of Catholic Trade Unionists, UA, WSU.

Brown, Joe. Collection. Box 7; folder: Rev. Charles E. Coughlin, UA, WSU.

"Callahan Measure Hit by Reuther." 1947. *FDR* (June 5): 2. Walter Reuther. Collection. Box 65; folder, UA, WSU.

"Catholic Labor Leaders Oppose the ACTU." 1947. *FDR* (September 25): 4. Walter Reuther. Collection. Box 108; folder: Speed-up, UA, WSU.

"The Chaplain's Corner." 1941. *Michigan Labor Leader* (August 15): 1, 3, UA, WSU.

"Cheap Tricks." 1941. *Michigan Labor Leader* (March 28): 6, UA, WSU.

The Church and the Social Order. 1940. ACTU. Collection. Box 2; folder: A Statement of the Archbishops and Bishops of the Administrative Board of the NCWC, UA, WSU.

Clancy, Raymond. Collection. Box 1; folder 16, UA, WSU.

Clancy, Raymond. Collection. Box 1; folder 18, UA, WSU.

Clancy, Raymond. Collection. Box 1; folder 21, UA, WSU.

Clancy, Raymond. Collection. Box 4; folder 2, UA, WSU.

"Clergy of Three Faiths Back Strike for Wage-Price Balance." 1946. *Wage Earner* (March 22): 5, UA, WSU.

"Commie 'Spread Strike' Line 'Preposterous'—Murray." 1946. *Wage Earner* (January 11): 4, UA, WSU.

"Communist Leader Demands Strike." 1946. *Wage Earner* (January 11): 4, UA, WSU.

"Communists Offer Seniority by Quotas." 1947. *FDR* (September 1): 7. Walter Reuther. Collection. Box 65; folder 7, UA, WSU.

"Communist Threat to 'Blast' ACTU Flops Hard." 1941. *Michigan Labor Leader* (August 29): 1, UA, WSU.

"Comrades at Fords." 1946. *Wage Earner* (March 8): 9, UA, WSU.

"Convention Comments." 1946. *Wage Earner* (March 29): 6, UA, WSU.

"The Corporate State." 1947. *Wage Earner* (May 12): 6, UA, WSU.

Croft, John. Collection. Box 1; folder 15, UA, WSU.

"Curbing Commies." 1947. *Wage Earner* (March 28): 6, UA, WSU.

De Gaetano, Nick. Collection. UA, WSU.

Deverall, Richard. 1942. "Notes on Statement Issued by Harry Purdy." ACTU. Collection. Box 17; folder: Richard Deverall, UA, WSU.

"Editorial." 1946. *Wage Earner* (February 1): 2, UA, WSU.

"Expect Reuther Candidacy When Convention Starts." 1946. *Wage Earner* (March 15): 4, UA, WSU.

"An Explanation of the Steel Story." 1946. *Wage Earner* (January 25): 1, UA, WSU.

"A Fair Policy on Women in Industry." 1947. *Wage Earner* (October 5): 4, UA, WSU.

Frankensteen, Richard. 1961. Oral History. UA, WSU.

"Fr. Clancy Signs with CIO." 1941. *Michigan Labor Leader* (April 25): 1, UA, WSU.

"Fr. Coughlin Errs." 1939. *Michigan Labor Leader* (November 17): 1, UA, WSU.

"Gadfly." 1946. *Wage Earner* (March 15): 6, UA, WSU.

"Gadfly." 1946. *Wage Earner* (April 19): 6, UA, WSU.

Ganley, Nat. Collection. Box 1; folder 1–38, UA, WSU.

Ganley, Nat. Collection. Box 5; folder 20, UA, WSU.

Ganley, Nat. Collection. Box 6; folder: 1929, UA, WSU.

Ganley, Nat. Collection. Box 10; folder 21, UA, WSU.

Ganley, Nat. Collection. 1960. OH. UA, WSU.

"GM Fight Is Showdown on Labor's Claim to Profit." 1945. *Wage Earner* (October 26): 5, UA, WSU.

"GM Strikers Won Ford, Chrysler Pay Raises." 1946. *Wage Earner* (February 1): 2, UA, WSU.

Goode, Bill. Collection. U.S. Army Intelligence, UA, WSU.

Goode, Bill. Collection. Army Intelligence, Walter Reuther, UA, WSU.

Goode, Bill. Collection. FBI ACTU file, UA, WSU.

Goode, Bill. Collection. FBI File, Nat Ganley, UA, WSU.

Goode, Bill. Collection. FBI, Reuther file, UA, WSU.

Haessler, Carl. 1959. Oral History, UA, WSU.

"I Will Never Witch Hunt." 1941. *Michigan Labor Leader* (September 29): 4, UA, WSU.

"It Is No Accident." 1947. *Wage Earner* (October 10): 3, UA, WSU.

"Keep Them Out in the Open." 1947. *Wage Earner* (March 21): 9, UA, WSU.

"Let the People Know Who the Communists Are." 1947. *Wage Earner* (February 21): 11, UA, WSU.

Mattson, Joe. UAW IEB Minutes, Special Session, October 18–20, 1946, UA, WSU.

Mooney, Archbishop Edward. 1939. *Michigan Labor Leader* (October 20): 1, UA, WSU.

"Murray Urged Reuther to Drop Price Claim." 1946. *Wage Earner* (January 21): 2, UA, WSU.

"The Other Party." 1940. *Michigan Labor Leader* (September 27): 5, UA, WSU.

"Quill Assails Views of Church on Labor." 1947. *Wage Earner* (January 24): 3, UA, WSU.

"Report of the Bargaining Committee." Walter Reuther. Collection. Box 36; folder 13, UA, WSU.

"Reuther Holds Key to Politics in UAW." 1946. *Wage Earner* (March 1): 2, UA, WSU.

"Reuther Leading in Unofficial Tally." 1946. *Wage Earner* (March 22): 1, UA, WSU.

"Reuther's Speedup Policy." 1947. *FDR* (September 25): 4. Walter Reuther. Collection. Box 65; folder 7, UA, WSU.

Reuther, Walter. Collection. Box 3; folder 5, UA, WSU.

Reuther, Walter. Collection. Box 3; folder 6, UA, WSU.

Reuther, Walter. Collection. Box 5; folder 8, UA, WSU.

Reuther, Walter. Collection. Box 12; folder 16, UA, WSU.

Reuther, Walter. Collection. Box 36; folder 9, UA, WSU.

Reuther, Walter. Collection. Box 36; folder 10, UA, WSU.

Reuther, Walter. Collection. Box 36; folder 13, UA, WSU.

Reuther, Walter. Collection. Box 36; folder 14, UA, WSU.

Reuther, Walter. Collection. Box 64; folder 3, UA, WSU.

Reuther, Walter. Collection. Box 65; folder 7, UA, WSU.

Reuther, Walter. Collection. Box 88; folder 3, UA, WSU.

Reuther, Walter. Collection. Box 93; folder 8, UA, WSU.

Reuther, Walter. Collection. Box 93; folder 9, UA, WSU.

Reuther, Walter. Collection. Box 93; folder 10, UA, WSU.

Reuther, Walter. Collection. Box 107; folder: Convention 1947, UA, WSU.

Reuther, Walter. Collection. Box 108; folder: Factional Statements on Convention Issues, UA, WSU.

Reuther, Walter. Collection. Box 108; folder: FE–UAW Merger, UA, WSU.

Reuther, Walter. Collection. Box 108; folder: News Clips, September 1947, UA, WSU.

Reuther, Walter. Collection. Box 108; folder: Speed-up and Un-Marked, UA, WSU.

Reuther, Walter. Collection. Box 108; folder: Taft-Hartley Issue, UA, WSU.

Reuther, Walter. Collection. Box 143; folder 4, UA, WSU.

Reuther, Walter. Collection. Box 143; folder 8, UA, WSU.

Reuther, Walter. UAW IEB Minutes, August 12, 1946, UA, WSU.

"Right to Strike Upheld in Strong Clergy Statement." 1946. *Wage Earner* (March 22): 5, UA, WSU.

"Scholle Wins But Reuther Loses." 1947 *FDR* (July 1): 4. Walter Reuther. Collection. Box 65; folder 6, UA, WSU.

"Steel 'Doublecross' Reduces Pay Level 18 Cents and $4 per Ton." 1946. *Wage Earner* (January 18): 3, UA, WSU.

Sugar, Maurice. Collection. Box 1; folder 8, UA, WSU.

Sugar, Maurice. Collection. Box 1; folder 24, UA, WSU.

Sugar, Maurice. Collection. Box 8; folder 8, UA, WSU.

Sugar, Maurice. Collection. Box 32; folder 5, UA, WSU.

Sugar, Maurice. Collection. Box 42; folder 5, UA, WSU.

Sugar, Maurice. Collection. Box 42; folder 15, UA, WSU.

Sugar, Maurice. Collection. Box 45; folder 15, UA, WSU.

Sweet, Sam. Collection. Box 5; folder 19, UA, WSU.

Taft-Hartley Act. Labor Laws, Vertical Files, UA, WSU.

"That's Democracy." 1946. *Wage Earner* (March 15): 6, UA, WSU.

"They Won Their Wage Battles." 1946. *Wage Earner* (January 11): 2, UA, WSU.

Thomas, R. J. Collection. Box 4; folder 5, UA, WSU.

Thomas, R. J. Collection. Box 10; folder 7, UA, WSU.

Thomas, R. J. Collection. Box 14; folder 4, UA, WSU.

"Thomas Charges Plot by Dubinsky." 1946. *Wage Earner* (March 22): 1, UA, WSU.

"Thomas Replies." 1947. *FDR* (September 25): 6. Walter Reuther. Collection. Box 108; folder: Speed-Up, UA, WSU.

"Too Much Hysteria and Too Few Facts." 1947. *Wage Earner* (April 4): 9, UA, WSU.

UAW Convention Proceedings, 1935, UA, WSU.

UAW Convention Proceedings, 1936, UA, WSU.

UAW Convention Proceedings, 1936, 2nd (Special Convention), UA, WSU.

UAW Convention Proceedings, 1937, UA, WSU.

UAW Convention Proceedings, 1940, UA, WSU.

UAW Convention Proceedings, 1941, UA, WSU.

UAW Convention Proceedings, 1942, UA, WSU.

UAW Convention Proceedings, 1943, UA, WSU.

UAW Convention Proceedings, 1944, UA, WSU.

UAW Convention Proceedings, 1946, UA, WSU.

UAW Convention Proceedings, 1947, UA, WSU.

UAW Convention Proceedings, 1980, UA, WSU.

"UAW Heads Demand Hearing on UE–GM 18½ Cent Betrayal." 1946. *Wage Earner* (February 15): 2, UA, WSU.

UAW IEB Minutes, July 14, 1941, UA, WSU.

UAW IEB Minutes, August 16–18, 1946, UA, WSU.

UAW IEB Minutes, December 9–18, 1946, UA, WSU.

UAW IEB Minutes, March 17–26, 1947, UA, WSU.

UAW IEB Minutes, Special Session, April 15, 1947, UA, WSU.

UAW IEB Minutes, April 28, 1947, UA, WSU.

UAW IEB Minutes, June 14, 1947, UA, WSU.

UAW IEB Minutes, June 20, 1947, Special Session, UA, WSU.

UAW IEB Minutes, September 22–24, 1947, UA, WSU.

UAW IEB Minutes, March, 1948, UA, WSU.

"UAW Factionalism." 1947. *Michigan Chronicle* (September 27): 6.

UAW Local 9. Collection. Box 97; folder: Pre-Convention Propaganda, 1947, UA, WSU.

UAW Local 51. Collection. Box 8; folder 8, UA, WSU.

UAW Local 51. Collection. Box 14; folder 12, UA, WSU.

UAW Local 51. Collection. Box 22; folder 12, UA, WSU.

UAW Local 51. Collection. Box 24; folder 11, UA, WSU.

UAW Local 51. Collection. Box 26; folder 8, UA, WSU.

UAW Local 174. Collection. Box 21; folder: Factionalism, UA, WSU.

UAW Research Department. Collection. Box 4; folder 4, UA, WSU.

UAW Washington Office. D. Montgomery Collection. Series 9, box 25-c-3 (1); folder 80-16: FE Merger with UAW, 1945–1947, UA, WSU.

"Was His Letterhead Red." 1947. *Wage Earner* (October 10): 6, UA, WSU.

Weber, Paul. 1947. *Wage Earner* (April 11): 6, UA, WSU.

incl Dept Papers + Daily Wkr United Auto Wkr

gd thorough research incl Key books

BOOKS, PERIODICALS, AND NEWSPAPERS

"AFL Link to Reuther Is Scented." 1946. *Detroit News* (March 24): 9.

Allan, William. 1946. *Daily Worker* (March 21): 5.

Aronowitz, Stanley. 1974. *False Promises.* New York: McGraw-Hill.

"The Auto Union Convention." 1946. *Daily Worker* (March 24): 3.

Bernard, John. 1983. *Walter Reuther and the Rise of the Auto Workers.* Boston: Little, Brown.

Bernstein, Irving. 1970. *Turbulent Years: A History of the American Worker, 1933–1941.* Boston: Houghton Mifflin.

Bettan, Neil. 1976. *Catholic Activism and the Industrial Worker.* Gainsville: Florida State University Press.

"Big Auto Local Opposes Proposal to Outlaw CP." 1947. *Daily Worker* (April 4): 4.

Blackwood, George D. 1951. "The United Automobile Workers of America." Ph.D. dissertation, Department of History, University of Chicago.

Blanchard, Paul. 1958. *American Freedom and Catholic Power.* Boston: Beacon Press.

"Blow to UAW." 1946. *Business Week* (February 16): 100.

Browder, Earl. 1943. *Detroit News* (May 14): 19.

Browder, Earl. 1945. *Daily Worker* (January 7): 8.

"Catholic Infiltration Disturbs Unions." 1945. *Christian Century* (May 9): 573.

"Churchill: Home View." 1946. *Newsweek* (March 18): 49.

Cochran, Bert. 1977. *Labor and Communism.* Princeton, NJ: Princeton University Press.

"Communists Call on Gov't. . . ." 1943. *Daily Worker* (June 2): 1.

Cormier, Frank, and William J. Eaton. 1970. *Reuther.* Englewood Cliffs, NJ: Prentice-Hall.

Cort, John C. 1944. *Commonweal* 40 (September 29): 42.

Cort, John C. 1947. *Labor Leader* (February 28): 5.

Crellin, Jack. 1943. *Detroit Times* (May 13): 9.

Crellin, Jack. 1943. *Detroit Times* (May 15): 5.

Curran, Joe. 1943. *The Pilot* (May 28): 5.

Davies, Joseph A. 1942. *New York Times Magazine* (April 12): 3.

De Caux, Len. 1970. *Labor Radical.* Boston: Beacon Press.

"Detroit Proves It—Fink Is the Name for Stalinist." 1943. *Labor Action* (May 31): 8.

"Dubinsky Ties Strings to Relief for GM Workers." 1946. *Daily Worker* (February 27): 5.

"Education Department." 1942. *United Automobile Worker* (September 15): 6.

Fardella, Joseph A. 1981. "The Catholic Church and the American Working Class: Three Embodiments of Papal Social Teachings." M.A. thesis, Wayne State University.

"Father Coughlin." 1934. *Fortune* (February): 34–37.

"*FDR.*" 1947 "Report to the Membership." *Automobile Worker* (September): 5–8.

"The Fight Inside the Auto Union." 1947. *Militant* (October 13): 1.

Fine, Sidney. 1969. *Sit Down.* Ann Arbor: University of Michigan Press.

Fountain, Clayton. 1949. *Union Guy.* New York: Viking Press.

Ganley, Nat. 1960. *Oral History.* University Archives, Wayne State University.

Garrett, Manny. 1946. *Labor Action* (March 11): 4.

Geschwender, James A. 1977. *Class, Race, and Worker Insurgency.* London: Cambridge University Press.

Glaberman, Martin. 1973. *Radical America* (Nov./Dec.): 114–116.

"GM Workers Re-Examining Reuther's Strike Strategy." 1946. *Daily Worker* (February 17): 4, 10.

Green, James R. 1980. *The World of the Worker.* New York: Hill and Wang.

Hall, Ben. 1947. *New International* (September): 198.

Halperin, Martin. 1982. "Disintegration of the Left-Center Coalition in the UAW, 1945–1950." Ph.D. dissertation, University of Michigan.

Halperin, Martin. 1988. *UAW Politics in the Cold War Era.* Albany: State University of New York Press.

Harrington, Michael. 1960. "Catholics in the Labor Movement: A Case History." *Labor History*: 231–263.

Harrison, Selig. 1948. "Political Program of the United Automobile Workers." M.A. thesis, Harvard University.

"Hate, Greed, Stupidity, Block Return to Prosperity." 1946. *Detroit Free Press* (January 21): 6.

"Here Is the Issue." 1945. *Detroit News* (December 30): 9.

"How They Bargain at Ford." 1941. *Business Week* (December 6): 92–96.

Howard, Milton. 1941. *Daily Worker* (August 16): 5.

Howe, Irving, and Lewis Coser. 1957. *The American Communist Party.* Boston: Beacon Press.

Keeran, Roger. 1980. *The Communist Party and the Auto Workers Unions.* Bloomington: Indiana University Press.

Klehr, Harvey. 1983. "American Communism and the United Auto Workers: New Evidence on an Old Controversy." *Labor History* (Summer): 404–413.

Klehr, Harvey. 1984. *The Heyday of American Communism: The Depression Years.* New York: Basic Books.

"Labor." 1941. *Time* (January 27): 16–18.

"Labor Priests." 1949. *Fortune* (January): 150–153.

"Labor Trends." 1946. *Newsweek* (March 11): 75.

Lahey, Edwin. 1943. *Saturday Evening Post* (December 18): 17, 105–106.

Lauren, Asher. 1946. *Detroit News* (March 22): 34.

Levenstein, Harvey A. 1981. *Communism, Anti-Communism and the CIO.* Westport, CT: Greenwood Press.

Lichtenstein, Nelson. 1974. "Industrial Unionism Under the No-Strike Pledge: A Study of the CIO During the Second World War." Ph.D. dissertation, pt. 2, University of California at Berkeley.

Linton, Thomas E. 1965. *An Historical Examination of the Purposes and Practices of the Education Program of the United Automobile Workers of America, 1936–1959.* Ann Arbor: University of Michigan School of Education.

"A 'Look at the Books' or 'A Finger in the Pie'?" 1946. *Detroit News* (January 7): 6.

"Lovestone Home Is Burglarized." 1938. *Workers Age* (August 13): 1.

Magil, A. B. 1943. *New Masses* (June): 12–15.

"Martin Puppet of Lovestone in Drive to Disrupt CIO." 1938. *Daily Worker* (August 4): 1.

"Master Strategy Cost GM Workers." 1946. *Daily Worker* (March 24): 3.

McWethy, James A. 1946. *Wall Street Journal* (September 21): 1,2.

Meier, August, and Elliot Rudwick. 1981. *Black Detroit and the Rise of the UAW.* New York: Oxford University Press.

"The Mine Strike and Its Lessons." 1943. *Detroit News* (May 14): 19.

Morris, George. 1946. *Daily Worker* (February 19): 9.

Morris, George. 1946. *Daily Worker* (March 3): 9.

Morris, George. 1947. *Daily Worker* (March 15): 7.

Morris, George. 1950. "The Vatican Conspiracy in the American Trade Union Movement." *Political Affairs* (June): 46–57.

"Murray UAW Talk KOs Reuther Tales." 1946. *Daily Worker* (March 26): 2.

O'Shea, Arthur. 1946. *Detroit Free Press* (March 22): 1.

Preis, Art. 1964. *Labor's Giant Step.* New York: Pioneer Publishers.

Rayback, Joseph G. 1966. *A History of American Labor.* New York: The Free Press.

"Red Baiters Sweep UAW Convention." 1947. *Militant* (November 17): 1.

"Report on the State of Your Union." 1947. *Automobile Worker,* Special Edition (October): 1–4.

"Report to the Membership." 1947. *Automobile Worker* (September): 5–8.

"Reuther: FOB Detroit." 1945. *Fortune* (December): 149, 288.

"The Reuther-Dubinsky Intrigue That Prolonged the GM Strike." 1946. *Daily Worker* (March 17): 12.

"Reuther Plans A-Bomb Scare." 1947. *Michigan Herald* (October 6): 1.

"Reuther's Role." 1946. *Militant* (March 23): 2.

Robinson, Archie. 1939. *Detroit News* (November 16): 10.

Rovere, Richard. 1941. "Labor's Catholic Bloc." *The Nation* (June): 13.

The Searchlight. 1986. UAW Local 659 (February 6): 1.

Seaton, Douglas P. 1981. *Catholic and Radicals.* Lewisburg, PA: Bicknell University Press.

Sevostyanov, G. N. 1979. *Recent History of the Labor Movement in the United States 1939–1965.* Moscow: Progress Publishers.

Sexton, Patricia Cayo. 1991. *The War on Labor and the Left: Understanding America's Unique Conservatism.* Boulder, CO: Westview Press.

Silverman, Suzanne. 1982. "Unionization as a Social Movement. A Case Study of the UAW, 1945–1950." Ph.D. dissertation. Columbia University.

"Slight Rift in Solidarity Forever." 1946. *Detroit News* (March 26): 18.

Spender, Steven. 1951. *World Within World.* Berkeley: University of California Press.

"Statement from Ford and CIO on Plant Vote." 1941. *Detroit Free Press* (May 24): 3.

Stiler, Robert. 1946. *Labor Action* (January 7): 2.

Stolberg, Benjamin. 1938. *The Story of the CIO.* New York: Viking Press.

"A Strange Bird Is the Pelican." 1947. *Detroit Free Press* (November 15): 6.

Sugar, Maurice. 1980. *The Ford Hunger March.* Berkeley, VA: Meiklejohn Civil Liberties Institute.

Taft, Philip. 1949. "The Association of Catholic Trade Unionists." *Industrial and Labor Relations Review.* (June): 210–218.

"Target and the Victims." 1947. Cartoon, *Milwaukee Sentinel* (January 24): 1.

"Thomas Blames Reuther Jump-Gun Policy for Length of GM Strike." 1946. *Daily Worker* (March 19): 5.

"28,000 Still Idle . . . . " 1943. *Detroit Times* (May 21): 1, 3.

"UAW Factionalism." 1947. *Michigan Chronicle* (September 27): 6.

"UAW Leaders Ask . . . ." 1943. *Daily Worker* (June 2): 5.

UAW Local 659, *The Searchlight,* February 6, 1986.

"UAW Local Upholds Ban on Trotskyite Rag." 1941. *Daily Worker* (August 16): 5.

"UAW OK's 50-Cent Dues Increase." 1946. *Detroit Free Press* (March 27): 3.

"UNIONS: Three Headed UAW." 1946. *Newsweek* (April 8): 67.

"Up Comes a New Issue." 1945. *Detroit News* (November 12): 10.

Ward, Richard. 1958. "The Role of ACTU in the American Labor Movement." Ph.D. dissertation. University of Michigan.

"Warplanes to Cost Average Family $100 Annually." 1941. *Daily Worker* (January 6): 3.

Wattel, Harold L. 1947. "The Association of Catholic Trade Unionists." M.A. thesis, Columbia University.

Westcott, Ray. 1948. "Priests, Workers and Communists." *Harper's Magazine* (November): 50–56.

Weybright, Victor. 1941. *Survey Graphic* (November): 554–559, 651–653.

"Whither Reuther." 1946. *Time* (February 25): 20.

Wilson, Jack. 1946. *Labor Action* (March 4): 2.

MISCELLANEOUS

American Steel Foundries v. Tri-City Central Trades Council, 257 US 184.

Conway, Jack. 1986. Interview, February 14.

Cort, John C. n.d. Unpublished manuscript; copy in this writer's possession.

Hitchman Coal and Coke Company v. Mitchell, Individually, et al, 245 US 229.

Reuther, Victor. 1988. Interview, May 24.

Sexton, Brendan. 1986. Interview, February 14.

Sheffield, Horace. 1986. Interview, October 27.

Strachan, Stuart. 1982. Interview, September 29.

Tappes, Shelton. 1986. Interview, December 4.

Weber, Paul. 1982. Interview, February 20.

Widick, B. J. 1987. Comments at North American Labor History Conference 9, October 22.

Wolf, Elinor. 1987. Interview, August 8.

Woodcock, Leonard. 1987. Interview, September 29.

INDEX

About the Author

BILL GOODE is retired from Empire State College, where he was an Associate
Professor of Labor Studies and former Dean of the Center for Labor Studies. He
has been the Director of Educational Activities for the UAW, the Director of the
International Brotherhood of Teamsters Labor Institute, and has been associated
with other labor and civil rights groups.